The Battle of Dyrrhachium (48 BC)

The Battle of Dyrrhachium (48 BC)

Caesar, Pompey, and the Early Campaigns of the Third Roman Civil War

Gareth C Sampson

Pen & Sword
MILITARY

First published in Great Britain in 2022 by
Pen & Sword Military
An imprint of
Pen & Sword Books Ltd
Yorkshire – Philadelphia

ISBN 978 1 52679 358 4

Typeset by Mac Style
Printed and bound in the UK by CPI Group (UK) Ltd,
Croydon, CR0 4YY.

MIX
Paper from
responsible sources
FSC
www.fsc.org   FSC® C013604

Pen & Sword Books Limited incorporates the imprints of Atlas,
Archaeology, Aviation, Discovery, Family History, Fiction, History,
Maritime, Military, Military Classics, Politics, Select, Transport,
True Crime, Air World, Frontline Publishing, Leo Cooper, Remember
When, Seaforth Publishing, The Praetorian Press, Wharncliffe
Local History, Wharncliffe Transport, Wharncliffe True Crime
and White Owl.

For a complete list of Pen & Sword titles please contact

PEN & SWORD BOOKS LIMITED
47 Church Street, Barnsley, South Yorkshire, S70 2AS, England
E-mail: enquiries@pen-and-sword.co.uk
Website: www.pen-and-sword.co.uk

Or

PEN AND SWORD BOOKS
1950 Lawrence Rd, Havertown, PA 19083, USA
E-mail: Uspen-and-sword@casematepublishers.com
Website: www.penandswordbooks.com

In loving memory of Geoff Sampson (1947–2019)

Contents

Acknowledgements

As always, the first and greatest acknowledgement must go out to my wonderful wife Alex, without whose support and understanding none of this would be possible. Next must come Thomas and Caitlin, who are a constant source of joy and anxiety.

Special thanks go out to my parents who always encouraged a love of books and learning (even if they did regret the house being filled with books). My father Geoff is no longer with us, and his loss is still felt by us all.

There are a number of individuals who through the years have inspired the love of Roman history in me and mentored me along the way; Michael Gracey at William Hulme, David Shotter at Lancaster and Tim Cornell at Manchester. My heartfelt thanks go out to them all.

A shout goes out to the remaining members of the Manchester diaspora: Gary, Ian, Jason, Sam. Those were good days; we will not see their like again.

As always, my thanks go out to my editor Phil Sidnell, for his patience and understanding.

It must also be said that as an Independent Academic, the job of researching these works is being made easier by the internet, so Alumnus access to JSTOR (Manchester and Lancaster) and Academia.edu must get a round of thanks also.

List of Illustrations

1. Possible bust of C. Marius.
2. Bust of L. Cornelius Sulla.
3. Bust of Cn. Pompeius Magnus.
4. Possible bust of M. Licinius Crassus.
5. Bust of C. Iulius Caesar.
6. Bust of M. Tullius Cicero.
7. Bust of M. Antonius.
8. Bust of Cato.
9. Bust of Sextus Pompeius.
10. Coin of Metellus Scipio.
11. Bust of Juba I.
12. Illyrian coastline.
13. Ruins of Amphitheatre of Dyrrhachium. (*Adobe Stock*)
14. Roman ruins of Apollonia. (*Pudelek via Wiki Commons*)
15. Corcyran coast.
16. Modern harbour of Massilia. (*Adobe Stock*)

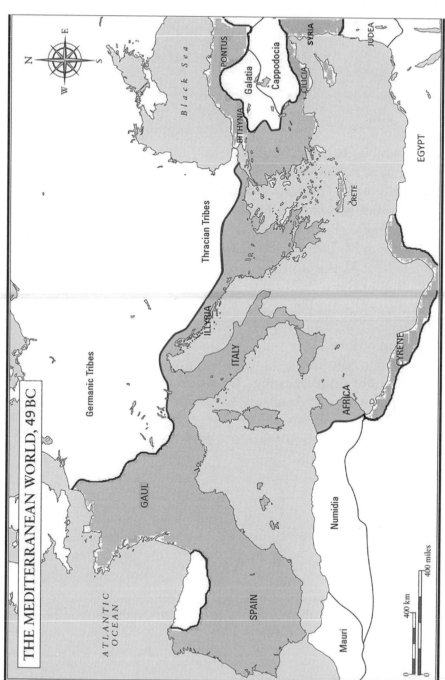

THE MEDITERRANEAN WORLD, 49 BC

Germanic Tribes

ATLANTIC
OCEAN

GAUL

SPAIN

Mauri

Numidia

ILLYRIA

ITALY

AFRICA

Thracian Tribes

Black Sea

BITHYNIA

PONTUS

Galatia

Cappodocia

CILICIA

SYRIA

CRETE

CYRENE

EGYPT

JUDEA

N
W   E
S

0   400 km
0   400 miles

Map 1.

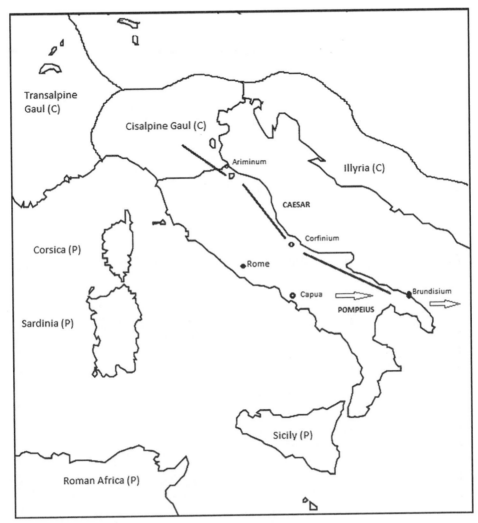

Map 2. The Italian Campaign.

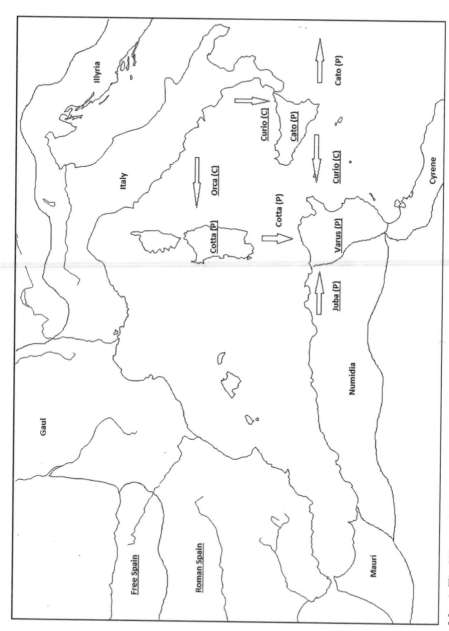

Map 3. The Western Mediterranean Campaigns.

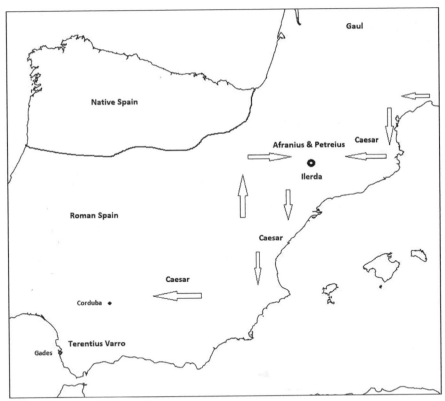

Map 4. The Spanish Campaigns.

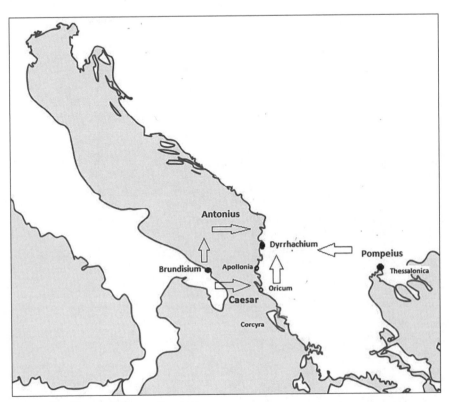

Map 5. The Epirote / Illyrian Campaigns.

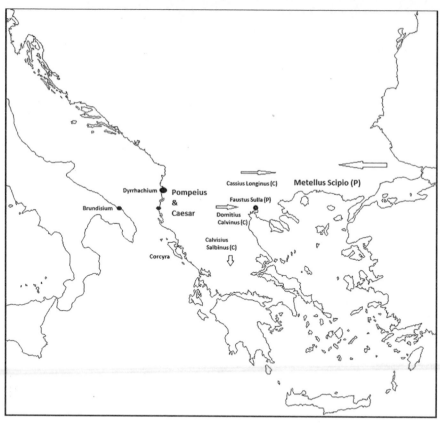

Map 6. The Greek & Macedonian Campaigns.

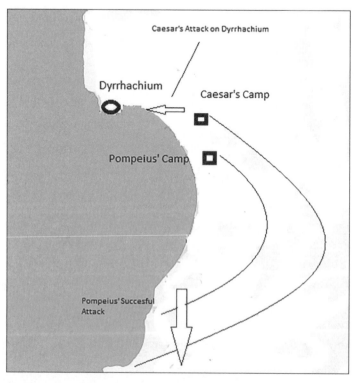

Map 7. The Dyrrhachium Campaign.

Introduction

The Defeat that Never Was

When is a defeat in battle not a defeat in battle? When the loser gets to write the history books. This sums up nicely the situation that we find in July 48 BC when the Roman Republic's two greatest living generals met in battle for the first time, in the Republic's Third Civil War. The two men in question were none other than Cn. Pompeius 'Magnus' (Pompey the Great) and C. Iulius Caesar. Having fought each other by proxy for over a year the two generals finally met in battle at the Epirote city of Dyrrhachium (modern Durres in Albania).

The outcome was clear at the time: Caesar was defeated by Pompeius and had his army routed, and was lucky to escape with his life. Appian best sums this up with the statement *'they fought one great battle in which Pompeius defeated Caesar in the most brilliant manner and pursued his men in headlong flight to his camp and took many of his standards'*. Thus, in the first major clash between these two legendary rivals, Pompeius defeated Caesar.

Yet, subsequent events – namely the Battle of Pharsalus the following month, and Caesar's own attempts to write the history of the campaign – have obscured this defeat and relegated it to its modern status of a minor reversal before the main event. This work seeks to reverse this process, overcome the Caesarian propaganda, both ancient and modern, and restore the battle to its rightful place in the history of the civil wars; namely a Caesarian defeat, and one that clearly highlighted both the defects in Caesar's own generalship, namely a rashness on the battlefield, and the abilities of Pompeius.

Even without the final outcome, the battle itself is a most noteworthy one, with this clash not being a 'traditional' open battle between two Roman armies but taking the form of a months' long siege and counter siege between two armies that had both dug in on the Bay of Dyrrhachium and were conducting an ancient form of trench warfare. The battle itself was the result of a month-long period of manoeuvre and counter manoeuvre in Epirus and Illyria between the two generals, with Caesar eager to give battle and Pompeius preferring to wait until he judged the time to be right.

This process neatly encapsulates the whole preceding eighteen months of campaigning which had begun when Caesar had been manipulated into famously crossing the Rubicon and confirming his status as an enemy of the Senate and People of Rome. The campaigns that followed highlighted the two totally opposing styles of Rome's two leading generals – slow and calculating versus bold and impetuous – and completely showcased each man's talents and flaws in one conflict, with control of the Republic going to the winner.

This work will not only analyse the background to and tactics of the Battle of Dyrrhachium itself but will seek to place it in its proper context as the culmination of an eighteen-month series of tactical campaigns across the Western Mediterranean between the Caesarian and Pompeian armies, ranging from Spain to Africa to the Adriatic. It will also showcase the differing tactical abilities of the two commanders in their battle for supremacy in the Roman Republic.

Ultimately, this work will attempt to restore the Battle of Dyrrhachium to its proper place as one of the four key battles between the Caesarian and Pompeian forces and forms the first in a series of four books analysing each key battle in this struggle for supremacy.

Timeline

Pre-Third Civil War (70–49 BC)

91–70: First Roman Civil War

72 Pompeius victorious in Spain against Perperna
71 Crassus victorious in Italy against Spartacus
   Formation of the Duumvirate between Pompeius & Crassus
70 Consulship of Pompeius & Crassus – Constitutional Reforms Enacted
68 Pompeius is appointed to command the war against the Mediterranean Pirates
67 Pompeius is appointed to command the Eastern War against Armenia & Pontus
65 Crassus as Censor tries to annex Egypt
64 Pompeius annexes the remnants of the Seleucid Empire

63–62: Second Civil War

62 Pompeius returns to Italy
60 Reformation of the Duumvirate between Pompeius and Crassus
59 Consulship of Caesar – passes Duumvirates' legislation
   Marriage of Pompeius to Caesar's daughter
58 Tribunate of Clodius – street violence in Rome
   Caesar launches the Romano-Gallic War
57 Tribunate of Milo – street violence escalates
56 Pompeius is appointed to a command to take charge of Rome's grain supply
   Conference at Luca – Formation of the Triumvirate
55 Consulships of Pompeius & Crassus
54 Crassus takes command of the First Romano-Parthian War
53 Battle of Carrhae – Crassus defeated by the Parthian Surenas. Killed in the retreat.
   Violence in Rome prevents Curule elections

Timeline

The Early Years of the Third Roman Civil War (49 BC)

49 **Italian Campaign**
Caesar invades Italy
Battle of Corfinium
Pompeius withdraws to Brundisium
Battle of Brundisium
Pompeius withdraws across the Adriatic to Dyrrhachium
Caesar seizes Rome

49 **Gallic Campaign**
Caesarian forces lay siege of Massilia
Pompeian-Massilian fleet defeated twice off Massilia
Massilia surrenders to Caesar after the Fall of Spain

49 **Spanish Campaign**
Caesarian forces cross Pyrenees and invade Pompeian Spain
Battles of Ilerda – Caesar trapped in a deteriorating position
Caesar convinces more Spanish tribes to back him
Pompeian forces decide to retreat and are routed by Caesar
Caesar wins over the Pompeian army and allies in Southern Spain

49 **Western Mediterranean Campaigns**
Pompeian forces evacuate Sardinia after a local revolt, Caesarian forces occupy island
Caesarian forces invade Sicily, Cato withdraws without a fight
Caesarian forces invade Roman Africa
Siege of Pompeian held Utica
Caesarian victory at the Battle of Utica

Timeline

The Early Years of the
Third Roman Civil War (48 BC)

48 **Epirote / Illyrian Campaign**
Caesar crosses the Adriatic and lands in Epirus, Pompeius moves to intercept
Pompeian Fleet cuts Caesar off, skirmishes between Pompeius and Caesar
Pompeian attack on Brundisium
Political disorder in Italy
Antonius crosses the Adriatic with Caesarian reinforcements
Caesar marches on the city of Dyrrhachium, Pompeius follows
Caesar lays siege to Pompeius' army in the Bay of Dyrrhachium
Failed Caesarian attack on the city of Dyrrhachium
Failed Pompeian attack on Caesar's siege lines
Pompeius breaks through Caesar's sieges lines to the south of the Bay
Caesar launches a counterattack on the Pompeian bridgehead
Pompeius launches a counterattack on Caesar
Caesarian army is routed, with thousands of casualties
Caesar regroups his army, breaks off the siege and marches inland to Macedonia, to join up with his other forces and face Metellus Scipio
Pompeius follows

48 **Greek / Macedonian / Thessalian campaigns**
Metellus Scipio crosses into Thessaly from Asia Minor
Caesarian forces spread into Greece, Thessaly, and Macedonia
Metellus Scipio defeats Caesarian forces in Thessaly, but is slowed down
Caesarian forces defeated in Macedonia by Faustus Sulla
Caesarian forces secure Aetolia and Acarnania
Pompeian forces fall back to the Isthmus of Corinth

Notes on Roman Names

All Roman names in the following text will be given in their traditional form, including the abbreviated first name. Below is a list of the Roman first names referred to in the text and their abbreviations.

A.	Aulus
Ap.	Appius
C.	Caius
Cn.	Cnaeus
D.	Decimus
K.	Kaeso
L.	Lucius
M.	Marcus
Mam.	Mamercus
P.	Publius
Q.	Quintus
Ser.	Servius
Sex.	Sextus
Sp.	Spurius
T.	Titus
Ti.	Tiberius

Section I

Rome, Blood & Politics:
The Background to the Third Civil War

Chapter One

Out of the Ashes, The Rise & Fall of the New Republic (70–49 BC)

Before we can move onto any study of the campaigns between Pompeius and Caesar, it is first necessary to understand how this Third Civil War had arisen and the respective position of the two rival commanders. I have already written about this at some length,[1] but what follows is a summary of the key events that helped to shape this conflict, set between the crucial years of 70 and 50 BC, from the creation of a New Republic in the aftermath of the First Civil War down to the outbreak of this war.

Rome 71 BC – The Rivals

In the summer of 71 BC, two great battle-hardened armies stood at the gates of Rome, their commanders being the two foremost generals of their generation, but both steeped in the blood of their fellow Romans. Given that the Republic had been locked in a civil war that had lasted for two decades and had seen Rome attacked on no less than four separate occasions,[2] one of which ended in a bloody sacking (87 BC), then the Senate and People had much to be worried about.[3]

Furthermore, just eleven years earlier both men had been part of the army that had marched victoriously into Rome having just defeated their enemies at the very gates of Rome itself (the Battle of Colline Gate) as commanders in the victorious army of the Roman general/warlord Sulla, another conquest that brought about bloodletting. However, despite this common background, tensions between the two armies and within Rome itself were high, due to the fact that both men were rivals, and both had just completed victorious campaigns over significant enemies and were thus expecting the rewards of these victories and further advancements.

The two men in question were none other than Cn. Pompeius 'Magnus' and M. Licinius Crassus, the two rising (or 'upstart', depending on your perspective) stars of the Sullan faction which had captured Rome in 82 BC, and which by 71 BC now had control of the whole of Rome's empire. Furthermore, both men had just completed campaigns that secured the Sullan faction's control of the Republic.

In truth however neither man's victories had been as glorious as their propaganda made out. Pompeius had not been able to defeat the leading Cinnan faction general Sertorius but had been able to wear him out over several years, backed as he was by the full might of Rome's empire. However, a final victory for Pompeius over the man who had a claim to be another of his generation's greatest generals had been denied him when his opponent was murdered by a disloyal deputy, who proved to be no match for either his former leader or Pompeius himself.

Equally Crassus' masterplan to be the man who saved the Republic from the seemingly existential threat posed by the slave army roaming Italy and its near mythical leader Spartacus, had been thwarted to a degree by the arrival of Pompeius in Italy and his destruction of a smaller slave force, followed by his attempt to usurp bragging rights on having defeated the slaves. Thus, for both men, the arrival of a victorious rival seriously endangered their own respective plans for progression.

The Breakdown of the Republican system (133–71 BC)

The previous sixty years of Roman politics had seen an increasing breakdown of the cohesion of the Republic's ruling oligarchy, which for more than two hundred years (since the ending of the Struggle of the Orders – 367 BC) had successfully managed political tensions within the oligarchy, whilst militarily dominating the Mediterranean. This cohesion was based on a total control of the key pillars of the Republic, both political and military, combined with a policy of open admission to new families into the oligarchy (providing they had sufficient money or talent) and an ever-shifting pattern of alliances within the families that made up the oligarchy, all ensuring that no one person would gain dominance. This can be best seen in the so called 'Fall of the Scipios' (184 BC), when the other families combined to bring down Rome's most successful general P. Scipio Africanus, the conqueror of Hannibal.

Yet, as the years passed and Rome's military successes multiplied, along with a burgeoning empire (and its resultant wealth), this successful system came under increasing strain, in particular from Scipio Africanus' grandson (P. Cornelius Scipio Aemilianus). This strain culminated in 133 BC and the Tribunate of one of Scipio's supporters Ti. Sempronius Gracchus. Gracchus was not the cause of the shattering of this cohesion but merely a symptom, the roots of which are analysed elsewhere.[4] It was Gracchus' Tribunate and subsequent murder that set the ruling oligarchy on a slide towards its own destruction, albeit one that they could have arrested at any time.

This strain ultimately manifested itself in many ways, the most important being the expansion of the powers of the Tribunate of the Plebs, the widening of the political game the oligarchs played to include other groups of Roman society, from the Equestrian Order of businessmen to the Italian allies, but most importantly in the failure of individuals or factions to back down. One of the strengths of the Roman system lay in its limitation to annual offices, limiting an individual's ability to political power, which in turn led to the political family or faction becoming the mainstay of the Republic. Yet as the years passed, individuals came to find ways to circumnavigate this restriction and refused to see the danger it posed in the eyes of their enemies. Thus if an individual could not be restrained by the normal levers of the Republican system, their opponents turned to the one weapon they had left: violence.

Though this cycle could have been averted, the whole process began to feed upon itself, with each example offering a lesson in the risks and the rewards of this behaviour. After two cycles of bloodshed, both involving the Gracchi brothers (Tiberius in 133 BC and Caius in 121 BC) the Republic had seemingly pulled back from the brink, but an unfortunate combination of two failing wars, one on Rome's northern European borders and one in North Africa,[5] were exploited by a junior Roman nobleman of Italian descent, who manipulated the situation for extraordinary personal advancement and in doing so laid a clear blueprint for others to follow. The man was C. Marius (Cos. 107, 105–100, 87 BC) and by 100 BC he was the most dominant politician and general Rome had seen. Yet, at the height of his power, Marius still realised that he needed to work within the Republican system and as the military crisis eased, so did the political ones.

Another decade ensued but the period 91–88 BC saw a twin collapse of the Republican system, with the Roman factions inflaming Rome's

Italian allies into open civil war and the personal breach between none other than Marius and his protégé, Sulla, which saw the pupil out-escalate the master when Sulla responded to Marius' political treachery (the usurpation of a prestigious eastern command) by marching his army on Rome itself (along with his Consular colleague) and using it to 'restore order', which in Sulla's eyes meant the deaths of his old mentor and his closest allies. The subsequent events that followed saw a total collapse of the Republic system and its empire, and the rise of Roman warlords, each controlling a separate part of it, men such as Marius, Cinna, Carbo and the Valerii Flacci.[6]

By 81 BC a victorious Sulla had united the majority of Rome's empire, thanks to military victories, political bloodshed and, in one case, negotiation with a rival warlord.[7] In place of a failing old system Sulla created a new Republic, one that saw his faction in total control, and the elimination of his enemies in a vicious bout of political bloodletting, aided by his lieutenants Pompeius and Crassus (and many others). All power was to be centralised in the Sullan Senate and the evolution of the previous fifty years was to be artificially turned back, by legislation.

Yet at the heart of this new Republic we can detect the Sullan belief that legislation would not be enough, and that one individual needed to moderate the Republican system; a Princeps if you will, and thus Sulla resigned his formal powers (the office of the Dictator) and 'retired' into private life, intervening where necessary in the running of the New Republic, backed up by a distribution of Sullan veterans throughout Italy.[8] Yet this 'Sullan Principate' was to be a short lived one, with Sulla dying of disease in 78 BC, and within a year, without this moderating hand, the Republic collapsed into civil war once more, with another attack on Rome (foiled on this occasion) and the resurgence of the defeated factions in Spain under a new commander.

The Rise of The Duumvirate and the End of the First Civil War (71–70 BC)

Thus, it was against this backdrop of collapse, bloodshed, and attempted recovery that Pompeius and Crassus sat facing each other at the gates of Rome. Yet these two men were not only the finest generals of their generation but were the finest political operators of their generation and both realised that further bloodshed was not necessary. Just as Marius and Sulla had built on the examples of those that came before them, so did Pompeius and Crassus. With the Republic having been subject to twenty years of bloody civil warfare, the very threat of further civil bloodletting was enough to scare their opponents into caving in. In fact Pompeius had used this tactic on serval previous occasions, including against Sulla himself.

We can see that both men realised that if they pooled their resources and formed a (temporary) alliance then they could (temporarily) take over the Republic. It was at this point that the Duumvirate of Pompeius and Crassus was formed, with both men being elected to the Consulship for 70 BC and using it to effectively overthrow the Sullan Republic and institute a new (Pompeian-Crassan) one in its place.[9]

Central to the vision that Pompeius and Crassus had for their 'new' Republic, was to effectively abolish the Sullan 'reforms' to the constitution and restore key 'Republican' foundations; most notably surrounding the offices of the Tribunate of the Plebs and the Censorship, both of which were recognised as too valuable a tool to be discarded. The prohibition of the Tribunate, especially its power of legislation, had naturally become a cause of political dissatisfaction in Rome itself,[10] yet the restoration of its powers once again created a fresh source of instability in the Republic. Pompeius and Crassus would have been all too aware of this, but both would have realised that the Tribunate was too useful a political weapon not to be used, especially when faced with a Senate dominated by the Sullan faction, many of whom would now be opponents of the two men.

To combat their opponents in the Senate, the two men restored the office of Censor and it is no surprise that the two men elected (both allies of at least Crassus) immediately set about purging the Senate, with sixty-four Senators removed, all of whom we can be sure were opponents of Pompeius and Crassus. Again, to serve as a counterbalance, the two men had a Tribune (Plautius) pass a law (*plebiscitum*) awarding an amnesty and restoring citizenship to the surviving followers of the Sertorian and Lepidian factions. Not only did this amnesty create a clear signal that the era of persecuting your opponents was over but signalled a clear end to the Civil War. It also had the added bonus of allowing opponents of the ruling Sullan faction back into Rome. In the field of judicial reform they had a Praetor (L. Aurelius Cotta) pass a law reforming the juries of the law courts, again another bone of contention and source of political tension in the pre-civil war Republic.

Thus, in political terms, this New Republic looked in from like the pre-civil war one, but in practice removed power from the Sullan dominated Senate. We hear little of Sullan faction opposition to these reforms, but then our sources are poor for this period. Furthermore, one of the leading Sullans, L. Licinius Lucullus, one of Sulla's closest supporters, was away from Rome, fighting a Great Eastern War against the Pontic and Armenian Empires, along with many of his supporters.[11] Perhaps the most notable leading Sullan was Q. Caecilius Metellus Pius, an old rival of Pompeius from Spain, but we hear nothing about his position in this period.

Yet it is clear that some key elements of the Sullan Republic survived, most notably the Sulla prohibition on the descendants of the proscribed and the Sullan veteran settlement programme in Italy and abroad. Thus those cities and peoples that had lost land to Sulla and had seen Sullan colonies placed on their doorstep remained disaffected. Ironically the same could have been said for many of the Sullan veterans themselves, many of whom seem to have not prospered on these new veteran colonies.

Thus the total effects of these reforms were to undermine the control of the Sullan faction, and the Senate in general, of the levers of power in the Republic and to reintroduce many elements which, as everyone would have been aware, would create greater instability. However at the heart of these reforms lay the best interests of the two leading men, Pompeius and Crassus, who moulded the Republic in their image.

Instability & Opportunity (69–64 BC)

What is interesting to consider is what these two oligarchs thought about this potential instability and whether they could control it? Certainly both men wished to become the most dominant figures in this new Republic, but neither was in position to do so yet, as they were equals.

With their year in office ending, both men stepped down from the Consulship and seemingly dissolved their partnership. Yet interestingly neither took a Proconsular command or seemingly left Rome for the next two years. Whilst this anomaly has puzzled many, the most logical conclusion is that both men took the opportunity to ensure that their reforms were not overturned by their opponents and thus became (temporary) guardians of this 'New Republic'. Certainly, they could ensure compliant Consuls were elected in their place, but only by their actual presence, along with their accompanying patronage (in both the Senate and Assemblies) could they block any attempts by their opponents to undo their changes.

Of the two men, it is clear that their short-term interests would soon diverge, with Pompeius eager to take up military command and Crassus preferring to remain in Rome, both pursing their own paths to becoming the leading man of the Republic. Even with his enforced stay in Rome, we can detect Pompeius' hand in the lessening of Lucullus' command in the east. By 67 BC, Pompeius made his move with a two-pronged approach, both spearheaded by a Tribune (A. Gabinius), using the office's newly restored powers of legislation. One law removed the majority of Lucullus' commands and handed them onto a third party (the Consul M. Acilius Glabrio), clearly a Pompeian caretaker, whilst the second law created the greatest command the Republic had seen, against an unusual foe: the pirates of the Mediterranean.

The Mediterranean had always seen a level of piracy, but the chaos of the civil war period, and the Pontic invasion and temporary annexation of the Eastern Republic, along with the annexation of the Seleucid Empire by Tigranes II of Armenia had seen piracy escalate from a nuisance to a positive danger, with attacks on Roman cities now a regular occurrence. More importantly, the Roman food supply was based on imports from overseas, such as Egypt and the Crimea and as Roman history showed, a hungry voting populace soon became a political issue. Yet for Pompeius, the worse the situation, the greater the opportunity.

Thus was born the proposal to grant Pompeius an extraordinary military command, over the entire Mediterranean for three years, with this command extending for fifty miles inland from any Mediterranean coastline and powers superior to any other Roman commander. The practical effect therefore, was to make Pompeius temporary commander in chief of the Roman world.

Thus once again the Tribunate had been deployed by a leading oligarch to further his own political ends. Naturally, Gabinius' law was opposed, and history repeated itself when Gabinius overcame the veto of a colleague by threatening to depose him (as had happened in 133 BC). Furthermore, one of Gabinius' colleagues (C. Cornelius) also used his Tribunate to pass reform measures leading to violence in the Assembly. So we can see that within just three years of the Tribunate being restored, the office was again at the centre of controversial political reform and violence, spurred on by one of the architects of the New Republic.

Naturally enough Pompeius set about this in a methodical way, carving up the Mediterranean into various zones, each with its own deputy commander, organising simultaneous attacks on the various pirate groups, accompanied by land attacks on their bases. In what was not a coincidence Pompeius chose to base himself in Cilicia, not only the heart of the pirate fleets, but a short march away from the campaigns being fought in the Great Eastern War, which had again swung back to Asia Minor.[12] Within a year Pompeius had defeated the majority of the pirate fleets and in 66 BC, usurpingly, another Tribune (C. Manilius) passed a law (*plebiscitum*) giving Pompeius command of the Eastern War against the Pontic and Armenian Empires, the greatest eastern war Rome had fought to date.

The year 66 BC also saw two other noteworthy political issues arise, both centring on elections. The first was Crassus' move to have himself elected as one of the Censors for 65 BC, again an office he helped to reinstate. Normally an honorific position, Crassus would use the office (in 65 BC) in an extraordinary way, proposing the annexation of Egypt, the last remnant of the once great Ptolemaic Empire and the Mediterranean's richest region, thus empire by administration. This bold move was blocked by Crassus' Censorial colleague (Q. Lutatius Catulus) and presumably Pompeius' supporters under instruction.

The second election was that of the Consuls for 65 BC, which saw a joint ticket elected, the mainstay of which was a certain P. Cornelius Sulla, the nephew of the former Dictator, and head of the Sullan family, if not the faction (Sulla's own son Faustus, still being a young man). Thus we can see the rise of the Sullan faction, which had been under additional pressures (see below) in domestic politics. Yet in an extraordinary move both Sulla and his colleague P. Autronius Paetus were prosecuted (successfully) for bribery, a common practice at Roman elections and stripped of their offices before they could take power. It can be no coincidence that this was the only such occurrence of this drastic step happening despite bribery being commonplace. One of their accusers (and successor) was none other than L. Aurelius Cotta, who had been Praetor in 70 BC under Pompeius and Crassus, the clear conclusion being that the anti-Sullan factions combined to keep the new head of the Sullan family from power in Rome.

The year 65 BC also saw another office holder of note, the Aedileship of a certain C. Iulius Caesar. At this point Caesar was more known for his anti-Sullan heritage and stance.[13] He was a nephew by marriage to C. Marius himself and had once been married to the daughter of another civil war warlord, L. Cornelius Cinna, who had ruled Rome between 87 and 84 BC. Given the slaughter of the Marian family during the civil war,[14] Caesar was de-facto inheritor of Marius' legacy and used his Aedileship to restore monuments to the man himself, in a very visible challenge to the Sullan faction.

More tangible challenges came in the form of prosecutions of members of the Sullan faction for actions committed under Sulla, which had all been legitimised by Sulla as Dictator and upheld by the Sullan Senate. Yet by 66 BC, we hear of the first prosecution of a Sullan supporter (Lucullus' brother) for acts committed under Sulla and although he was acquitted more prosecutions followed, particularly of the lesser members of the faction. There were two headline grabbing cases in 64 BC, one prosecuted by none other than Caesar himself, the other by another up-and-coming Roman aristocrat, M. Porcius Cato (the Younger). Thus, whilst only junior members of the faction were under threat, this, combined with the loss of the Consulships of 65 BC, would have made many believe that their faction was clearly under attack and in decline.

The Reaction and the Second Civil War (63–62 BC)

As with physics, every political action can lead to an opposite rection and matters came to a head in 63 BC, when the New Republic faced its biggest challenge to date in what we must describe as a Second Civil War. The events of this year have traditionally been referred to as the Catilinarian Conspiracy, a serious misnomer, which dated from the words of one of the participants, none other than M. Tullius Cicero, and have been perpetuated ever since. The events of this year have been obscured by the focus on one individual, which allowed the Senatorial oligarchy to ignore the deeper routed causes of this civil conflict. There were two distinct groupings of Sullan supporters, those amongst the oligcrahy and those settled veterans and by 63 BC both were upset with the position they found themselves in. The Sullan faction within the oligarchy found themselves shut out from office, with another Sullan candidate (M. Sergius Catilina) failing to be elected for 63 BC, and resentful at their colleagues. At the same time, many of the Sullan veterans had found themselves impoverished, having failed at their farms and angry that their plight was being ignored, despite them having been the backbone of their faction's success in the First Civil War.

This was an unfortunate turn of events as it provided dissatisfied veterans with a political leadership and provided dissatisfied politicians with armed supporters. The final turning point (unsurprisingly) was centred once again on the proposed Tribunician legislation. We find several measures being put forward, some attacking the Sulla's legacy but others supporting them:

> For the Tribunes united with Antonius, the Consul, who was very much like themselves in character, and one of them supported for office the sons of those exiled by Sulla, while a second wished to grant to Publius Paetus and to Cornelius Sulla, who had been convicted with him, the right to be members of the Senate and to hold office; another made a motion for a cancelling of debts, and yet another for allotments of land to be made both in Italy and in the subject territory.[15]

Thus, on the pro-Sullan side we see proposals to redeem P. Cornelius Sulla and admit him back into the Senate and some measure of the alleviation of debts and a further distribution of land, all of which would have benefited the veterans. By the end of the year the failure of these proposals seems to have cemented in the minds of a portion of the Sullan faction and a portion of the Sullan veterans that they were not benefiting from the new Republican order and in fact were being downtrodden. When combined with an attitude of being the victors of the civil war, this brought the feeling of anger to the surface and thus was born a plot to restore what they saw as their rightful place in both Roman politics and Roman society.

This 'conspiracy' seems to have centred on two men, each leading one of the two Sullan groupings (political and veteran). Respectively they were P. Cornelius Lentulus Sura and C. Manlius. It is Lentulus we know the most about. He hailed from one of Rome's oldest and most noble families; the Cornelii and his branch of the family had been one of the most successful. In his youth Lentulus had followed Sulla and held the Questorship in 81 BC when Sulla himself was Consul.

Thus, Lentulus was part of the Sullan oligarchy which ruled the Republic in the aftermath of Sulla's victory, a point confirmed when he was elected to the Consulship of 71 BC. Yet he had clearly fallen foul of either Pompeius or Crassus as he was immediately purged from the Senate during the Censorship of 70 BC. It is unsurprising that a man of his character took this humiliation lying down and he stood for and won one of the Praetorships for 63 BC and thus was a serving Praetor this year. Furthermore, it is reported, though with what accuracy we will never know, that Lentulus firmly believed in the purported Sibylline Oracle:

> *These recited forged oracles in verse purporting to come from the Sibylline books, which set forth that three Cornelii were fated to be monarchs in Rome, two of whom had already fulfilled their destiny, namely, Cinna and Sulla, and that now to him, the third and remaining Cornelius, the heavenly powers were come with a proffer of the monarchy, which he must by all means accept, and not ruin his opportunities by delay.*[16]

C. Manlius by contrast was a different character altogether. We are told that he was a Sullan veteran, who became leader of the Sullan veterans in Etruria. The main surviving sources portray him as nothing more than an agent of Catilina, yet he seems to have been a power in his own right.

The plan seems to have been a coordinated action, with an army of Sullan veterans rising up in Italy, with no Roman army to oppose them, whilst the Sullan faction in Rome staged a coup and seized the Consulships for the following year (62 BC). The faction would then pass legislation ensuring their own position and that of their followers, thus turning the clock back to the Sullan Republic. What they thought they would do with regards to both Pompeius (overseas with a massive army), or Crassus is not known. Subsequent sources have accused both men of either allowing the plot to develop or even encouraging it, so they could reap personal benefit from it. At this time Pompeius had successfully won the Great Eastern War and was preparing to return to Rome which may well have spurred the plotters into action (before he and his army returned to Italy).

Yet on this occasion, the 'New' Republic held firm; neither of these two leaders being of the calibre of the warlords of the First Civil War and certainly not a 'new Sulla'. The plot in Rome was inevitably betrayed and arrests were made, followed swiftly by extra-judicial murders, most notably that of Lentulus. The Sullan veteran army was never of a significant size and the Senate was able to muster sufficient forces both to challenge the main force and to put down various small rebellions that broke out in Italy. The military campaign came to a head in January of 62 BC at the Battle of Pistoria, the only large-scale battle of the Second Civil War and the destruction of the army of Manlius, followed by his death (and that of Catilina).

The Golden Years of the 'New' Republic (62–60 BC)

As always, the events of 63–62 BC can be viewed in many ways. On the one hand, it did not say much about the stability of the 'New' Republic that it collapsed into a Second Civil War, just seven years after the end of the First. On the other hand, however, it did say a lot about the ability of the 'New' Republic that it was able to emerge from this Civil War unscathed. In many ways the 'New' Republic faced its first serious challenge and passed with flying colours. Disaffected elements of the oligarchy and the veteran community had attempted to use armed force to overthrow the state and set themselves up as the new ruling order (or re-establish the old ruling order) and had been defeated and without recourse to relying on the leading oligarchs.

Pompeius naturally attempted to use this crisis to his advantage and (unsurprisingly) a Tribune (Q. Caecilius Metellus Nepos) was instructed to place a bill before the people recalling Pompeius from the East to take charge of the Civil War and a second to allow him to be elected Consul in absentia. However, again the strength of the Republic was shown in the fact that both motions were defeated when the rest of the oligarchy (presumably including Crassus) combined in opposition. However, again there were shades of the Old Republic when there were attempts to override Tribunician vetoes and armed force was used in the Forum, resulting in bloodshed. Once again, the Senate exhorted the Consuls to defend the city, though the *senatus consultum ultimum* does not seem to have been deployed. The upshot was that both motions were defeated and

Metellus fled the city (thus breaking his oath of office) and made his way to Pompeius in the East.

With Pompeius in the East, one would have thought that the time was right for Crassus to rise up again and ensure he was called on to defend the Republic, as he had been in 72 BC when another hostile army was in Italy (that of Spartacus). However, again the Senatorial oligarchy closed ranks, and were happy that the elected Consuls could deal with the threat, especially given the rumours circulating in Rome that Crassus himself was behind the conspiracy (rumours that were impossible to verify then, let alone now).

Thus the Senatorial oligarchy not only combined to defeat the rogue Sullan faction and its veteran army but were also able to stop both Crassus and Pompeius from exploiting the crisis for their own ends. If anything, this challenge seems to have emboldened the New Republic in particular to face down the two 'founders', an attitude that continued in the subsequent years which we now may well view as a golden period for the New Republican system.

Having spent the rest of the year putting down pockets of Sullan and local resistance, not to mention an associated rebellion in Gaul (from the Ambrones), the next clear challenge for the Republic was the return of Pompeius. Having taken command of the war against the Pontic and Armenian Empires, Pompeius had turned the campaign into a war of eastern conquest, establishing the Republic as the premier power of the Near and Middle East.[17] The Pontic and Armenian Empires were dismantled, the remnants of the Seleucid Empire were annexed, and the Ptolemaic and Parthian Empires humbled. Rome now controlled a swath of territory from the Crimea to the Red Sea, and from the Mediterranean to the Caspian, either by direct control of territory, or through vassal states. All of which allowed Pompeius to be labelled as a 'new Alexander'.[18]

The clear danger lay in this 'new Alexander' returning to Italy and finding himself once more a regular Senator, with both commands having expired. Having been thwarted in his plan to take a leading role in the Second Civil War, Pompeius saw no need to rush back to Italy and took his time in finishing his eastern settlement (which would need official ratification by the Senate and People) and made a leisurely trip back to Italy via Greece. Upon arrival he indulged in the grand gesture of disbanding his army, to prove he was no Sulla, and celebrating lavish

Triumphs. Without an emergency, he saw no need to hold the Consulship himself but ensured one of his officers was elected for next year along with the usual selection of lesser offices for his supporters (Praetors, Aediles and most importantly Tribunes).

If Pompeius imagined that his eastern successes would allow him to dominate the 'New' Republic as *primus inter pares* (first amongst equals) he found himself sorely mistaken. Here again we can see the underlying strength of the Republican oligarchy which reacted to this 'new Alexander', exactly as their ancestors had done over a hundred years earlier, with Scipio Africanus. Amongst the squabbling and political infighting of the various Senatorial families and factions there was only one thing that would bring them together, the thought of one of them gaining a lasting dominance over them all. Thus Pompeius found himself frustrated politically and could not even get his eastern settlement, which cemented an unprecedented Roman domination over the Near East ratified.[19] Even worse, he could not secure a land distribution programme for his discharged veterans. This continued into the year 60 BC, even though, again, Pompeius had a subordinate as a Consul (L. Afranius).[20]

The Counter Reaction and the Restoration of the Duumvirate (59 BC)

It is standard political axiom that every political action has a counter reaction and when the pendulum swings in one direction it brings it nearer to the opposite and the same was true at this stage of the Republic. The irony cannot have been lost on Pompeius that he had wanted to restore a stable Republic and done so only too well, and this very stability now thwarted his own ambitions, and was beginning to affect his powerbase (both in the east and even closer to home with his veterans). With his eastern settlement still not ratified and his power and prestige in the east waning and the comparisons to Alexander now looking hollow, and with his veterans restless, Pompeius clearly realised that it would be he who would have to undermine the stability of this 'New' Republic to save his own position.

We will never know how much of the opposition to Pompeius came from Crassus himself, as his very power lay in unseen political dealings behind closed doors, dealings that contemporary and especially later historians could only speculate over. Certainly, Crassus would never allow

Pompeius to be '*primus inter pares*', a role that he wanted for himself. We will never know which of the two men made the first move to rekindle the Duumvirate of 71–70 BC that had so dominated Rome, though given the position it is more likely that it was Pompeius. Nor do we know what Crassus' price was; the most common explanation involving Equestrian tax firms, seems a poor reason.[21]

As with much of Roman political history, we do not know the details, but we do know the outcome; Pompeius and Crassus renewed their temporary alliance after a gap of over a decade and installed one of Crassus' agents, none other than C. Iulius Caesar as one of the Consuls, though interestingly despite all their power they could not secure both. Caesar and Pompeius were further bound together by the marriage of Caesar's daughter Iulia to Pompeius.[22] As well as securing a Consulship, the three men also seem to have agreed that they would use all methods available to push through their legislation and overcome any legitimate obstacles. Thus the two 'founders' of the New Republic agreed to temporarily attack their own creation and hope that the damage was not too great.

The year of Caesar's Consulship (59 BC) saw all the fault lines of the Republican system brought back into sharp focus. Instead of powerful oligarchs using the Tribunate as their weapon they now used the Consulship, backed up by the Tribunate. Legitimate attempts at opposition by Caesar's colleague (L. Calpurnius Bibulus) were overturned or simply ignored as was Tribunician opposition. In a blueprint set under Marius, violence was used to drive their opponents away from the Assembly so there would be no opposition present at the vote, a simple but theoretically valid tactic.

Thus the Duumvirate (and their agent) drove through an agrarian law providing land for Pompeius' veterans, ratified his eastern settlement and even garnered favour with the Equestrian business cartels by amending an unwise tax collection contract they had entered into. They even found time to ratify the rule of Ptolemy XII in Egypt (for a sizable donation) another piece of business left over from Pompeius eastern campaigns.[23]

Once more, neither Pompeius nor Crassus chose to take up an overseas command, again to ensure they remained in Rome to oversee their legislation and also perhaps as there were no attractive commands immediately available, though a move against the Parthian Empire was an obvious possibility for the future. They did however create an extraordinary command for their agent Caesar; a five year command in Cisalpine Gaul, Transalpine Gaul and Illyria, perhaps not coincidentally the provinces nearest to Italy. Where the impetus for this campaign came from, we will never know. Certainly, Caesar wanted to establish his name as a military commander and this was the best available threat of conflict, with the east having been pacified and there being nothing of note in Africa. It would also allow Caesar to once again tap into the legacy of his uncle, the great Marius, whose greatest campaigns had been against the Germanic and Gallic tribes who had migrated towards Italy.

Nevertheless, we must not overestimate the significance of this command. Gaul had always been considered a backwater for military campaigning that lacked the prestige of an eastern command. For all Rome's domination of the Mediterranean and now the Near East, centuries of fighting had only established Roman control of the southern Gallic coastline, to secure the land route to Spain. A longer campaign in Gaul was probably considered folly and it is highly unlikely that anyone (but Caesar) took seriously the notion of conquering Gaul.

Nevertheless Caesar had his reward, and the Duumvirate got rid of him into the Gallic wilderness for up to five years (if he survived that long). There was also the outside possibility that Crassus may have harboured of the political usefulness of having an agent/ally in charge of the military of Rome's nearest provinces (Italy not being allowed to have armed forces present).

The final act of the Duumvirate was of course to secure sufficient magistracies for the forthcoming year (58 BC) for their supporters, as a matter of course and to secure their legislation. Another Pompeian commander (A. Gabinius) was elected Consul and an aspiring young Roman nobleman was elected to the Tribunate having taken the extraordinary (and Duumvirally supported) step of renouncing his Patrician status and becoming Plebeian (and thus eligible for election to the Tribunate); his name was P. Clodius (Claudius) Pulcher.[24] With their business concluded and with Caesar departing, Pompeius and Crassus broke up their Duumvirate and went their separate ways once more to continue their respective political and military schemes.

The Descent of the New Republic (58–56 BC)

Unfortunately for Pompeius and Crassus (at least in the short term) the forces they had unleashed in 59 BC proved unwilling to be put back in the bottle. In particular these came to be represented by none other than their agent in the Tribunate, Clodius, who let loose his own programme of legislative reforms backed up by the full armoury of dubious political tactics to push it through the Assembly, including armed gangs. Highlights of this programme were the annexation of Cyprus, another piece of the eastern jigsaw missing from Pompeius' settlement, Gabinius securing command in Syria, putting a Pompeian agent in charge of the eastern legions, the actual banishment of Cicero (for murdering the Sullan conspirators in 63 BC) and the effective exiling of Cato (to oversee the annexation of Cyprus).[25]

Clearly revelling in the power of his office, as the year passed, Clodius broke free of the patronage binds that tied him to Pompeius and turned both his legislation and his armed supporters against him; whether this was at the behest of Crassus is not known, but was always a distinct possibility. Naturally enough Pompeius was not going to take this lying down, and so turned to a new agent, T. Annius Milo, for whom he arranged election as one of the Tribunes for 57 BC. Milo was also supported to form his own street gangs who then fought fire with fire and met Clodius' men in open battle across the streets of Rome. We will never know for certain whether Clodius was his own man or Crassus' agent, or even a mixture of both.[26]

What we do know is that the Republic was plunged into bloody chaos with the Tribunician college split between allies of Milo (and Pompeius) and allies of Clodius (and possibly Crassus) (with a 5:2 split in favour of Milo, with three unknowns).[27] Whilst the civil war crisis of 63–62 BC had been graver, the Senatorial oligarchy had pulled together and deployed its military resources well, an option that was not available here. Thus, whilst Rome was dominating the Mediterranean and Gaul militarily, it could not control the streets of Rome itself.

Whilst Pompeius' actions had initially been in response to those of Clodius (and possibly Crassus), he would have soon realised that these events would work in his favour. Whilst he clearly had a duty as both a member of the ruling oligarchy and one of the 'founders' of the current Republic, to safeguard the new Republic and restore peace, the longer the chaos continued the more opportunities it presented. Before the year (57 BC) was out, we can clearly see Pompeius grasping one such opportunity.

On top of the political clashes and street violence, Rome was suffering from shortage of grain, due to poor harvests. As we have said above, food shortages amongst the (voting) populace of Rome soon became a major political issue. At one point the Urban Praetor (L. Caecilius Rufus) was attacked by a mob in broad daylight over the issue (whether sponsored or spontaneous is not known). As we have seen (above), some ten years earlier when Rome's grain supplies were threatened by the pirates of the Mediterranean, Pompeius skilfully exploited the crisis and gained an extraordinary command. Thus in 57 BC, history repeated itself and a newly recalled Cicero (thanks to the efforts of Pompeius' Tribunes) proposed to the Senate another empire wide command for Pompeius to secure Rome's grain supply. This was shortly augmented by a proposal passed by one of Pompeius' Tribunes. Although at first glance such a command seemed beneath Rome's greatest general, the details dispel that notion:

> *The Consuls drew up a law by which complete control over the corn-supply for five years throughout the whole world was given to Pompeius. A second law was drawn up by Messius, granting him power over all money, and adding a fleet and army, and an imperium in the provinces superior to that of their Governors.*[28]

Thus Pompeius once more held a superior imperium, with troops and a fleet, all of which could be held whilst he remained in Rome, at the centre of the political storm. By 56 BC, Clodius was back in elected office (the Aedileship) and Milo was a private citizen, though both still with command of their armed street gangs and thus, with their political roles reversed, continued their clashes. Milo unsurprisingly found himself being prosecuted by Clodius and his new ally C. Porcius Cato. According to Cicero, Pompeius himself believed that Crassus was the mastermind behind both men which, if this were the case, meant that the 'New' Republics' two founders were tearing it apart:

> *For Pompeius understands what is going on, and imparts to me that plots are being formed against his life, that Caius Cato is being supported by Crassus, that money is being supplied to Clodius, that both are backed by Crassus.*[29]

The Rise & Fall of The Triumviral Republic (55 – 53 BC)

It was against this backdrop of political chaos, food shortages and street violence that a momentous event occurred in the history of the Republic. Again we will never know the precise details behind the event, but we do know the outcome. The event in question was a meeting between Rome's two most powerful men and a third party. The two men were obviously Pompeius and Crassus and the third party was none other than C. Iulius Caesar himself.

Whilst Pompeius and Crassus had been fighting each other by proxy with the Republic descending into chaos, Caesar had unexpectedly proved to be a general of some note. In 59 BC most members of the oligarchy would have considered a five-year command in Gaul a vanity project that would either end in failure or death. Yet Caesar turned this notion on its head and by mid-56 BC had defeated the largest Gallic tribes of central and northern Gaul and pushed onto the Channel. Naturally, Caesar had not been slow to trumpet his triumphs at Rome. Yet in contrast, Caesar's political position was far weaker than his military one. His command had been for five years, which would take him to until the end of 54 BC. However, he had already realised that to turn these victories into a lasting settlement would take time and political support in Rome, of which he had little. Furthermore, despite his victories, the People could easily pass a law transferring the command to another now that it had proved to be successful.

Thus Caesar reached out to his two former patrons and offered to broker a meeting, at Luca (modern Lucca) in what is now Tuscany, but what was then the southernmost point of Cisalpine Gaul. This meant that it was close enough to Rome, but still within Caesar's provinces, which he could not leave. There the infamous Conference of Luca took place, which saw Pompeius, Crassus and Caesar and their supporters, including over two hundred Senators, meet in private.[30] Though Pompeius had benefited from the chaos with his extraordinary command, both men would have realised that they had battled themselves into a stalemate through their proxies.

Furthermore, two excellent opportunities had arisen in the field of foreign affairs, both in the East, and both of which could be exploited, but only if the political chaos in Rome abated. The Eastern War left only two 'empires' standing, the Ptolemaic and the Parthian. By mid-56 BC, both had collapsed into political chaos and seen their rulers overthrown. In Egypt, Ptolemy XII's unpopular rule had been made worse by the tax he needed to extract from his people to pay both the Duumvirs for their recognition in 59 BC and had seen him ousted in a popular and palace coup. He was thus resident in Rome, with the Senate looking for a commander to 'restore' him and thereby regain access to Egypt's wealth. Further to the east, the ruler of the Parthian Empire, Phraates III, who had done so much to restore his empire's fortunes after a generation long civil war,[31] had himself been overthrown (and murdered) in a palace coup, by his sons, who had then promptly fallen out and collapsed the empire into another civil war. Thus both 'empires' were ripe for Roman exploitation.

It was perhaps these opportunities that focused the minds of Pompeius and Crassus who realised that once again it was perhaps time to put aside their rivalry and combine forces once more. Such a 'burying of the hatchet' would also bring about peace in Rome, a dividend they could both reap politically. However, the era of the Duumvirate was over and, in its place, stood a Triumvirate, with the admission of a junior member: Caesar himself. Here we must be careful not to overinflate Caesar's position. Though his military reputation was growing, as was his reputation amongst the People of Rome, this did not translate into political power, as we can see through his need for his former patrons. Key to Caesar's admission into this cabal was his battle-hardened legions in Gaul (including Northern Italy, a few days march way from Rome). This was something that the other two men could not yet compete with. If admitted these men were a powerful asset and threat, if omitted they were a serious danger. Thus was borne the First Triumvirate.

We need to be clear that the formation of this cabal and its subsequent seizure of power was effectively a coup, albeit one with a great deal of popularity. Though they used constitutional means, these three men seized control of the Republic and in particular its military assets and control of its foreign policy. Thus Pompeius and Crassus steamrollered their way to a second joint Consulship (in 55 BC), ensuring that their supporters filled the magistracies, and that their enemies were excluded. In Rome itself, Clodius and Milo were told to bring an end to the violence and political paralysis. In terms of foreign affairs, an ambitious programme of imperial expansion was envisaged with a war against the

Parthian Empire duly agreed; this was ostensibly to place a puppet ruler (Mithradates IV) on the throne, probably supported by the annexation of Mesopotamia, along with the restoration of another Triumviral puppet (Ptolemy XII) back on the Egyptian throne. Gaul was to be turned into a Roman province and Caesar was given another five years in command and the political support he needed in Rome.

Given so much support from within the Senatorial oligarchy itself, and from the People, and backed up by Caesar's legions, their opponents within the Senate could do little in practice to oppose them. Again, the Triumvirs did not obviously seize power and no new constitutional arrangement were made. The two men laid down their offices at the end of the year, but unlike in 69 BC, both men enhanced the control of the Triumvirate by effectively seizing control of the bulk of Rome's military forces. On top of Caesar's control of both Gallic provinces and Illyria, Pompeius was 'awarded' control of both Spanish provinces and their armed forces, crucially along with the right to rule through legates, meaning he could stay in Rome. The military forces of the East were awarded to Crassus, who took command of the First Romano-Parthian War. Aside from Macedonia, this put the bulk of Rome' s armed forces under Triumviral control.

With Caesar campaigning in Gaul and Crassus in the East, control of Rome fell to Pompeius himself who was finally able to take the role of informal Princeps that he had sought for so long, albeit with two absent partners. It is interesting to speculate what form this Triumviral oversight of the Republic would have taken. Unfortunately the experiment was cut short in 53 BC in the foothills of Mesopotamia when Crassus, having been unexpectedly defeated in battle (Carrhae) with a Parthian army, was subsequently murdered during the retreat.[32] Thus the Triumvirate, only formed in 56 BC, became a Duumvirate once again, but not one of long standing allies and equals, but an uneven one between a patron and his former agent.

The Rise of the Pompeian Republic (53–51 BC)

Crassus' defeat and death had been totally unexpected and threw the Senatorial oligarchy into a panic. Rome's eastern armies had been defeated by a supposedly weaker foe and their eastern empire now lay virtually defenceless. Yet for Pompeius himself this Roman defeat was a gift from the gods. His long-term rival and sometimes partner had been killed, and thus removed from the political scene. Furthermore, Crassus' eldest son (Publius) had been killed along with him (in the Battle itself), leaving just one son (Marcus) alive, but in Gaul serving under Caesar. Thus the whole of Crassus' political network in Rome was now lacking a patron and available for Pompeius to sweep up. Caesar himself was campaigning on the Rhine and thus in no position to interfere with Pompeius' plan.

Despite (or perhaps because of) Pompeius' presence in Rome, the old political feuds and accompanying street fighting, which had marred the years before the Triumvirs seized power, resurfaced, again focussed on the clashes between Milo and Clodius. With Pompeius' backing, Milo, although elected Tribune a year after Clodius, had actually overtaken him in the *cursus honorum* and was now a candidate for the Consulship, whilst Clodius was only a candidate for the Praetorship. Naturally both men's supporters attempted to prevent the other from being elected, with the result that the elections were consistently disputed and delayed. Furthermore, the conflict was not solely related to these two rivals but also saw other ambitious politicians such as P. Plautius Hypsaeus and Q. Caecilius Metellus Scipio using similar methods in their bids for the Consulship.

Even before news of Crassus' death reached Rome, with Crassus campaigning on the Euphrates and Caesar on the Rhine, we can clearly see who was benefiting from this chaos; none other than Pompeius, with many in Rome (though not amongst Pompeius' opponents) clamouring for someone to be appointed to stop the political chaos and violence. Thus we should not be surprised to find that two Tribunes proposed that Pompeius be appointed Dictator, with a brief to bringing an end to this chaos.

It is unlikely that this proposal was a serious one on Pompeius' part; but a piece of stage-managed political theatre; firstly to raise the issue in people's minds that a strong man was required to quell the violence (and with it the association that the Republic was proving ungovernable without a strong figure at its head) and secondly to allow Pompeius to reject the offer of a Dictatorship, with all the connotations of Sulla, and bloody repression, that came with it. Thus the proposals came to nought, the elections failed to be held and Rome entered a new year without any elected officials other than the Plebeian ones (Tribunes and Aediles). At the centre of this chaos stood Pompeius, who still held his imperium to alleviate the grain issue, which he had done with his usual efficiency and with enough veterans in Italy to re-arm and impose peace if he wished, but sitting there watching the situation worsen.

If those in Rome thought the situation was bad at the end of 53 BC, matters deteriorated even further in January of 52 BC when Clodius was murdered in a fight between his and Milo's armed retinue outside of Rome. Clodius' funeral turned into a riot when his supporters burnt down the Temple being used as the Senate House. With no senior magistrates to call on, the Senate passed the *senatus consultum ultimum* (SCU), last used during the Second Civil War in 63 BC, and ordered their most senior available general (Pompeius) to levy troops in Italy, from his own settled veterans.

Caesar, clearly worried about events at Rome and his own position, had returned to Italy (Cisalpine Gaul) for the winter but could not intervene physically as he could not leave his province. Furthermore, Caesar's whole conquest of Gaul was thrown into doubt as the year progressed when the Gallic chieftain Vercingetorix rose up in revolt plunging Gaul into chaos and forcing Caesar to spend the year campaigning rather than monitoring, or trying to influence, events in Rome.

For Pompeius though, being named by the Senate as the man to restore peace in Rome was not enough. Gathering the Senate in his newly built theatre outside the sacred boundaries of Rome, and under armed guard (for their own 'protection') he pushed for a formalisation of his new position. With few options even his opponents caved in and agreed to nominate Pompeius as (temporary) 'Head of the Republic'. With all sides wishing to avoid the bloody connotations of the office of Dictator, a new constitutional solution was found: Pompeius would be sole Consul, with the right to eventually nominate his colleague.[33] Thus the New Republic admitted that its stability rested on having a supreme figure ensuring peace and an end to political violence.

Having been appointed as the (temporary) 'Princeps' of the New Republic, Pompeius set about his task with ruthless efficiency. Pompeius used two main tools to restore peace in Rome, establishing new courts to try political violence and corruption with a swifter judicial process, all backed up by his armed veterans on the streets of Rome. Thus a judicial purge of the troublemakers was enacted, with the highest profile casualty being none other than Milo himself, who realised too late that he was to be a sacrifice to Pompeius' ascent to power.[34] Again, learning from the past issues with judicial murders under both Sulla (82–81 BC) and Cicero (63 BC), these men were exiled from Rome and Italy but not put to death, thus enhancing Pompeius' reputation for clemency and a wise 'rule'.

One of the key troublemakers of 53 BC had been none other than Q. Caecilius Metellus Scipio, scion of Rome's two most noble houses. Not only was Metellus too senior to exile, but one of his daughters was the widow of Publicus Crassus (Crassus' eldest son). Thus Pompeius offered Metellus an alliance, with Pompeius marrying Metellus' daughter (himself being a widower since the death of Caesar's daughter in 54 BC) and Metellus becoming the new Consul, technically ending Pompeius' sole rule.

Having ended the crisis and restored peace, Pompeius again confounded his critics and stepped down from his Consulship at the end of the year, ensuring compliant successors were elected. He further strengthened his position by gaining a further five-year extension to his command in the Two Spains. Thus, with legions at his command (albeit in Spain), veterans available in Italy and a Rome purged of the worst offenders (except those closely connected to him), Pompeius sat back and took up the role of quiet arbiter for the Republic.

The Pompeian Masterplan (50–49 BC)

Though Pompeius had been called on to restore peace to the Republic, which he had done, he would have realised that his victory was fleeting. He had cured the very crisis that had propelled him to his leading role in the Republic. He was certainly *primus inter pares* but his opponents amongst the Senatorial oligarchy would never allow him the position he sought (the role of Princeps).[35] Furthermore, he still had a rival and a heavily armed one at that, Caesar in Gaul. News of the major Gallic rebellion against Caesar's attempted conquests must have come as a gift from the gods for Pompeius, much as the news of the Battle of Carrhae had. At a stroke, Caesar's attention had been pulled away from matters in Rome and his reputation as the 'Conqueror of Gaul' thrown into serious question. He must have secretly hoped that history would repeat itself and that a foreign foe would remove his rival for him, as had happened with Crassus. By late 52 BC, however, news of Caesar's great victory at the Battle of Alesia reached Rome, securing Rome's/Caesar's conquest of Gaul, and foreshadowing the return of a problem.

Clearly in Pompeius' eyes, Caesar was an upstart, one with no background comparable to his and someone that had even been his agent. It is equally clear that Caesar saw himself as a rival to Pompeius and filling the vacant role that Crassus' death had created. The two men could have settled down to a partnership like the Duumvirate, especially given Caesar's desire for further campaigns and Pompeius' desire to rule in Rome, or they could have clashed like so many First Civil War oligarchs had.

Yet we can perhaps detect the signs of a 'Pompeian masterplan' here. Whilst he could 'cut a deal' with Caesar and ensure his swift departure for the East and command of the First Romano-Parthian War (hoping for a similar outcome as Carrhae), Caesar perhaps represented something else; an opportunity. Pompeius had grown up as a young man during the First Civil War and had built a career on the implied threat of further civil war. Political chaos and street violence in Rome had briefly propelled him to the role of Princeps; to make this role permanent would need a far greater challenge to the Republic. Whilst he had supporters in the magistracies, support amongst the Equestrians and the People, his veterans and even a good portion of the Senatorial oligarchy, as it stood, he would forever face opposition from the majority of the oligarchy who would sooner or later transfer their (temporary) support to Caesar as a counterweight. Furthermore, if Caesar was to prove as successful in the East as he had been in Gaul then he would eclipse Pompeius.

Yet the events of 52 BC had proved that when faced with a threat to their position the rest of the oligarchy had no option but to turn to him. Thus if the threat increased then so would the 'payoff'. It is with this framework in mind that perhaps we can view the events that led to the rupture between Pompeius and Caesar during 50 BC.

The key issue was Caesar's Gallic command, renewed in 55 BC for five years and so coming to an end.[36] For Caesar, the Gallic revolt had undone much of his conquests of the previous six years but by late 52 and into 51 Roman control had been restored. Gaul would now become a Roman province, but would Caesar reap the political rewards? In the years he had been fighting in Gaul, Crassus had been killed and Pompeius had cemented his position as being the most dominant force in the Republic. That being the case, would he brook a rival? Caesar always seemed to have been far more comfortable in the field than in Rome and a second Consulship would simply be the stepping stone for a Proconsular command, the greatest of which would be the Romano-Parthian War, currently in abeyance following Cassius' successful defence of Syria from a Parthian invasion. Such a war would allow him to become the new Alexander and march Roman armies across the Middle East and up to India.

Clearly, given the respective roles the two men wished to play, there was an opportunity for a deal to be done. However, as we can see from the events that followed, it is apparent that Pompeius was in no mood to compromise. Having grown up in the First Civil War, both men had seen first-hand what happened when a senior Roman commander (Sulla) had his command (for an Eastern War) snatched from him by his former mentor (Marius). Just under forty years later another senior Roman commander (a nephew of Marius) again faced having his current command snatched off him by a former mentor (and Sulla's former son in law).

In the first case, it is obvious that Marius had no idea that Sulla would march his army on Rome. In this latest case however, with the first example to call upon, it is clear that Pompeius must have considered this a possibility. Unfortunately for the stability of the New Republic, and the lives of many of its citizens, it seems equally clear that Pompeius did not consider this to be a bad outcome, but quite the reverse. If Caesar were forced into attacking his own state to defend his position, then he could be painted as a new Sulla, which would have been more than little ironic given Caesar's family ties and opposition to the latter. If Caesar became this clear threat to the very existence of the Republic, not helped by the latter's autocratic tendencies, then Pompeius could be the saviour of the Republic and, having defeated Caesar, adopt the position he had sought all his life as Princeps of the New Republic.

Thus in late 50 and early January 49 BC, Pompeius abandoned the art of compromise, which he had utilised since the beginning of the New Republic and goaded his opponent into either backing down or declaring civil war. Had Caesar backed down then Pompeius' masterplan would have been foiled as perhaps he could see himself being goaded into attacking Rome. However, had he backed down, he would have perhaps destroyed his own position forever enhancing Pompeius' further, and though there many have been fresh opportunities he would have to fight for them as a private citizen.

Throughout late 50 BC, the various attempts at compromise, from both the Caesarian faction and the worried neutrals were rebuffed. Matters came to a head in early January 49 BC; the newly elected Consuls were both supporters of Pompeius, though Caesar did have two supporters elected as Tribunes (M. Antonius and Q. Cassius Longinus). They naturally tried to veto any anti-Caesarian motions but were overruled and fled Rome to join Caesar. The Senate voted to pass the *senatus consultum ultimum* and Caesar was ordered to disband his legions or face being an 'enemy of the state'.

Having been given the direct ultimatum, Caesar could not realistically back down, and it must be argued that Pompeius did not want him to. Though Caesar declared civil war by marching his legions into Italy proper in January 49 BC (across the River Rubicon) triggering the Third Roman Civil War, it seems most likely that it was Pompeius who orchestrated it, thus ending the New Republic he had helped to create. In its place would be a Pompeian Republic, as long as he ensured he defeated Caesar on the battlefield.

Section II

The Battle for the Western Republic: The Early Campaigns of Third Civil War (49 BC)

Chapter Two

The Italian Campaign –
The Phoney War (49 BC)

C aesar's invasion of Italy proper, with the crossing of the Rubicon has become one of the most famous acts of the ancient world, along with his supposed utterance of *alea jacta est* (let the die be cast).[1] This, along with the fact that his subsequent career is so well known, makes it problematic to examine this act dispassionately. Yet this is just what we must attempt if we are to understand this crucial first year of the war.

Aims and Tactics – Caesar

Ultimately, we must ask ourselves what were Caesar's aims in this invasion of Italy?[2] Here we can see the problem of having a primary source written by the main protagonist. Caesar wrote his account after his victory and to subsequently justify his actions. It does not give us an insight into his thinking. Having been declared an 'enemy of the state', Caesar clearly had little option but to turn to the military or face complete ruin, and possibly death at the hands of his political enemies. He would have been struck by the parallels of recent history, with his (at the time) more famous uncle both being declared an enemy of the state and being undone by the swift use of military force (by his former protege L. Cornelius Sulla).

Nevertheless, having taken the military option, there is still the question of how he was going to use his forces, and again recent history had provided two clear possibilities. On the one hand there were the examples of Sulla and Marius in 88 and 87 BC respectively, both of whom used their armies to storm Rome, accompanied by increasing bloodshed. On the other hand there were the examples of Caesar's two former colleagues, Pompeius and Crassus, who in 71 BC, camped their armies under the walls of Rome and intimidated the Senate into granting their political demands.

It must be noted that in each of the previous occasions however, the general had access to far greater forces than Caesar had at his disposal. Nevertheless, Caesar was faced with two options; all out civil war or negotiated settlement. In truth Caesar had probably intended to keep his options open, with a negotiated settlement, which removed his 'enemy' status and restored his political position as his preferred option, backed up by a willingness to go to an all-out civil war if it proved necessary.[3]

Key to this strategy was the need to reach Rome before Pompeius could mobilise his forces and thus secure the levers of power, in particular the Assemblies and have the SCU overturned, and his commands restored by popular legislation. To those ends he soon met up with the two exiled Tribunes (Antonius and Cassius) who would be crucial in passing such legislation. Thus the key to Caesar's strategy was speed, hence the use of a small number of troops ('three hundred horsemen and five thousand legionaries'[4]). If he reached Rome quickly then it would hardly likely to be defended and would fall without a fight.

The second key factor in Caesar's strategy was to ensure that he could remove any obstacles in his pathway, most notably the scattering of forces that lay between him and Rome, primarily those of his replacement in the Gallic command, L. Domitius Ahenobarbus. The obvious unknown factor in this whole plan however was his opponent, Cn. Pompeius 'Magnus'; would he fight or negotiate? Though Caesar had worked both for (in 60–59 BC) and with Pompeius (56–55 BC), the two men had never been close. Having been politically outmanoeuvred by Pompeius, Caesar must have hoped that his invasion of Italy and threat to Rome itself would bring Pompeius to the negotiating table. Nevertheless, if the worse was to happen and Pompeius would not negotiate, then Caesar's clear final objective would have been to seize Pompeius himself. Caesar would have been all too aware of the example set in 88 BC (during the First Civil War) when Sulla seized military control of Rome but allowed his opponent, Marius (Caesar's uncle) to escape and rally support, thus transforming a coup into a long civil war. Thus, as well as seizing Rome, Caesar needed to seize Pompeius himself, if he were to stop this attempted coup turning into another full-scale civil war.

Aims and Tactics – Pompeius

We find ourselves in an even worse position when it comes to using the sources to ascertain Pompeius' tactics in this situation. Not only do we not have an equivalent account written by the man himself, but all the histories we do have, have been written in hindsight, with the ultimate result of this conflict known and therefore seemingly predestined. Nevertheless, we need to put aside all thoughts of a predetermined outcome and try to view the situation as it was at the time and using what we know about Pompeius' history and tactical acumen.

Having totally outmanoeuvred Caesar politically, he would have known that there were only two outcomes; Caesar capitulating or Caesar following the now well-trodden path of using his military to restore his position. Having employed Caesar as his agent (in 60–59 BC) and then acknowledging him as an ally (56 BC), Pompeius would have been well aware of which route Caesar would likely have taken. Yet Pompeius now found himself a victim of his own success. Having successfully forced Caesar into adopting the role of 'enemy of the state', a man who would attack his own city, and thus underline his own role, as the 'saviour of the Republic', he now actually had to stop Caesar.

In theory, Pompeius had more forces in Italy than Caesar's invasion force but there were two key problems, both of which Pompeius understood all too well. We know Pompeius was given command of the two legions in Italy, which were destined for reinforcing the eastern provinces against Parthian attack.[5] Yet these were in southern Italy and not between Rome and Caesar. Furthermore, these legions had been transferred from Caesar's command and so it could be argued that there may have been a suspicion as to their loyalty at the time, though they later proved their worth to Pompeius in Greece. Additional forces were being raised (as detailed below) which soon again outnumbered the Caesarian forces but even if veterans were being recruited these were freshly levied legions and no match for battle-hardened veterans, even if they wanted to get involved in a civil war campaign (which as events showed many did not).

Furthermore, although it fits the adventurous image of Caesar invading Italy with just one legion, he had in fact already ordered two others from Transalpine Gaul to cross the Alps and rendezvous with him in northern Italy. Another three legions were left in Narbonensis (Southern) Gaul, to protect Caesar's flanks from any advance from Spain of Pompeius' legions.

Thus, whilst the key to Caesar's strategy was speed, the opposite was true for Pompeius; he needed to slow Caesar down and buy himself time to mobilise his forces, to defend the Republic. As Dio points out, Pompeius had access to quality intelligence on Caesar's military aims in this campaign, from one of his own senior legates, T. Labienus, who defected from Caesar when the latter invaded Italy.[6]

> *Pompeius, perceiving this, became afraid, especially when he learned all his rival's intentions from Labienus; for this officer had abandoned Caesar and deserted to the other side, and he announced all Caesar's secrets to Pompeius.*[7]

Thus, Pompeius could be left in no doubt as to Caesar's aims and his tactics. Armed with this knowledge, in theory Pompeius had two options, to fight or negotiate. Throughout his political career he had always opted for the latter, whether dealing with Sulla, the Senate or Crassus. Yet those tactics belonged to the earlier phase of his career. In the meantime he had consolidated his position as the most powerful man in the Republic, exemplified by his sole Consulship in 52 BC. In his own mind, Pompeius now had no equals, with both his old mentor (Sulla) and old partner (Crassus) dead. Caesar's invasion of Italy had given him the crowning crisis of his career: saving Rome from another Sulla, the irony of which could not have been lost on him.

To cement his position as 'Princeps' of the Republic he needed this crisis and he needed to ensure that it did not end in a shabby negotiation, but in a career-defining victory. Pompeius would have clearly realised that there would have been many in the Senate hoping to settle this matter by negotiation, to avoid the horrors of the First Civil War, yet for him to succeed there could be no successful negotiation, though he certainly needed to be seen to be 'making an effort'.

Therefore, rather than defuse the situation, he needed it to escalate and become a full-blown civil war. Thus, we have the paradox that the aggressor was probably hoping for a negotiated settlement, but the defender aiming for a full-scale civil war. In military terms Pompeius would have readily realised that Caesar had the short-term military advantage, with his forces closer to Rome and that Rome had never successfully been defended, especially in a civil war (his own father being involved in the siege of 87 BC). That left only two strategies: delay Caesar long enough to mobilise his forces in Spain, or draw Caesar further on, by surrendering Rome. Furthermore if the Senate could be persuaded to flee Rome, rather than stay and negotiate, it would only enhance Caesar's disgrace and his own elevation.

Thus, Pompeius seems to have entered into a cynical calculation. Certainly losing control of Rome, and the Electoral and Legislative Assemblies was a clear risk and would allow Caesar to overturn his official 'enemy' status and become the 'official' voice of Rome. Yet as Pompeius himself had seen first-hand, Rome changed hands frequently in the 80s BC during the First Civil War; what mattered was victory in the war, not the battle. Sulla had turned from Consul to enemy and back again several times before he was ultimately elected as Dictator and 'saviour' of Rome. With Caesar dead in battle, Pompeius could then re-enter Rome as the hero and Princeps of the Republic. This would no doubt be followed by a programme of propaganda, including the writing of histories, blackening Caesar as the renegade who betrayed his country, much as happened with Catilina, no doubt eagerly supported (in public at least) by Cicero.

Thus Pompeius prepared a two-stage strategy, slow Caesar down, but ultimately evacuate Rome and Italy if necessary, to ensure a wider victory in the war which must now inevitably follow. Most interestingly, we have corroboration of this theory from Cicero. Whereas his early letters had Pompeius abandoning Rome and then Italy for fear of Caesar's' armies, he later confessed that it was part of a wider, and preconceived, Pompeian 'masterplan':

> *Nor, indeed, did he* [Pompeius] *abandon the city because he was unable to protect it, nor Italy because he was driven from it; but his idea from the first was to stir up every land and sea, to rouse foreign princes, to bring barbarous tribes in arms into Italy, to collect the most formidable armies possible. For some time past a kind of royalty like Sulla's has been the object in view, and this is the eager desire of many who are with him. Do you suppose that some understanding between the two, some bargain has been impossible? Today it is still possible. But the object of neither is our happiness: both want to be kings.*[8]
>
> *This 'disgraceful' measure our friend Cnaeus* [Pompeius] *had contemplated two years ago.*[9]

This is a point that Syme himself found convincing:

> *Furthermore, the whole strategy of Pompeius, distasteful if not inexplicable to many of his allies and associates, was simple and masterly. Caesar would be entrapped in Italy or entangled in a guerrilla war in Spain, while Pompeius returned to victory with all the armies and fleets of the eastern lands. Pompeius should have won.*[10]

The Campaign in Italy (49 BC) – Caesar's Advance and the Failure of Negotiations

Having briefly covered both protagonist's objectives, we can now turn to the conflict itself. Caesar himself provides a commentary on the progression of his campaign (see Map 2). Having crossed the Rubicon, with one legion (the Thirteenth), Caesar made for the Roman colony of Ariminum (modern Rimini) on the Adriatic coast. The city fell without a fight and Caesar made it his temporary headquarters, which is where the two Tribunes (M. Antonius and Q. Cassius Longinus) met him. From there he issued orders to the rest of his army in Gaul, to cross the border and join him.

It was here that two emissaries of the Senate reached him, one a Praetor named L. Roscius Fabatus, the other a kinsman named L. Iulius Caesar, and a man whose father was one of Caesar's legates.[11] Though sent on the Senate's orders, L. Caesar apparently came with a personal message from Pompeius, stating that he was not Caesar's enemy:

> *He says that Pompeius wishes to be cleared of reproach in the eyes of Caesar, who should not construe as an affront to himself what he had done for the sake of the state. He had always placed the interests of the Republic before private claims. Caesar, too, considering his high position, should give up for the benefit of the state his partisan zeal and passion, nor be so bitterly angry with his enemies as to injure the commonwealth in the hope that he is injuring them. He adds a few other remarks of this kind, at the same time making excuses for Pompeius.*[12]

Even if we accept Caesar's account that Pompeius sent this message, we can question the sincerity behind. Pompeius had manoeuvred Caesar into this position and had nothing to gain from a de-escalation. The proposal from the Senate was the same one that had been issued at the height of the political crisis, namely that both men should disband their armies and return to civilian status. Caesar dispatched both men with a counter proposal:

> Let Pompeius go to his own provinces, let us disband our armies, let everyone in Italy lay down his arms, let fear be banished from the state, let free elections and the whole control of the Republic be handed over to the Senate and the Roman People. That this may be done more easily and on definite terms and be ratified by an oath, let Pompeius himself come nearer or allow me to approach him. In this way a conference will settle all disputes.[13]

Thus Caesar would disband his army and be allowed to return to Rome with an unblemished character and be allowed to stand for the Consulship of 48 BC, whilst Pompeius would be exiled from Rome to Spain and his legions, with the details thrashed out at a face-to-face conference (such as the infamous one at Luca). Naturally, there was no chance that Pompeius would accept these proposals, but Caesar was probably aiming over the head of Pompeius to those in the Senate and People who were not strong supporters of Pompeius and wanted peace. Interestingly the emissaries found Pompeius and the two Consuls (C. Claudius Marcellus & L. Cornelius Lentulus Crus) at Capua, not Rome, showing that Pompeius had no wish to conduct negotiations under the eyes and ears of the Senate and the People. Unsurprisingly, in these circumstances, a more strongly worded counter demand was made in the name of the Senate and People:

> the main purport of which was that Caesar should return to Gaul, quit Ariminum and disband his forces; if he did this, Pompeius would go to the Spanish provinces. Meanwhile until a pledge was given that Caesar would carry out his promise, the Consuls and Pompeius would not interrupt their levies.[14]

With neither man willing to exile themselves back to their province and thus abandon the centre of political power in Rome, this offer effectively ended negotiations and again shows that Pompeius had no interest in diffusing the situation nor in buying himself more time. Had he truly wanted to buy more time to organise an effective military response in Italy, then he could have organised such a conference and even made an effort at considering the proposals. Having received Pompeius and the

Consuls' demand, Caesar clearly understood that Pompeius had no wish to end this conflict with a negotiated settlement and that it was war. Having achieved a clarity in his objectives Caesar then set forth with his military campaigns.

Caesar's Advance Through Northern Italy

With the die having now been truly cast, Caesar set out to secure the immediate region, recruit additional forces and clear any opposition forces from his march on Rome itself. To those ends, M. Antonius, despite holding the Tribunate, which precluded holding a military command, was given command of a force and dispatched southwards to Arretium (modern Arezzo – see Map 2) whilst Caesar himself, after holding a local conscription, garrisoned the cities of Pisaurum (Pesaro), Fanum (Fano), and Ancona, each with one cohort. We hear of no opposition to these forces, which given the nature of the civil war was not surprising, with most locals caring neither one way or the other, only trying to ensure that they avoided any damage or injuries to the populace.

The nearest forces to oppose Caesar's advance were stationed in the city of Iguvium (Gubbio) in Umbria. Here was stationed a Propraetor, Q. Minucius Thermus, who commanded five cohorts (roughly two and a half thousand men, depending on their readiness). Caesar dispatched one of his commanders C. Scribonius Curio with only three cohorts, presumably to test the willingness of Thermus to stand and fight. For whatever reason (Caesar states that the city supported him, though most likely they didn't care one way or another) Thermus refused this offer to stand and fight and withdrew from the city, with his forces. Most likely, not being a strong supporter of Pompeius, he calculated that it was better not to take sides, than risk finding himself on the losing one.

Caesar's own narrative informs us that Thermus' men deserted him on the retreat and returned to their homes.[15] We are not told whether these forces had been recently levied, but they too seemingly had no appetite to fight fellow Romans and would rather not take sides. Thus the quality of his troops may well have swayed Thermus' decision. With Curio securing Iguvium, Caesar's advance continued, strengthening his forces by withdrawing the garrisons of the cities named above.

The next city in Caesar's path was the port of Auximum (modern Osimo) in Picenum which seemed to be a centre of Pompeian recruitment, lying in the traditional heartlands of the Pompeian family. Again, having sent Curio to Iguvium and himself moving towards Auximum, Caesar did not take an obvious and immediate route to Rome itself, but was eliminating the centres of opposition that lay in the region. Auximum was held by a P. Attius Varus, with a force of unknown size.

Once more, a similar pattern emerged (if we are to believe Caesar's own narrative) that Varus' forces refused to engage with Caesar, forcing Varus to withdraw rather than fight. On this occasion whilst a number of Varus' men deserted to return home, some joined Caesar (according to his own account[16]). Though there does seem to have been a brief skirmish between Caesar's forces and some of Varus' men, though the numbers involved must have been negligible. Varus himself escaped but remained committed to the Pompeian cause (see Chapter Four).

Again, following Auximum, Caesar chose to subdue the region of Picenum, a long-standing region of Pompeian support rather than strike at Rome. There seem to have been a number of reasons for this. Firstly, it is likely that Caesar wanted the Senate (though not Pompeius) to offer more agreeable terms without the need to attack the city itself. Secondly, he still had too few forces and needed to bolster them with local recruits and fresh supplies. Thirdly, he sems to have believed that he could not afford to leave Pompeian forces in his rear if he did move on Rome and fourthly and finally, he seems to have been awaiting his other legions from Gaul. As Caesar himself notes, it was in Picenum that his Twelfth Legion caught up with him, doubling the size of his army.[17]

Naturally, the towns and cities of the region did not put up a fight and capitulated to avoid destruction. With his forces doubled, Caesar set his sights on the regional capital of Asculum (modern Ascoli Piceno), site of some of the fiercest fighting in the early years of the First Civil War.[18] Asculum was being held by the Pompeian commander P. Cornelius Lentulus Spinther (Cos. 57 BC), with a force of ten cohorts (roughly five thousand men, though still recruiting). Again, rather than stand and fight, Spinther retreated from Asculum towards Corfinium, the stronghold held by L. Domitius Ahenobarbus. Yet again Caesar informs us that the bulk of his forces melted away.

Again, we find another Pompeian commander, and an ex-Consul at that, falling back rather than facing Caesar. In this case, though he had upward of five thousand men at his disposal, the bulk of them seem to have been new recruits (even if many were from the veteran community), and he was still outnumbered, facing two battle hardened veteran legions of Caesar. Thus far, each of the commanders Caesar had faced had only been present on recruitment missions, not with orders to face Caesar and try to slow him down. Not only had Caesar successfully disrupted the Pompeian recruitment process but was developing momentum in his progress throughout North-Eastern Italy. It also showed that the bulk of freshly levied troops had little appetite to fight in a civil war.

Nevertheless, whilst on his retreat (rout), Spinther ran into another Pompeian commander, L. Vibullius Rufus, sent direct from Pompeius himself to verify the recruitment process. Vibullius seems to have restored some order to the retreat and then gathered as many freshly levied forces as he could (Caesar informs us that it was thirteen cohorts, some six to seven thousand men) and marched toward Corfinium to reinforce Domitius Ahenobarbus and inform him of Caesar's approach, now with two legions.

Caesar meanwhile had continued with his capture of the key cities of the region, including Camerinum (modern Camerino) and Firmum (modern Fermo), expelling the Pompeian commander C. Lucilius Hirrus and a Lentulus respectively. Having levied additional forces from those recruited by the Pompeians, Caesar set off to confront Ahenobarbus at Corfinium.

The Siege of Corfinium (49 bc)

The Battle of Corfinium represents the first major conflict of the war.[19] To date, Caesar had only faced either very junior commanders (and one former Consul) who had been in the region on recruitment drives and with no orders, nor sufficient forces, to engage with Caesar. In L. Domitius Ahenobarbus, he faced an equal. Ahenobarbus had long been a political opponent of both Caesar and Pompeius and was the brother in law of M. Porcius Cato. Consul in 54 bc, the Senate had appointed him as the successor to Caesar in the Command of Transalpine Gaul.

Caesar himself tells us that Ahenobarbus had recruited twenty cohorts from the region (roughly ten thousand men) and now had the additional thirteen cohorts (roughly six to seven thousand men) that Vibullius brought with him. Thus Ahenobarbus commanded some sixteen to seventeen thousand men, as opposed to Caesar's ten thousand (at least two legions, plus any local levies) and seems to have outnumbered him. In terms of experience though, the majority of Caesar's legions were battle-hardened after fighting in Gaul for nearly a decade whilst Ahenobarbus, men were fresh recruits (even if there were veterans amongst them).

Ahenobarbus had chosen his regional base well. The city had been the regional capital of the Paeligni tribe of Italy and was a capital for the Italians in the early stages of the First Civil War (91–89 BC). The site was a strong defensible one, approached by a bridge over the Aternus (Aterno) river. The initial clash took place at the bridge over the Aternus river, which Ahenobarbus' men were attempting to demolish:

> *On his arrival there five cohorts dispatched from the town by Domitius [Ahenobarbus] were breaking down the bridge over the river, distant about three miles from the town. A conflict taking place there with Caesar's skirmishers, the Domitian troops were quickly driven from the bridge and withdrew into the town. Caesar, leading his troops across, halted outside the town and pitched camp close to the wall.[20]*

Having lost the initiative, Domitius set himself to defending the city from Caesar, whilst dispatching a message to Pompeius calling for reinforcements:

> *[Domitius sent men] with dispatches to Pompeius in Apulia to beg and beseech him to come to his assistance, pointing out that Caesar could easily be cut off by two armies operating in the narrow passes and so be prevented from foraging. If Pompeius does not do this, Domitius says that he himself and more than thirty cohorts and a great number of Senators and Roman knights will be imperilled.[21]*

Caesar also reports the encouragement Domitius gave to his men:

> *[Domitius] placed engines on the walls and assigned each man a definite duty for the protection of the town. In a speech he promised the troops lands out of his own possessions, four acres apiece, and in like proportion to the centurions and reserves.[22]*

Caesar again seems to have been content to wait, especially as he was expecting further reinforcements from Gaul. To further secure his position he dispatched M. Antonius with five cohorts (roughly two and a half thousand men) to the nearby city of Sulmo (some seven miles away), held by then Pompeian commanders Q. Lucretius Vespillo and C. Attius Paelignus, along with seven cohorts (roughly three and a half thousand men). Again, showing the ineffectiveness of freshly levied men, the town surrendered to Antonius and the seven cohorts were recruited by him. Lucretius and Attius attempted to flee, with Lucretius escaping and Attius being captured and subsequently freed by Caesar. Caesar's position was further strengthened by the arrival of more of his forces from Gaul:

> *Three days after, the Eighth Legion joined him* [Caesar] *and twenty-two cohorts from the new levies in Gaul and about three hundred horsemen from the Noric king.*[23]

Thus Caesar now had three battle hardened legions (upward of fifteen thousand men) along with those new recruits taken from the Pompeian commanders (upward of another ten thousand men) and another ten thousand fresh recruits from Gaul. This comfortably gave Caesar the larger force and one more than sufficient for his campaign. Nevertheless, he could not afford to leave Ahenobarbus at his rear, if he advanced to Rome and thus, he set about besieging Corfinium.

> *On their arrival* [Caesar] *pitched a second camp the other side of the town and put Curio in charge of it. On the subsequent days he set himself to surround the town with an earthwork and redoubts.*[24]

Being outnumbered both in terms of quantity and quality of his forces, Ahenobarbus' plan was seemingly to withstand the siege and thus tie Caesar up until fresh Pompeian forces could arrive from the south. On the face of it this was a sound tactic as it stopped Caesar from advancing on Rome and gave Pompeius more time to levy his forces. Unfortunately for Domitius, he had not understood Pompeius' tactics. Pompeius had neither the forces nor the desire to attack Caesar in northern Italy. He would have been well aware that even if he could match Caesar's numbers then freshly levied troops would be no match for battle hardened veterans.

Furthermore, as detailed above, the crisis was not yet of a sufficient magnitude to suit Pompeius' plan. The crisis had only been in place for a month at most and Rome was not yet threatened. Defeating Caesar now would not bring the ultimate reward which Pompeius desired, to save the Roman state from its enemy; the bogey man which Pompeius had done so much to create. He needed the situation to get much worse before he could reap the rewards. If anything, his plan called for the fall of Corfinium and the defeat of Ahenobarbus. Thus Ahenobarbus was sacrificed for Pompeius' greater good and Pompeius, reply to Ahenobarbus was as follows:

> For Pompeius had sent back word that he would not utterly imperil the whole situation, and that it was not by his advice or consent that Domitius had betaken himself into the town of Corfinium and bade him therefore come to him with all his forces if there should be any opportunity of doing so. This, however, was being rendered impossible by the blockade and investment of the town.[25]

Having been sacrificed by Pompeius, Ahenobarbus publicly stated that Pompeius was on his way to relieve the siege whilst privately making plans to sacrifice his own forces and flee the city. However rumours of Ahenobarbus' plans leaked, and his forces realised that they were being sacrificed and set about their own plot, the upshot of which was the arrest of Ahenobarbus and his surrender, along with that of the city to Caesar. With their forces no longer willing to fight it was left to the next highest-ranking Roman nobleman, none other than P. Cornelius Lentulus Spinther to negotiate the terms of surrender. Having received the due assurances about their personal safety, Spinther surrendered Corfinum.

> As soon as day dawned Caesar ordered all Senators and their sons, Military Tribunes, and Roman knights to be brought before him. There were fifty of them: of the Senatorial order, L. Domitius [Ahenobarbus], P. Lentulus Spinther, L. Caecilius Rufus, Sex. Quintilius Varus the Quaestor, L. Rubrius; also the son of Domitius with many other youths, and a large number of Roman knights and decurions whom Domitius had summoned from the municipal towns.[26]

In a consistent display of public clemency and with an eye to countering Pompeian propaganda that Caesar would be a new Sulla (and slaughter his opponents) Caesar ordered the release of the Senators, including Spinther and Ahenobarbus. However he ensured that the thirty-plus cohorts in Corfinium swore allegiance to him and not Pompeius and the Senate, thus nearly doubling the size of his invasion force. Caesar himself tells us that siege had lasted just seven days.

In many respects, Corfinium met the aims of both Caesar and Pompeius. Caesar had removed the only major obstacle between him and Rome (the Pompeian forces) and had done so without bloodshed and actually added these forces to his own. The road to Rome now lay open. Paradoxically that served Pompeius' purposes as well. With the fall of Corfinium, Caesar's march on Rome was now unstoppable and he now had the crisis he needed to cement his new position. In practical terms he had only lost freshly levied men and unreliable commanders, none of which were necessary for his campaign. He must have believed it was a small price to pay.

The Withdrawal from Rome

The collapse of resistance in Northern and Central Italy had the expected effect in Rome amongst the anti-Caesarian elements of the state; namely panic. However, there were still four theoretical options available, two that involved military force and two that did not. In military terms, the options were that Pompeius would advance from the south and block Caesar's advance on Rome or that Rome itself would have to be reinforced to be defended from a siege. In terms of the first, Pompeius had made it clear that he would not do so. Aside from any political reasons, Caesar had the momentum and battle-hardened forces, and Pompeius was never a general to rush into battle ill prepared. In terms of the second option, everyone would have had in mind the bloody siege of 87 BC, which had proved that Rome could not be defended for long. It had also fallen without a fight in both 88 and 82 BC.

In terms of the non-military options, there were only two: retreat, or stay and come to an accommodation with Caesar. Of all the remaining sources it is Dio that provides the best picture of the fear within the populace of Rome itself, both noble and commoner, and describes the genuine mood that many would have had believing Caesar to be a new Sulla.

A bloodthirsty tyrant at the head of an army of men who had been used to fighting Gauls for the last decade. No doubt many would have played on the myths surrounding the Gallic invasion of Italy in the fourth century (c.390–386 BC) which led to the sack of Rome itself. Here was another army invading from Gaul and naturally this was a view which Pompeius would have encouraged.

Prior to 49 BC, there would have been three rough groupings within the Senate: those who strongly supported Caesar, those who strongly supported Pompeius and those who strongly supported neither. The Caesarians seem to have withdrawn already; now it was the time of the Pompeians and those neutrals who would not tolerate a man marching on his own city. Here it seems that Pompeius' stratagem had paid off, as with Caesar approaching, the majority of the Senatorial oligarchy evacuated Rome, turning even the moderates against Caesar, for this unconscionable act.

When these events were announced at Rome such consternation seized at once on the inhabitants that when the Consul Lentulus had come to open the treasury for the purpose of providing a sum of money for Pompeius in accordance with a decree of the senate, as soon as ever he had opened the inner treasury he fled from the city; for news was falsely brought that Caesar was on the very point of arriving and that his cavalry had already come. Lentulus was followed by his colleague Marcellus and by most of the magistrates. Cn. Pompeius had left the city the day before and was on his way to the legions which he had taken from Caesar and distributed in winter quarters in Apulia. The levying of troops round the city is broken off; no one thinks there is any safety this side of Capua. It was at Capua that they first rally with renewed courage and begin to raise a levy among the colonists who had been planted there under the Julian law, while Lentulus brings the gladiators, whom Caesar kept in a training school there, into the forum and encourages them by the prospect of liberty, gives them horses, and orders them to follow him; but afterwards, on the admonition of his followers, because such a proceeding was censured by the general judgment, he distributes them for safe keeping among his friends in the elites at Capua.[27]

[Pompeius] *issued an edict declaring a state of anarchy, and forsook the city, commanding the senate to follow, and forbidding any one to remain who preferred country and freedom to tyranny.*

Accordingly, the Consuls fled, without even making the sacrifices usual before departure; most of the Senators also fled.[28]

He [Pompeius] *also commanded the whole senate together with the magistrates to accompany him, granting them permission for their absence by a decree, and announcing to them that he would regard anyone who remained behind in exactly the same light as those who were working against him.*[29]

Those Romans well versed in their history would have drawn obvious parallels with the evacuation of Athens in the face of the advance of the Persian armies under the Emperor Xerxes (another 'bloodthirsty tyrant'). Moving aside from the oligarchy, Dio is the only surviving source to address the fears of the majority of the populace, many of whom could not afford to flee their homes and businesses.

The ones left behind were experiencing different, but equally painful emotions. Those who were being sundered from their relatives, being thus deprived of their guardians and quite unable to defend themselves, exposed to the war and about to be in the power of him who should make himself master of the city, not only were distressed themselves by the fear of outrages and of murders, as if these were already taking place, but they also either invoked the same fate against those departing, through anger at being deserted, or, condoning their action because of their necessity, feared that the same fate would befall them.[30]

Thus the Consuls and the majority of the other magistrates evacuated Rome and withdrew to Capua on the western coast of Italy, where Pompeius had already set up a temporary base. This was where the emissaries Caesar and Roscius found them. Having determined not to defend Rome, Pompeius chose not to defend Capua either, having no wish to be hemmed in on the western side of Italy and so transferred his forces to the port of Brundisium (modern Brindisi) on Italy's eastern coast, the main transfer point to Greece.

This was an interesting move given that Pompeius' main legions were to the west in Spain which we would have assumed to have been his destination, to join up with his legions. Furthermore, such a move would have had echoes of the First Civil War, when Spain became the centre of the anti-Sullan forces, under the command of Sertorius, who even set up a rival Senate. Ironically, it was Pompeius (along with Metellus Pius) who had been sent by the Sullan Senate to crush Sertorius. Thus Pompeius was all too aware that he had been able to bottle Sertorius up in Spain and isolate him from the rest of Rome's Mediterranean empire and allies.

Thus, if Pompeius had withdrawn to Spain, he too could have been bottled up by a Caesarian army guarding the Pyrenees, made easier by Caesar having Gaul as a powerbase. Thus the logical choice was to withdraw to Greece, leaving him access to the whole of Rome's eastern empire, the majority of which had been conquered by him a decade earlier.[31] Furthermore, it would mean that he had Caesar surrounded and contained in Italy (along with Gaul) with Pompeian legions to his east and west.

Not only would Caesar be bottled up militarily, but politically as well. As the First Civil War had shown, whichever faction had military control of Rome itself, could pass itself off as the legitimate voice of Rome, with control of the Senate and Electoral and Legislative Assemblies. With Pompeius holding Greece he could cut off the main conduit of transmission of orders from Rome to the rest of the Mediterranean World, thus negating that advantage. Naturally with Caesar holding Gaul and Italy, and Pompeius holding Spain and Greece, the obvious regions to contest would be Sicily and Africa (see Map 3).

The Siege of Brundisium

It is clear that Caesar soon found out that Pompeius had withdrawn from Capua to Brundisium, most likely from various elements of Pompeius' forces that either deserted or had been captured. Pompeius had ordered a general muster of all the forces his officers were levying to meet at Brundisium. Caesar had ordered his cavalry to try to intercept more of the Pompeian officers levying forces in the regions ahead of him and one, under the command of a Vibius Curius, intercepted the forces of P. Rutilius Lupus, one of the Praetors, and again his freshly levied forces deserted to Caesar. They would have informed him of their new muster point. This news would have greatly alarmed Caesar, as the whole point of the march on Rome was to secure both the organs of state and Pompeius himself. If Pompeius and his armies eluded him then Caesar's whole plan of stopping the outbreak of a long and empire wide civil war were ruined.

Thus Caesar changed his plan, abandoned the march on Rome and headed south-eastwards towards Brundisium, hoping to cut Pompeius off, a task made the more difficult by not having naval control of the Adriatic. Interestingly Caesar himself mentions that he dispatched the forces he captured at Corfinium to Sicily to try to secure the island before the Pompeian faction could.[32] Furthermore, Caesar dispatched another important prisoner he had taken to Brundisium, again to offer Pompeius a face-to-face conference at which they could sort out their differences and come to an arrangement (again another method to try to prevent Pompeius from leaving Italy). The downside of this tactic was that it confirmed Caesar himself was making straight for Brundisium and not stopping at Rome:

> *N. Magius of Cremona, Pompeius' chief engineer, is captured on the route and brought back to Caesar, who sends him back to Pompeius with instructions to the effect that, since up to the present no opportunity of a conference has been allowed and he himself is on the way to Brundisium, it is to the interest of the state and the common welfare that he should have a conference with Pompeius.*[33]

Duly forewarned, Pompeius made his plans accordingly and dispatched half of his army (thirty cohorts, roughly fifteen thousand men[34]) across the Adriatic, under the command of the Consuls C. Claudius Marcellus and L. Cornelius Lentulus Crus,[35] whilst he remained where he was with another thirty cohorts. The Pompeian army crossed the Adriatic and landed at the city of Dyrrhachium (modern Durres in Albania), a key Epirote port and the start of the Via Egnatia, the Roman road which cut across Greece and Macedonia. According to Plutarch he also dispatched his father-in-law Q. Caecilius Metellus Pius Scipio Nasica (Cos. 52 BC) and his son Cnaeus to raise a fresh fleet.[36]

Caesar reached Brundisium with six legions, three veteran ones from Gaul and three thrown together from freshly levied recruits in Italy, giving him some thirty thousand men, roughly equal in number to Pompeius, if not superior in quality. The key question is of course why Pompeius stayed to face Caesar? Here there were four possibilities, two political and two military. In terms of the political ones, the first is that he wanted to parlay with Caesar away from the eyes and ears of the bulk of the Senate, who he had shipped off to Epirus. The other possibility is of course, that Pompeius had to be the last to withdraw from Italy to preserve his military reputation – a tactical retreat and not a flight. If he had been first across the Adriatic the many would have wondered. Yet by staying and fighting Caesar, Pompeius was making a statement.

In terms of the military ones, the first is purely practical, namely that he did not have sufficient ships to evacuate his whole army and the number of his ranking passengers in one trip. This is explicitly stated by Dio and seems to be borne out by Pompeius waiting until his fleet returned from disembarking at Dyrrhachium (see below).[37] Nevertheless, he could have chosen to be on the first crossing. The other possibility is that, whilst withdrawing from Italy, he still wanted to keep possession of Brundisium, the largest of the Italian ports on the Adriatic to ensure his control of both the crossing point and the Adriatic in general. Yet given the speed with which Pompeius evacuated the city, this does not seem to have been a long-term military objective.

Thus it seems that Pompeius chose to make a deliberate stand, to bolster his reputation and be seen to be the last man to leave Italy, brought about by his fleet not having sufficient numbers to evacuate his whole army in one go. As it was, with so few forces at his command, Pompeius, military options were limited, so he settled down to defend the city from a Caesarian siege (by land) and awaited the return of his fleet. Pompeius clearly felt comfortable enough being able to defend the city for a short period, especially with control of the Adriatic. We must assume that even if there were not sufficient boats to transport the remaining ten thousand men, there were enough for him and his command staff in the event of an emergency (such as Caesar breaching the city). Thus, the first actual clash between Caesar and Pompeius in the Third Civil War was a siege. Naturally, Caesar provides an excellent description of his own siege efforts:

Where the mouth of the harbour was narrowest, he [Caesar] threw out piers and a dam from the shore on each side because the sea was shallow there. As he proceeded further out, since the mole could not hold together where the water was deeper, he placed two rafts thirty feet square over against the end of the breakwater. He fastened these by four anchors, one at each of the four angles, to prevent them being shifted by the waves. When they were finished and placed in position, he attached in order other rafts of a like size. These he covered with soil and a raised causeway that there might be no obstacle in the way of approach or ingress for the purpose of defence. In front and on each side, he protected them with fascines and screens; on every fourth raft he ran up towers of two stories that he might thus more conveniently defend them from an attack by ships and from fire.

> *To meet this Pompeius fitted out some large merchant-ships which he had seized in the port of Brundisium. On them he erected towers of three stories each, and when, they were equipped with a number of engines and weapons of every kind he brought them up close to Caesar's works so as to break through the rafts and destroy the works. Thus fighting went on every day, each side discharging slings, arrows, and other missiles.[38]*

If nothing else, Caesar had helpfully restored to Pompeius his chief engineer, to oversee the defence of the city, not the last time that one of Caesar's demonstrations of clemency backfired on him. According to Caesar, he continued to attempt negotiations with Pompeius throughout the siege but was rebuffed with the excuse that as the Consuls were not present then Pompeius could not officially negotiate (something that had never stopped him before). This first clash between the two men came to a frustrating conclusion after just nine days, when the return of Pompeius' fleet signalled the end of his stay in Italy:

> *When nearly half the work had been completed by Caesar and nine days had been spent on it, the ships which had conveyed to Dyrrhachium the first part of the army and had been sent back thence by the Consuls return to Brundisium. On the arrival of the ships Pompeius, either because he was perturbed by Caesar's siege-works or else because he had originally intended to quit Italy, begins to prepare his departure, and in order to delay with greater ease any sudden attack on the part of Caesar, and prevent his troops breaking into the town at once after his departure, he blocks the gates, barricades lanes and streets, draws transverse trenches across the thoroughfares, and fixes therein stakes and blocks of wood sharpened at the ends. These he levels over with light hurdles and earth, while he shuts off the approaches and the two routes which led outside the wall to the harbour by planting in the ground huge balks of timber also sharpened to a point. Having made these preparations, he bids the soldiers embark in silence, and places light-armed men, drawn from the reserves, the archers, and the slingers, at intervals along the wall and in the towers. These he arranges to recall at a given signal when all the troops had embarked and leaves some merchant-vessels for them in an accessible place.[39]*

Thus Pompeius completed his withdrawal to Epirus, leaving Caesar with a port (which fell without a fight) but no ships with which to give chase, a point which Caesar himself admitted.[40] According to the dating in Cicero's letters (from a letter he received) this happened on 15–16 March:

> *Matius and Trabatius to Cicero Imperator:*
>
> *After leaving Capua we heard, while on the road, that Pompeius, with all the forces he had, started from Brundisium on the 15th of March: that Caesar next day entered the town, made a speech, hurried thence for Rome, intending to be at the city before the 1st of April and to remain there a few days, and then to start for Spain.*[41]

With his main prize having eluded him, Caesar divided his army, between garrisoning the major Adriatic ports, in an attempt to prevent Pompeius from seizing them, dispatched forces to seize Sardinia and Sicily (see Chapter Four) and then himself set out to Rome, to secure both his political and financial position.

> *He now divided his forces into five parts, one of which he left at Brundisium, another at Hydrus, and another at Tarentum to guard Italy. Another he sent under command of Quintus Valerius to take possession of the grain-producing island of Sardinia, which was done. He sent Asinius Pollio to Sicily, which was then under the command of Cato.*[42]

> *After I had despatched the letter informing you that Caesar would be at Capua on the 26th [March], I received one from Capua saying that he would be in Curio's Alban villa on the 28th.*
>
> *Caesar, as he has informed me, has stationed a legion at Brundisium, Tarentum, and Sipontum respectively. He appears to me to be closing up exits by sea, and yet himself to have his eyes on Greece rather than on Spain.*[43]

Caesar and the Consolation Prize of Rome

Having thus dispensed with his army Caesar made for Rome, which he would have reached towards the end of March. He then used Antonius and Cassius, the two Tribunes who had fled Rome (thus breaking a central tenet of their office[44]) to use their Tribunician power to assemble first the Senate and then the Assembly outside of the Pomerium (the sacred boundary of Rome, which according to law and tradition, he himself could not cross, whilst holding a military command). Caesar immediately attempted to allay the fears of the remaining Senators and the People that he was not about to unleash fresh horrors on the city, as had happened in the First Civil War. Here we can see the contrasting statements for Appian and Plutarch, which we must assume come from different traditions at the time (pro- and anti-Caesar):

> *He found the city more tranquil than he was expecting, and many Senators in it.*[45]

> *He found the people shuddering with recollection of the horrors of Marius and Sulla, and he cheered them with the prospect and promise of clemency.*[46]

Caesar thus put on a show of moderation. The meeting of the Senate was scheduled for 1 April and Caesar used it to explain/excuse his actions, to bemoan the situation that had forced him to act as he had and got them to agree to send a Senatorial delegation to Pompeius. We are not told how many of the Senate were left in Rome; many of the neutrals, such as Cicero, had fled to their summer villas to see how the situation would play out. What we are told is that though Caesar was a model of moderation, there seemed to be little enthusiasm amongst the remaining Senators for his actions, and as always Caesar's actions spoke louder than his words, as seen by his talk of clemency and the presence of his soldiers at the meeting. As always Dio summed up the situation well:

> *He saw that they were displeased at what was going on and suspicious of the multitude of soldiers.*[47]

Furthermore, though the Senate accepted his proposal to send Senatorial envoys to Pompeius in Greece to discuss peace, no volunteers could be found:

> *The Senate approves his proposal about the sending of envoys, but no one was found to be sent, each refusing for himself the duty of this embassy mainly through fear. For Pompeius when quitting the city had said in the senate that he would regard in the same light those who remained at Rome and those who were in Caesar's camp.*[48]

> *But no one would listen to him, either because they feared Pompeius, whom they had abandoned, or because they thought that Caesar did not mean what he said, but was indulging in specious talk.*[49]

Caesar seemed to fare no better with the People. As Dio states, Caesar again promised toleration and peace and even bribes of free grain and three hundred sesterces for each citizen, none of which were forthcoming.[50]

> *Recalling also the behaviour of Marius and Sulla, how many benevolent phrases they had often addressed to them and then what treatment they had accorded them in return for their services, and furthermore perceiving Caesar's need and seeing that his armed forces were many and were everywhere in the city, they were unable either to trust his words or to be cheered by them.*[51]

Again, Caesar's actions spoke louder than his words and he undid all the promises of toleration and respect for the law by his next action: the ransacking of the state treasury and threatening to kill a Tribune. Having failed to prevent the collapse of the political situation into a full-blown civil war and needing to fight campaigns on multiple fronts, Caesar clearly needed money for his existing forces and to raise fresh ones. The state treasury held in a Temple was a tempting target, being an emergency repository of monies, but one that no one had touched.

> *He took away money hitherto untouched, which, they say, had been deposited there long ago, at the time of the Gallic invasion, with a public curse upon anybody who should take it out except in case of a war with the Gauls. Caesar said that he had subjugated the Gauls completely and thus released the commonwealth from the curse.*[52]

> *On entering Rome, Caesar broke down the doors of the treasury and took the money he had been refused. He carried off 4,135 pounds of gold and almost 900,000 pounds of silver.*[53]

> *Caius Iulius Caesar, on first entering Rome during the civil war that bears his name, drew from the treasury 15,000 gold ingots, 30,000 silver ingots, and 30,000,000 sesterces in coin.*[54]

Thus not only did Caesar ransack the scared state treasury, with his men having to break their way in, but this action was opposed by one of the Tribunes. Of the Tribunes of 49 BC we know that two of them (Antonius and Cassius) were staunch supporters of Caesar. We also know the identities of another five, with the other three remaining anonymous. The central restriction of a Tribune's power was that it could only be exercised within the sacred boundaries of the Pomerium and that he could not leave the city (except possibly overnight) for the entirety of his year of office (unless sanctioned on exceptional occasions by the Senate[55]). It was this restriction that Antonius and Cassius had broken by fleeing to Caesar. With Pompeius and the Consuls withdrawing from Rome and passing a decree ordering all magistrates to evacuate Rome, and that any who stayed would be regarded as an enemy, we do not know how many of the running eight Tribunes (possibly ten if Antonius and Cassius had been replaced[56]) left the city.

What we do know is that at least one Tribune stayed true to his oath of office and remained in Rome: L. Caecilius Metellus. Metellus naturally opposed the ransacking of the state treasury for the purpose of fighting a civil war. When Metellus physically intervened to prevent them, as was his right to do so, the following happened:

> *Metellus once more opposed him and was commended by some for so doing; but Caesar, raising his voice, threatened to kill him if he did not cease his troublesome interference. 'And you surely know, young man,' said he, 'that it is more unpleasant for me to say this than to do it.'*[57]

Thus, despite his rhetoric of clemency and moderation, Caesar threatened, in public, to kill a Tribune of the People, one merely fulfilling the duties of his role. This, despite all the rhetoric about having gone to war in the first place in defence of the rights of the Tribunes.[58] Caesar himself mentions Metellus, but naturally omits the death threats:

> *Also L. Metellus, the Tribune, is put up by Caesar's enemies to thwart this proposal and to hinder everything else that he proposed to do.*[59]

A more revealing account can be found in one of Cicero's letters, when Cicero narrated an account he had received first-hand from a friend who was one of Caesar's officers and present in Rome (Curio):

> *that in an excess of anger Caesar had really wished the Tribune Metellus to be killed, and that it was within an ace of being done: if it had been done, there would have followed a serious massacre: that a great many people advised one: that Caesar himself was not by taste or nature averse from bloodshed, but thought clemency would win him popularity: if, however, he once lost the affection of the People, he would be cruel: he was,*

again, much disturbed by finding that he had caused ill-feeling among the populace itself by taking the treasury, and therefore that, though he had quite made up his mind to address the people before leaving Rome, he had not ventured to do so, and had started with very disturbed feelings.[60]

Thus it seems that Caesar narrowly averted a massacre of the People, but whilst he secured his financial position with a massive influx of monies, soured his political position and confirmed to many within both the Senate and People that he was acting tyrannically. Having spoken to the Senate and People and having secured the treasury, Caesar soon left Rome to go on campaign, apparently wishing to spend no more time in Rome itself and playing politics than he had to, which rather summed up Caesar's later career. He himself referred to it thus:

Thus three days are spun out with discussion and excuses. Also L. Metellus, the Tribune, is put up by Caesar's enemies to thwart this proposal and to hinder everything else that he proposed to do.

When his design was understood, several days having been already wasted, Caesar, in order to avoid throwing away any more time, having failed to do what he had proposed, leaves the city and goes into further Gaul.[61]

Before he left, he set out his dispositions for ruling the chunk of the Western Republic he controlled and set out his commanders to recover elements he did not (see Chapter Four):

He then placed Aemilius Lepidus in charge of the city, and the Tribune, Marcus Antonius, in charge of Italy and of the army guarding it. Outside of Italy he chose Curio to take command of Sicily in place of Cato, and Quintus Valerius for Sardinia. He sent Caius Antonius to Illyria and entrusted Cisalpine Gaul to Licinius Crassus. He ordered the building of two fleets with all speed, one in the Adriatic and the other in the Tyrrhenian sea, and appointed Hortensius and Dolabella their admirals while they were still under construction.[62]

Thus Rome was entrusted to the Praetor (and future Triumvir) M. Aemilius Lepidus, son of the civil war general who had himself marched his army on Rome (in 77 BC). Italy was entrusted to M. Antonius, despite his still holding a Tribunate, leading to him holding the newly created position of *tribunus plebis pro praetore*; a Tribune with Praetor's powers, and instruction to guard the east coast against a Pompeian invasion.[63]

He also seemed to leave Antonius with instructions to bring legislation before the People, in particular measures to restore the rights of the sons of those proscribed by Sulla, a long standing Caesarian political goal (since the 60s BC) and overturn the recent lex Pompeia of 52 BC which had exiled a number of disruptive (anti-Pompeian) members of the Senatorial oligarchy and their supporters.[64] How successful these proposals were is unclear and they may only have been passed when Caesar returned to Rome later in the year. Antonius would have faced the veto of his colleague Metellus, though the presence of Caesarian forces in the city may have swung any vote. Though he had secured temporary control of Rome and Italy, the lack of success in Caesar's political dealing can be seen by the defection of a number of previously neutral members of the Senatorial and Equestrian oligarchy to Greece, including Cicero.

> *Meanwhile Cicero and other Senators, without even appearing before Caesar, retired to join Pompeius, since they believed he had more justice on his side and would conquer in the war. For not only the Consuls, before they had set sail, but Pompeius also, under the authority he had as Proconsul, had ordered them all to accompany him to Thessalonica, on the ground that the capital was held by enemies and that they themselves were the Senate and would maintain the form of the government wherever they should be. For this reason most of the Senators and the knights joined them, some of them at once, and others later.*[65]

Summary – Stalemate

Thus, we can see that the first campaign of this Third Civil War was something of an anti-climax, with Pompeius refusing to give battle and allowing Caesar to capture Italy and Rome itself. Yet as we have discussed above, we can see these prizes as merely being consolations in the wider strategic game the two men were playing. Of the two men, it seems that it was Caesar who wanted a short campaign, to restore his position and avoid a long drawn-out civil war, whilst Pompeius' political objectives called for an escalation of the crisis, which he ultimately succeeded in.

It was neither in Pompeius' military nor political objectives to face Caesar in Italy. Though in theory he had the greater number of troops in Italy proper, they were scattered across the peninsula and most were freshly levied. Pompeius was also correct in his assumption that more of Caesar's battle-hardened legions would soon be following him from Cisalpine Gaul. Given their respective positions, Pompeius had no wish to jeopardise his whole campaign by rushing northwards to meet Caesar in battle before these reinforcements arrived.

Thus, Pompeius had nothing to gain and everything to win by letting Rome and Italy fall without more than token resistance, leaving Caesar trapped between Pompeian armies to both the West (Spain) and the East (Greece) with Pompeian fleets in control of the Adriatic and wider Mediterranean. Pompeius now had the crisis he needed to cement his position as 'saviour of the Republic' and the time he needed to build an army of sufficient size and quality to face Caesar in battle. As Plutarch himself comments: *Other people, now, count this sailing away of Pompeius among his best stratagems.*[66] Caesar on the other hand, now faced a dilemma about what to do next about been forced to re-think his strategy.

Chapter Three

The Gallic and Spanish Campaigns (49 BC)

L acking the ability to cross the Adriatic in force and lacking the patience to spend the rest of the year in Italy building up his forces to anticipate any Pompeian invasion from either the east or the west, Caesar chose to abandon Italy, just three months after he invaded it and march on Pompeian-held Spain. Spain had been a Pompeian stronghold since the latter stages of the First Civil War, when the Sullan faction dispatched Pompeius to reconquer Spain from the Cinnan general Sertorius. This long-standing association had been strengthened recently when Pompeius chose the two Spanish provinces as his Consular command after his Consulship in 55 BC, receiving the right to rule it via legates, meaning he could remain in Rome (see Chapter One).

At this point Caesar only held the two territories of Italy and Gaul, both of which were vulnerable to attack: Gaul from the west (Pompeian Spain) and Italy from the east (Pompeian Greece and Epirus). Knowing Pompeius as he did, he would have been aware that he was unlikely to attack Italy before he had assembled his forces from across the east (see Chapter Five), judging the main danger to be the threat from Pompeian Spain. Whilst Gaul was his powerbase, he had only just finished a decade-long programme of conquest and had already suffered a recent significant rebellion. This left the province vulnerable to any Pompeian armies marching into it from Spain and stirring up discord among the recently conquered Gallic tribes.

Pompeius and Massilia

Given the interconnectivity of the Roman oligarchy, on both sides of the civil war divide, it is clear that Caesar's intentions were well known and thus word soon reached Pompeius, who naturally sought to slow his opponent down and divert him from an attack on Spain. To those ends, Pompeius made contact with the city of Massilia (Marseilles), a long-standing Roman ally and persuaded them to oppose Caesar's march to Spain. He even promised them reinforcements by sea (on which the Pompeian fleet had the advantage). Thus unlike all the other cities Caesar had encountered, when his armies approached Massilia, the key city of the southern Gaul, he found his way barred.

> *Receiving these instructions, the people of Massilia had closed their gates against Caesar, and had called to their aid the Albici, a barbarian tribe, who owed allegiance to them from olden times, and inhabited the hills above Massilia; they had collected and brought into their town corn from the neighbouring districts and from all the strongholds; they had set up manufactories of arms in the town, and were engaged in repairing their walls, gates, and fleet.[1]*

Whist Caesar was negotiating with the elders of the city, the Pompeian fleet arrived with the new Pompeian commander for the city; none other than L. Domitius Ahenobarbus, the Senatorially appointed commander of Transalpine Gaul. As we have seen (see Chapter Two), Ahenobarbus had faced Caesar in Italy, at Corfinium, and been forced to surrender, upon which Caesar let him go, in what would become a long-standing policy of clemency.

This policy seems to have reflected Caesar's upbringing, to avoid the slaughter of the First Civil War and the deep-seated enmities that lingered for over a generation. Yet throughout these campaigns, whatever benefit he hoped it would bring in the long term, it always seemed to backfire in the short term. We have already seen that he released Pompeius' chief engineer N. Magius back to Pompeius in time for him to mastermind the defence of Brundisium (see Chapter Two). No sooner had he released Ahenobarbus than he retired to his Etrurian estates, raised a fresh force, and made contact with Pompeius who dispatched him by sea to take command in Massilia. Thus Caesar faced an opponent he had already beaten and captured, within the space of a few weeks. This would not be the last time that Caesar's policy of clemency failed; that final time would come five years later, on the Ides of March 44 BC.

Thus Caesar now faced a Pompeian stronghold in the middle of the key route between Spain and Italy, with the ability to disrupt his campaign. Clearly Pompeius was counting on either delaying Caesar's arrival in Spain, to give his commanders more time to prepare, or more likely knowing Caesar's impatient streak, forcing him to detach a portion of his army and tying them down in a siege. Dio reports that Caesar did indeed launch an attack on Massilia himself:

> For Caesar had persisted in his attempt for some time, thinking to capture them easily, and regarding it as absurd that after vanquishing Rome without a battle he was not received by the Massaliots; but when they continued to hold out, he left them to care of others and himself hastened into Spain.[2]

Thus, it seems he soon realised that he was wasting valuable time, and allowing the Pompeian commanders in Spain further time to mobilise and so he split his army, leaving behind one third to conduct the siege:

> Caesar conducts three legions to Massilia; he determines to bring up towers and penthouses for the siege of the city and make twelve warships at Arelate. These having been made and equipped within thirty days from the day on which the timber was first cut down, and having been brought to Massilia, he puts D. Brutus in command of them, and leaves his legate, C. Trebonius, to conduct the siege of Massilia.[3]

The Siege of Massilia (49 BC) – The First Naval Battle

The clear problem we have with the siege is that there is only one source that provides any detail (Caesar) and it is written by one of the protagonists and thus can hardly be labelled a dispassionate and balanced account. Nevertheless, from the detail we have, we can analyse the main themes of the campaign.

Any thoughts the Caesarians under Trebonius had about bringing the siege to a swift conclusion were soon dispelled, as the siege lasted for almost the rest of 49 BC. Massilia was an ancient Phoenician city which had resisted the local Gallic tribes for hundreds of years, with a near impregnable position on a coastal promontory, surrounded by sea on three sides. Given that and given the help that they could receive from the Pompeian controlled regions of the empire, if Massilia was to fall, then the Caesarian fleet had to gain mastery of the seas around the city and put it under blockade, otherwise face an endless stream of Pompeian reinforcements. Command of the newly constructed Caesarian fleet fell to D. Iunius Brutus Albinus.

The surviving sources record that there were two major naval battles fought off the coast of Massilia between the two fleets. Caesar's commentary provides a detailed account of both, but naturally with a pro-Caesarian slant.[4] The first clash came whilst Caesar was at Ilerda in Spain (see below), so was some months into the siege. This delay was down to the time it had taken Ahenobarbus to build up the Massilian fleet, as detailed by Caesar:

The Massilians, following the advice of L. Domitius, equip seventeen ships of war, of which eleven were decked. To these they add many smaller vessels, so that our fleet may be terrified by the mere multitude. On board they put a great number of archers and of the Albici, about whom I have explained before, and stimulate them by prizes and promises. Domitius demands special ships for himself and peoples them with farmers and herdsmen whom he had brought with him.[5]

Caesar provides further details about the various strengths and weaknesses of the two fleets, both in terms of numbers and skill levels, but naturally emphasises the superiority of his enemy's forces, both in terms of number and quality, thus making the Caesarian victory seem all the more impressive:

Our men had not only to employ less well-trained rowers and less skilled pilots who had suddenly been taken out of merchant ships, not yet knowing even the names of the various tackle but were also retarded by the slowness and heaviness of their ships. For, having been made in a hurry of unseasoned timber, they did not display the same handiness in respect of speed.[6]

Thus Ahenobarbus led the Massilian fleet out of harbour to engage with the Caesarian fleet. Given that he may well have been outnumbered, Brutus seems to have fallen back on an old Roman tactic, first seen in the First Punic War. When similarly confronted by a superior quality of Carthaginian ships and seamanship, the Romans turned the tables by effectively turning each ship-to-ship conflict into a land battle, by grappling onto the enemy's ship and allowing infantry (effectively marines) to board and engage in hand to hand fighting. Every young Roman (nobleman) would have been brought up on these stories and Brutus used a similar tactic:

And so, provided that an opportunity of fighting hand to hand were given them, with quiet courage they confronted two ships with one, and throwing aboard the iron claw and holding each ship fast, they fought on opposite sides of their vessel and so boarded the enemy's ships; and after slaying a large number of the Albici and the herdsmen they sink some of the ships, take others with their crews, and drive the rest into port. On that day nine ships of the Massilians are lost, including those that were captured.[7]

Again we have a shorter account in Dio, which seems to suggest that Caesar had the advantage going into the battle:

But just at this time the Massaliots were defeated in a naval battle by Brutus owing to the size of his ships and the strength of his marines, although they had Domitius as an ally and surpassed in their experience of naval affairs; and after this they were shut off completely.[8]

Thus, Brutus was apparently able to negate the numerical and quality advantages that the Massilian ships had by engaging at close quarters and holding on to them long enough for Roman infantry to board and slaughter the crews. According to Caesar, half of the Massilian fighting ships were lost and the others retreated back into harbour, providing the Caesarians with control of the seas and the ability to effect a blockade.

The Siege of Massilia (49 BC) – The Second Naval Battle

Despite the ability to place Massilia under a naval blockade, the reality seems to be that it was not a tight one and the defenders were able to send and receive messages from the outside world, with Domitius sending word of their setback to Pompeius in Epirus. Still wanting to ensure that Massilia remained a thorn in Caesar's side, whilst he campaigned in Spain, Pompeius dispatched a small relief fleet from his larger naval resources, composed of sixteen ships, commanded by L. Nasidius.

As Caesar himself details, not only was Nasidius able to sail past Caesarian-controlled Sicily without opposition (see Chapter Four) but he was actually able to capture an additional ship from the harbour at Messana, all showing the command of the seas which the Pompeian fleet had.[9] Sending a small fast boat to Massilia, Nasidius arranged with Ahenobarbus for a joint action against Brutus. Following the aftermath of the first defeats, Caesar again records that Domitius had committed to rebuilding the Massilian fleet:

> *After their previous disaster the Massilians had brought out of the docks and repaired an equivalent number of old ships and equipped them with the utmost industry, there was an abundant supply of rowers and helmsmen, and had added to them some fishing-vessels which they had furnished with decks, to protect the rowers from the blows of missiles while they also manned them with archers and catapults.*[10]

Again the effectiveness of Brutus's blockade must be called into question, as the Massilian fleet under Ahenobarbus was able to leave port and join forces with that of Nasidius:

> *Finding the wind favourable, they quit the port and reach Nasidius at Taurois, a Massilian fortress, and there get their ships into trim and again make up their minds to the struggle and join in arranging their plans. Operations on the right are assigned to the Massilians, on the left to Nasidius.*[11]

Receiving word of this combined force, Brutus took his fleet, which was still apparently outnumbered despite the additional ships he had captured during the first battle and gave chase, meeting the combined Pompeian-Massilian fleet in battle. On this occasion it seems that the Massilians had learnt from the first battle and kept their distance from the Caesarian ships, utilising their greater manoeuvrability. The battle was swung when, for whatever reason, the Pompeian ships refused to give battle and turned and retreated to Pompeian-held Spain. This 'fact' is provided by Caesar, but we have no other details and therefore must treat it with caution:

> *But the ships of Nasidius were of no use and quickly retired from the battle; for neither the sight of their fatherland nor the promptings of kinsmen urged them to incur the supreme peril of life.*[12]

Thus, if he did so, we are ignorant of why Nasidius refused to engage the Caesarian fleet and retreated to Spain. The obvious reasons are that either his nerve broke, or he was following orders to preserve the fleet and aid the Pompeian forces in Spain, which Pompeius may well have considered to be the priority, and not Massilia. Naturally enough, left on its own, the Massilian fleet fought on, but was overwhelmed:

out of the fleet of the Massilians five were sunk, four captured, and one fled with the Nasidian ships, and they all made for hither Spain.[13]

Thus, the second battle ended with Brutus emerging victorious and remaining in command of the seas around Massilia. Furthermore, a Pompeian relief fleet had apparently been beaten off, seemingly ending any hope of outside relief. We are not told whether Brutus' second naval 'victory' allowed him to place Massilia under a close enough blockade to cut them off from the sea completely or whether it was as seemingly ineffective as the first one.

The Siege of Massilia – The Land War

What is clear however, is that the naval victories were at best only a platform from which the Caesarians could build their successful siege strategy. The key to taking Massilia lay with the siege on land and there Caesarian success seemed much harder to come by. Certainly the Caesarian land commander (Trebonius) could not match his counterparts' success and by autumn 49 BC, Massilia's walls were still standing, and the siege had accomplished little. Again Caesar provides a flavour of the ongoing conflict:

> *In front went a tortoise sixty feet in height, for the levelling of the ground, also made of very stout timbers, and wrapped over with everything that could serve to keep off showers of firebrands and stones. But the greatness of the works, the height of the wall and the towers, the multitude of engines, hindered the whole of our operations. Moreover, frequent sorties from the town were made by the Albici, and firebrands were flung upon the earthwork and the towers, all of which assaults our troops repelled with ease, and kept driving back into the town those who had made a sortie, even inflicting great losses on them.*[14]

We also find a passage of Vitruvius which details the Caesarian mining operations and Massilian counters:

> *Similarly when Massilia was besieged, and the enemy had made more than thirty mines; the Massilians suspecting it, lowered the depth of the ditch which encompassed the wall, so that the apertures of all the mines were discovered. In those places, however, where there is not a ditch, they*

excavate a large space within the walls, of great length and breadth, opposite to the direction of the mine, which they fill with water from wells and from the sea; so that when the mouths of the mine open to the city, the water rushes in with great violence, and throws down the struts, overwhelming all those within it with the quantity of water introduced, and the falling in of the mine.[15]

Nevertheless, at some point during the siege, Trebonius' efforts began to pay off and one of the defensive towers was brought down along with a section of wall. At this point, the Massilians called for a truce, in order to seek terms with Caesar himself. Trebonius, apparently under orders not to sack the city, agreed and a temporary truce was arranged. Unfortunately for Trebonius, this was a ruse on the Massilians' part and after several days of peace, waiting for the Caesarian sentries to be off guard, a sortie left the city and attacked the siege works:

after an interval of several days, when our men were weary and slack in spirit, suddenly at noon, after some had gone away and others after their long toil had surrendered themselves to sleep among the siege works, and all their arms had been put away out of sight, broke forth from the gates and set fire to the works, the wind being strong and favourable. The wind spread the fire to such an extent that the mound, the sheds, the tortoise, the machines all caught fire at once, and they were all consumed before it could be ascertained how it had happened. Our men, alarmed by the sudden mischance, snatch up such arms as they can, others fling themselves from the camp. They charge the enemy but are prevented from following the fugitives by arrows and catapults from the wall. The foe retires beneath their wall, and there without hindrance set fire to the gallery and the brick tower. So the labour of many months perished in a moment through the perfidy of the enemy and the violence of the storm.[16]

Thus the Caesarian siege was set back, with their siege equipment destroyed by the fire. Despite this, it seems that Trebonius set his men to work rebuilding the siege equipment and managed again to reach the Massilian walls, but having conceded a respite to the defenders, giving them time to repair the damage and thus 'reset' the clock on the siege.

However, when the end came, it came through negotiation, not force. By the end of the year (October/November 49 BC), news reached Massilia of the fall of Spain to Caesar (see below). This converted their position from being an advance post of Pompeian-controlled Spain to being an isolated island surrounded by Caesarian territory. Furthermore, after over six months of being besieged, their food supply was dwindling, and disease had broken out. That, and the realisation that Pompeius had clearly no intention of coming to their aid, forced the Massilians to reconsider their position. Thus the Massilians sought terms with a returning Caesar, who spared the city, and left two legions as a garrison. L. Domitius Ahenobarbus, having no wish to test Caesar's policy of clemency again, was able to breach Brutus' naval cordon and sailed back to Dyrrhachium, and serve under Pompeius again.

Ultimately, in the grand scheme of the war, the siege of Massilia was simply a distraction for both sides. For Pompeius it gave him a chance to distract Caesar from his Spanish campaigns and reduce the size of the army that he took into Spain, and for Caesar it was an annoyance he could have well done without. As it was, even without the three legions (a third of his forces) Caesar was able to successfully complete his Spanish campaigns (see below). Had it turned out otherwise, then the Massilian distraction would have proved to have been more important in the long term.

The Spanish Campaigns (May to August 49 BC)

As discussed above, one of the key issues we face with analysing this Spanish campaign is that, although we have a detailed account of the manoeuvres and clashes, it is written by one of the commanders, and the victorious one at that. Furthermore, it was written for public consumption after Caesar's ultimate victory in the civil wars and thus used to justify its inevitability. The majority of the other surviving sources for the period gloss over the details of the campaign, though Dio preserves a useful overview of the key points of the campaign, which present an alternative view to the Caesarian one.

Spain was well used to civil war campaigns, having been a major battleground during the First Civil War in the 70s BC. On that occasion it was Pompeius who had been dispatched by the Sullan-controlled Senate to bring this last region back under their control. Now the Spanish found themselves backing a Pompeian-controlled Senate against Caesar. Upon hearing that Caesar was making for Spain, Pompeius dispatched a legate L. Vibullius Rufus to Spain to give orders to his commanders.

There were three Pompeian commanders in Spain, the most senior of which was L. Afranius (Cos. 60 BC). Afranius had been a long serving Pompeian commander who had seen action in both Pompeius' civil war campaigns in Spain during the 70s and during the Eastern Wars of the 60s BC. He had been sponsored by Pompeius for the Consulship of 60 BC, the year before Caesar, who replaced him as Pompeius' agent in the Consulship. Ever the loyal subordinate, Pompeius had entrusted him and the other two men with commands in Spain in 54 BC, thus giving them five years' experience commanding the province.

Though only of Praetorian rank, M. Petreius was another hardened Roman commander having fought in both the First and Second Civil Wars, including serving under Pompeius in Spain and commanding the Senatorial forces at the Battle of Pistoria in 62 BC (see Chapter One). The third commander was another former Praetor, M. Terentius Varro. By 49 BC, he was already in his mid-60s and had more of a reputation of an administrator than a general, as borne out by the Pompeian tactical dispositions.

Of the three commanders, Afranius held three legions, Petreius and Varro two each, bringing the total to seven legions (or more than thirty-five thousand men), all of whom had been serving in Spain for at least five years. They also had around ten thousand cavalry at their disposal. These were complemented by a large number of auxiliary troops from the natives of the region. As stated above, Pompeius sent the legate L. Vibullius Rufus with orders for his three commanders. Afranius was to meet the Caesarian invasion head on by intercepting the Caesarian army after they had cleared the Pyrenees. Petreius was to take his two legions to join him and Varro was to defend the interior with his two legions.

Ultimately, we must question what Pompeius' intentions were. Certainly, he wanted Afranius and Petreius to wear Caesar's army down, but there was always the danger that they could actually defeat Caesar. Pompeius' overall strategy however was centred on the need for it to be him who finally defeated Caesar and ended his threat to the Republic and that needed to be done in person, either in Greece or Italy. Only then would he become the 'saviour' of the Republic and its long-term guardian. If Caesar were killed in Spain, then this whole strategy would crumble, leaving him with a 'Pyrrhic' victory. Nevertheless, we must assume that Pompeius factored into his plans that Caesar would be delayed in Spain, perhaps into the year 48 BC, but not defeated. At the very least, Afranius and Petreius would hold Caesar up and buy Pompeius the time he needed to assemble his army in Greece.

Pompeius' view towards the Spanish campaigns can be seen by the striking fact that he sent no reinforcements to Afranius and Petreius despite having control of the seas. The same attitude was displayed to the other theatres of conflict in the Western Republic (see Chapter Four). As we have seen, Vibullius arrived with Pompeius' orders but no legions. Later, L. Nasidius arrived with sixteen ships, having been dispatched to break the Caesarian naval siege of Massilia (see above), but again no fresh legions were dispatched. Thus we can see that Pompeius did not want Caesar defeated in Spain, merely delayed. Interestingly Caesar's own commentary gives voice to the following rumour:

> *He had heard that Pompeius was marching at the head of his legions through Mauritania into Spain and would very soon arrive.*[17]

Cicero reports another rumour to his friend Atticus:

> *There is a certain hope, no great one in my mind, but warmly entertained in these parts, that Afranius has fought a battle with Trebonius in the Pyrenees; that Trebonius has been repulsed.*[18]

Despite these rumours, Caesar, having been detained at Massilia, dispatched the legate C. Fabius with three legions (half his army, having left another three legions at Massilia) to seize the crossing of the Pyrenees and establish a bridgehead in Spain. Afranius had stationed some men to guard the passes, but, along with Petreius, was mustering a five-legion army at Ilerda (modern Lleida in Catalonia). Afranius had chosen the city to make his defence of Spain, set as it was on the high ground situated between two rivers: the west bank of the River Sicoris (modern Segre) and the east bank of the River Cinga (modern Cinca) commanding the whole region. He seems to have only made a token effort to defend the Pyrenees, presumably on Pompeius' orders, in order to draw Caesar and his legions further into Spain.

Having fought a long campaign in Spain himself (admittedly against one of the First Civil War's greatest generals, Q. Sertorius) Pompeius presumably wanted Caesar to become 'bogged down' into a drawn-out affair. Thus Fabius secured passage over the Pyrenees and took his three legions into Spain to await the arrival of Caesar and the other half of the army. Caesar himself provides us with an estimation of the size and composition of the two armies:

> *There were, as I have explained above, three legions belonging to Afranius, two to Petreius, besides about eighty cohorts, some heavy-armed from the hither province, others light-armed from further Spain, and about five thousand cavalry from each province. Caesar had sent forward six legions into Spain, five thousand auxiliary infantry and three thousand cavalry which he had had with him during all his former wars, and an equal number from Gaul, which he had himself pacified, having specially called to arms all the men of conspicuous rank and bravery from every state; to these he had added men of the best class from among the Aquitani and the mountaineers who border on the province of Gaul.*[19]

Thus, even though Caesar had been forced to leave three legions behind to besiege Massilia, reducing his army by a third, he still had six legions to the five of Afranius and Petreius. With Afranius having chosen the city of Ilerda to make his stand, along with his three legions, Fabius took his three legions to the east bank of the River Sicoris and made camp, with both sides waiting for their reinforcements (Petreius with two legions and Caesar with three). Of the two it was Petreius who arrived first, thus giving the Pompeian forces a temporary five to three advantage in legions.

The Battle of Ilerda (49 BC) – The Initial Battle

It seems that, having chosen to defend the western bank of the River Sicoris, Afranius had ensured that there were insufficient supplies on the eastern bank, forcing Fabius to create two temporary bridges across the river (roughly four miles apart) and use them to forage on the western bank, and thus in range of Afranius' cavalry. Caesar reports that '*they were engaged in constant cavalry skirmishes*'.[20]

Soon after these initial clashes, Fabius chose to deploy two of his three legions on the western bank to protect his foragers. Unfortunately for him, a storm broke which demolished the bridge they had used to cross, exposing them on the western bank, having to march for the second bridge. When Afranius and Petreius learnt of this, they dispatched four of their legions and all their cavalry to catch and destroy the Fabian legions, who at the time were commanded by another legate L. Munatius Plancus. Caesar describes the clash that followed:

> On the news of his approach L. Plancus, who was in command of the legions, under the stress of necessity occupies the higher ground and draws up his lines facing in opposite directions that he might not be surrounded by cavalry. So going into action with unequal numbers, he sustains impetuous charges of the legions and cavalry. After the cavalry had engaged, the standards of two legions are seen by each side some little way off. These Fabius had sent by the further bridge to support our men, suspecting that what actually occurred would happen, namely, that the commanders on the other side would employ the opportunity which a kind chance afforded them of crushing our men. On their arrival the battle is broken off and each leader marches his legions back to camp.[21]

There is an obvious discrepancy in the description of the numbers of Caesarian legions involved, as Plancus had two legions on the western bank whilst Fabius brought another two in support, yet the total of the Fabian legions was meant to be three. It may well have been the case that some of Caesar's legions had arrived by then, or Fabius had been recruiting locally. Caesar's own commentary later states that he arrived with six legions but recruited a seventh locally and this may account for the disparity.[22] Again, Dio presents a shorter and less pro-Caesarian account:

> Fabius overcame the garrison upon the Pyrenees, but as he was crossing the river Sicoris the enemy fell upon him suddenly and killed many of his men who were cut off.[23]

Thus, in Caesar's account, disaster is averted thanks to the actions of both Plancus' staunch defence and Fabius' quick thinking, which saves two of his legions from destruction. Whilst it certainly seems that the legions were rescued, Dio's account certainly suggests that they suffered far higher casualties than we find in the Caesarian account.

Naturally the Caesarian account shifts the focus onto the 'heroic' recovery from adversity rather than the tactical blunder that nearly derailed his whole campaign from the beginning. Nevertheless, we do need to question Afranius' tactical decisions here. He had two Caesarian legions trapped, yet withdrew when faced with two more legions, even though he had deployed four of his. We are not told the exact tactical dispositions here and it may well have been the case that Afranius found himself trapped between Plancus' legions and Fabius', with his legions committed to attacking Plancus' legions on the high ground thus exposing his rear. Nevertheless, Afranius lost an excellent opportunity to destroy Caesar's advance guard before Caesar arrived.

The Battle of Ilerda (49 BC) – The Second Battle

As Caesar himself states, he arrived two days later, meaning that the Caesarian forces now outnumbered the Pompeian ones. Having assembled his combined force, and with the bridge repairs completed, with typical boldness, Caesar marched his whole army across the Sicoris and confronted Afranius, drawing his army up in battle formation on level ground near Afranius' camp, thus offering him battle. Afranius, perhaps as per his orders, remained holding the high ground, whilst Caesar began to fortify his position. Having surveyed the respective positions of the two armies, Caesar then set upon seizing a tactical advantage, by securing some high ground between the two armies and attempting to cut Afranius and Petreius off from the city of Ilerda itself:

> Between the town of Ilerda and the nearest hill on which Petreius and Afranius were encamped was a plain about three hundred paces in width, and in about the middle of this space was a rather high mound. Caesar was confident that if he occupied and fortified this, he would cut off his adversaries from the town and the bridge and from all the stores which they had brought into the town. In this hope he leads out of the camp three legions and having drawn up the line in a suitable position, he orders a picked advance guard from one legion to charge and occupy the mound. This movement being quickly discovered, the cohorts of Afranius which were stationed in front of the camp are sent by a shorter route to occupy the same position. A battle is fought, and as the Afranians had reached the mound first, our men are driven back and, fresh supports being sent up, are compelled to turn and retreat to the standards of the legions.[24]

Furthermore, Caesar goes on to analyse the different fighting styles of the two forces, with the Pompeians apparently greatly influenced by fighting the Spanish tribes:

> The method of fighting adopted by the enemy's troops was to charge at first at full speed, boldly seize a position, take no particular trouble to preserve their ranks, but fight singly and in loose order; if they were hard pressed they did not consider it a disgrace to retire and quit their position, for, waging a continuous warfare against the Lusitanians and other barbarous tribes, they had become used to a barbarous kind of fighting, as it usually happens that when troops have spent a long time in any district they are greatly influenced by the methods of the country. It was this system that now threw our men into confusion, unaccustomed as they were to this kind of fighting; for as the enemy kept charging singly, they thought that they were being surrounded on their exposed flank. As for themselves, they had judged it right to keep their ranks and not to desert their standards nor to give up without grave cause the position they had taken. And so when the vanguard was thrown into confusion the legion posted on that wing could not stand its ground and withdrew to the nearest hill.[25]

With the Caesarian forces in retreat, Caesar himself took to the field at the head of the Ninth Legion and drove back the Pompeian forces, who retreated to the fortified city of Ilerda itself. As Caesar himself details the Ninth then unwisely gave chase and found themselves harried from the high ground outside the city, which was occupied by the Pompeians. After five hours of fighting the Ninth charged the high ground and drove the Pompeians into the city, allowing the other Caesaerian forces to withdraw. Caesar placed his casualties at seventy dead and six hundred wounded, though again we may well distrust such light casualty figures. Nevertheless, the day ended with the Pompeians in charge of the hill that the battle was fought over, who then fortified it and placed a garrison there. Dio presents a shorter account of the battle, but one in which high Caesarian casualty figures are hinted at:

> Afranius and his followers, on perceiving this, occupied the place first, repulsed their assailants, and pursued them when they fled. Then, when others came out against them from the camp, they at first withstood them, then yielded purposely, and so lured them into positions which were favourable to themselves, where they slew many more of them.[26]

Thus, whilst Caesar claimed that his first battle with Afranius was a stalemate,[27] Dio records that it was a Caesarian defeat, with his men being lured into a trap and suffering heavy casualties. As we will see, downplaying his defeats was a standard Caesarian tactic in his account of the war. Clearly though Caesar had come off worst, as his plan to cut Afranius off from the city of Ilerda had failed and the Ninth Legion had had to be rescued from being cut off. Furthermore, the battle showed the tactical advantage which Afranius had by holding the various sites of high ground in the vicinity: his camp, the city of Ilerda and the route between the two.

The Battle of Ilerda (49 BC) – Caesar's Deteriorating Position

It was at this point during the conflict that nature, and poor engineering, intervened once more. Caesar's engineers had apparently not learnt the lesson from Plancus' earlier near disaster. Once again there was a heavy storm and, on this occasion, both bridges were swept away, trapping Caesar's army on the west bank, cut off from their initial position on the east bank, thus severing their supply lines. Thus Caesar's army faced a lack of supplies, whilst Afranius' was well provisioned. Furthermore, there was a long-standing bridge across the river at Ilerda itself, which was controlled by Afranius' force. This meant that he could traverse both banks and harry Caesar's rear whilst Caesar was trapped, at least until his engineers were able to build another bridge, not an easy task with the river in flood.

To further compound Caesar's problems, a large column of reinforcements (archers and cavalry from Gaul) had arrived, along with supplies and baggage, numbering more than six thousand. Sensing his chance to further inflict misery on Caesar's army, Afranius crossed the bridge with a large contingent of cavalry and three of his legions, to effectively circle around Caesar and cut him off. Afranius' cavalry attacked the reinforcement column at dawn. What followed was another skirmish between the two forces:

Nevertheless the Gallic horsemen quickly rally and join battle. Though few, they stood their ground against a great number of the enemy, so long as an encounter on equal conditions was possible; but when the standards of the legions began to approach, after the loss of a few men, they withdraw to the nearest hills. This period of the battle was of great moment for the safety of our men, for by getting free room they withdrew to higher ground. On that day about two hundred archers were lost, a few horsemen, and a small number of camp followers and beasts of burden.[28]

Again, as we have seen throughout, Dio's account paints a different picture:

And on one occasion when some [Caesarian] soldiers had crossed to the other side of the river and meanwhile a great storm had come up and destroyed the bridge which they had used, they [Pompeians] crossed over after them by the other bridge, which was near the city, and destroyed them all, since no one was able to come to their assistance.[29]

Thus again we find Caesar playing down the casualties he suffered and depicting a tactical reversal as a 'heroic defence'. Nevertheless, though his supply column may have avoided destruction, it was driven off and Caesar' army was effectively trapped with dwindling supplies, with Afranius now ensuring that there was no way out for Caesar's army and playing a waiting game. Caesar was seemingly paying for his bold incursion over the Sicoris. Caesar himself reports that Afranius and Petreius sent news of Caesar's plight back to Rome:

Afranius and Petreius and their friends wrote to their partisans at Rome an amplified and exaggerated account of these events. Rumour added much, so that the war seemed almost finished. When these letters and messages were conveyed to Rome great crowds thronged the house of Afranius and hearty congratulations were offered. Many set out from Italy for Cn. Pompeius, some that they might show themselves the first to bring him such news.[30]

Again, in Caesar's account it is Afranius and Petreius that are exaggerating the situation Caesar found himself in. Once more, Dio paints a different picture:

Caesar, when things were taking this course, fell into desperate straits; for none of his allies rendered him assistance, since his opponents met and annihilated the separate forces as often as they heard that any were approaching, and it was with difficulty that he managed to obtain provisions, inasmuch as he was in a hostile territory and unsuccessful in his operations.[31]

Thus it seems that Afranius and Petreius certainly had Caesar tied down in the stalemate that Pompeius had demanded. Pompeius himself must have heard of this, as seen in Dio, with news being borne from Rome:

> *The Romans at home, when they learned of this, renounced all hope of him, believing that he could hold out but a short time longer, and began to fall away to Pompeius; and some few Senators and others set out to join the latter even then.*[32]

Thus Afranius and Petreius were now seemingly confident that all they had to do was wait and let hunger and the pressure tell on Caesar's legions, until such point as they mutinied or were starved into submission. It is not known if they considered an attack on Caesar's position, but that would have meant abandoning the strategic advantage given to them by holding the high ground and exposing themselves to Caesars' greater numbers.

The Battle of Ilerda (49 BC) – The Turning Point – The Pompeian Retreat

With his military campaign having ground into a potential defeat, Caesar clearly needed to change tactics. This he did by constructing a fleet of troop transports and ferrying the bulk of his army back across the river unobserved and fortifying the opposite bank. Having thus extricated himself from that potently dire situation, he was able to use his larger cavalry contingent (which had been reinforced from Gaul) to harass Afranius' foragers and put pressure back on the defenders.

Furthermore, realising that he could not dislodge Afranius and Petreius from their position militarily, he set about undermining them politically and logistically. Freed from his position he was able to communicate with the various native cities and tribes of the region, all of whom owed their allegiance to Pompeius, something which he seems not to have done until then.

Nevertheless, despite his military setbacks, Caesar was now able to convince a number of them to change sides and the reasons for this are not clear in any surviving accounts. Dio puts it down to Afranius' boastful statements about his victories over Caesar, but this is far from convincing. Certainly on a personal level neither Afranius nor Petreius seemed to be what we would call charismatic and Petreius latter revealed a brutal streak which may well have been present.

There may well have been some element of the natural rebellious nature of the Spanish tribes, having earlier backed the rebel candidate in the First Civil War (Sertorius) against the 'official' Roman one (Pompeius). Furthermore, Pompeius having defeated Sertorius, there may well have been lingering resentment which Caesar could have stoked up. Naturally, Caesar himself does not state what inducements he offered them to switch. He does state however that the rumours of Pompeius coming to relieve Spain via North Africa were now widely believed to be false.[33] Thus if Pompeius was not coming to Spain, then the immediate danger of disloyalty to the man himself was removed; all that was left was disloyalty to his subordinates.

Furthermore, determined not to be caught out again and sensing another tactical advantage Caesar put his engineers to work creating a ford over the Sicoris by digging the equivalent of thirty feet wide drainage ditches to lower the level of the river. Caesar now had no need for bridges for his cavalry, meaning that they could cross the river far more easily and harry the Afranian force if they ventured out from their high ground.

Thus, from being on the brink of defeat, the momentum was now with Caesar, who was seemingly getting stronger with each day, whilst Afranius and Petreius were sat outside of Ilerda in a fixed and deteriorating position. Already outnumbered to begin with, if Caesar kept being reinforced and the native tribes of the region declared for him, then they would soon find themselves trapped in their previously secure position. With the waiting game seemingly ruled out (in their own minds at least), Afranius and Petreius only had two realistic options: attack or withdraw. With any attack meaning that they would have to sacrifice their high ground and the numbers in Caesar's favour, they chose the latter and began to plan a withdrawal to Celtiberia, another supposed hotbed of Pompeian loyalty. Again Caesar details both the logic of this move and their plan of action:

In this district they were expecting to find large reinforcements of cavalry and auxiliaries and were proposing to prolong the war into the winter in a place of their own choosing. Having formed this plan, they order ships to be sought for along the whole course of the Ebro and to be brought to Octogesa. This town was situated on the Ebro and was thirty miles from the camp.

They order a bridge to be made at this part of the river by coupling ships together and bring two legions over the Sicoris. A camp is entrenched with a rampart twelve feet high.[34]

Thus, the plan was a sound one, autumn was approaching (it was c. July 49 BC) and if the withdrawal could be properly managed then they could retreat into Celtiberia, gain reinforcements and adhere to Pompeius' plan to keep Caesar tied down in Spain until the next year. Caesar's scouts would have left him in no doubt that Afranius and Petreius' five legions were planning a withdrawal. The move naturally offered Caesar an opportunity to harass and attempt to stop the withdrawal, otherwise the war would continue into the new year, stalling Caesar's momentum and handing Pompeius the advantage. With his legions still having to use the bridges, Caesar sent his cavalry forces to attack the withdrawing Pompeian forces whilst they were on the march:

He [Caesar] sends horsemen who cross the river and, although Petreius and Afranius had moved camp about the third watch, suddenly show themselves in the rear of the column and begin to delay them and impede their march by pouring a great number of men around their flanks.

At early dawn it was observed from the higher ground adjacent to Caesar's camp that the enemy's rear was being hard pressed by the attack of our cavalry, and that sometimes the end of the column was being held up and even being cut off from the rest, while at other times their colours were pushed forward and our men were driven back by a charge of the cohorts in a body, and then again wheeled round and pursued the foe.[35]

Nevertheless, it soon became clear that the Caesarian cavalry would not be able to do anything more than delay Afranius' legions from their withdrawal. Thus Caesar again made another of his bold and innovative moves and took the risk of sending his legions straight across the Sicoris.

He leaves one legion to guard the camp. The rest of the legions he leads out lightly equipped, and after placing a great number of packhorses in the river above and below leads across his force. A few of these men were carried away by the strength of the current but were caught and supported by the horsemen; not one, however, was lost.[36]

With a forced march Caesar's more lightly equipped legions were able to catch up with those of Afranius and Petreius:

When his army had been led across without loss, he draws up his forces and proceeds to lead his battle in three lines. And there was such zeal in the soldiery that though a circuit of six miles was added to their route and a long delay was interposed at the ford; they overtook by the ninth hour of the day those [Pompeians] who had gone out at the third watch.[37]

Having been caught by Caesar's army, Afranius and Petreius chose to halt and pitch camp on high ground to negate Caesar's greater cavalry forces. Caesar himself states that his men were in no condition for battle, having been marched hard all day.[38] Again Afranius and Petreius were faced with the decision whether to fight or continue the withdrawal, but on this occasion, they chose neither and sat there, drawing criticism from Caesar himself:

The enemy [Pompeians] pitched their camp earlier than they had intended, for the hills were close by and difficult and narrow routes awaited them only five miles off. These hills they were eager to penetrate in order to escape Caesar's cavalry and by placing outposts in the defiles to stop the march of his army, and themselves to conduct their forces across the Ebro without danger and alarm. This they should have attempted and carried out by every possible means but worn out by a whole day's fighting and the toil of their march, they postponed the business till the next day.[39]

Afranius and Petreius apparently decided to lead their army out of their camp and into the hills at night, but Caesar seemed to have been alerted to this move by some prisoners that were taken and used his cavalry to prevent this. The next day, Afranius and Petreius chose not to give battle or force a withdrawal but kept their position and sent out scouts to reconnoitre the vicinity and a potential escape route. Whilst Afranius and Petreius debated their position and next course of action, Caesar acted decisively once more and sent his cavalry via a circuitous route to cut off the Afranian line of retreat to the River Ebro.

Finally realising the danger, that they were being cut off, Afranius and Petreius ordered their army to break camp and march for safety, with, as Caesar himself states, it effectively becoming a race between the two armies,[40] the key difference between the two forces being that Caesar's cavalry were continuing to harass the Afranian legions from the rear, slowing them down. Thus it was that Caesar's army was able to reach the passes that went through the hill first and cut off Afranius army, which now faced Caesar's legions ahead of them and Caesar's cavalry to their rear. Naturally enough, Afranius sought high ground for his army (to negate Caesar's cavalry) and dispatched a force to find an alternative route through the mountains. Caesar's cavalry however put paid to this plan:

> *When the light-armed men were making for this by an oblique route, Caesar's horsemen, perceiving it, charged the cohorts; nor could they, with their small shields, hold out for ever so short a time against the cavalry attack, but are all surrounded by them and slain in the sight of both armies.*[41]

The Pompeian Retreat and Collapse

Thus Afranius and Petreius were effectively trapped on a hilltop with their legions surrounded by Caesar's army and without an adequate water supply, leaving them with only three options: fight, retreat, or surrender. Caesars's legions blocked their path to the Ebro (their intended withdrawal route) and his cavalry roamed the plains below. Caesar naturally turned the screws on them by dispatching cavalry to cover any routes of escape and began to dig in for a siege. Again, Afranius and Petreius came to the conclusion that being outnumbered, especially in cavalry and fighting on a flat plain, would result in their destruction and so they attempted to carve out a fourth option and tried to secure access to fresh water, whilst their reviewed any viable escape routes.

Here Afranius and Petreius made their final mistake as, whilst on the one hand it was a good idea to personally scout various escape routes, it was also a bad idea for both commanders to leave their trapped legions without senior command. Naturally enough, the rank and file of the trapped army soon sent emissaries to Caesar seeking terms of surrender, with Caesar himself pointing out that both armies contained numerous men who had friends in the opposing army (both Roman and Spanish). Caesar, having no wish to be seen spilling Roman blood, happily guaranteed the safety of all his opponents. When the two commanders discovered this, their reactions were opposite; Afranius returned to camp, apparently accepting he had been outmanoeuvred, but Petreius went on the offensive and attempted to break up the fraternisation between soldiers of the two forces:

He arms his retinue; with this and his official staff of light-armed men and with a few barbarian horsemen, his own retainers, whom he had been able to maintain to guard his person, he makes a sudden onset on the rampart, interrupts the soldiers' colloquies, drives our men from the camp, and slays all he catches.[42]

Having summoned the army, Petreius attempted to restore discipline in the Pompeian forces:

When this action was over Petreius goes the round of the maniples and calls on his men, beseeching them with tears not to hand over himself or their commander Pompeius to the foe for punishment. A crowd quickly gathers at the general's headquarters. He demands that all should swear not to desert or betray the army and its officers, nor to take measures for their own safety apart from the rest. He first takes this oath himself, and also compels Afranius to take the same. Next come the Military Tribunes and Centurions; the rank and file come forward and take the oath century by century. They issue orders that any soldier of Caesar who is in the company of one of their men should be brought forward by him. When produced they kill him publicly at the headquarters. But many of them are concealed by those who had entertained them and are let go at night through the ramparts.[43]

Thus, the attempted surrender was forestalled, but the Pompeian forces still remained trapped on the hill, and without an adequate supply of water and naturally enough, as Caesar himself notes, the Pompeian army suffered from an increasing number of desertions, from both legionary and auxiliary forces.[44] Nevertheless, with overall morale temporarily holding, Afranius and Petreius determined that the only course of action available was to retreat back to Ilerda, fighting their way through Caesar's cavalry, rather than his legions, which blocked their path ahead. Thus the Pompeian legions retreated, fighting a rearguard action against Caesar's cavalry along the way, with Caesar and his legions in pursuit.

This game of cat and mouse continued throughout the first day, as described by Caesar,[45] with the Pompeians being forced to make camp wherever they could and then spending the night and the subsequent two days pushing forward from one temporary camp to another in a slow crawl forwards. On the third day and with their forces exhausted from this inexorable harassment, Afranius and Petreius drew up their army for battle, presumably intending to make a last stand, outnumbered as they were. Caesar provides an account of the battle formations:

The Afranian line was a double one of five legions. The third line of reserves was occupied by the auxiliary cohorts. Caesar's line was threefold, but the first line was held by four cohorts from each of the five legions, next to these came three reserve cohorts, and again three more, each from its respective legion; the bowmen and slingers were enclosed in the centre of the force, while cavalry protected the flanks.[46]

Yet neither side seemed willing to end the standoff, with Caesar calculating he could accomplish his victory without giving battle (and being seen to spill Roman blood) and Afranius realising that to attack would invite destruction. Thus, with all day spent in this stand-off, the two sides faced each other until sunset and then returned to their camps.

A brief account can be found in Frontinus:

In the Civil War, when Caius Caesar held the army of Afranius and Petreius besieged and suffering from thirst, and when their troops, infuriated because of this, had slain all their beasts of burden and come out for battle, Caesar held back his own soldiers, deeming the occasion ill-suited for an engagement, since his opponents were so inflamed with wrath and desperation.[47]

By this point both sides had reached the River Sicoris again and Afranius attempted to make use of Caesar's ford, but was blocked by Caesar's cavalry ahead of them. Thus Afranius now faced the same natural barrier that Caesar had some weeks before. On the fourth day of the retreat, and with Caesar's legions behind him and the River Sicoris (and Caesar's cavalry) in front of him, and with dwindling supplies, Afranius gave into the inevitable and called for a conference with Caesar. The terms for the surrender of the Pompeian army were as follows:

The final result was that those who had a domicile or holding in Spain should be discharged at once, the rest at the River Varus. Pledges are given by Caesar that no wrong should be done to them, and that no one should be compelled to take the oath of allegiance against his will.

Caesar promises to provide them with corn from that time while on their way to the River Varus. He also adds that whatever any one of them has lost in war, when such property is in the hands of his own soldiers, should be restored to the losers; after making a fair valuation, he pays the men a sum of money for these effects.[48]

Thus the five Pompeian legions of Afranius and Petreius were disbanded by mutual agreement:

About a third of the army having been discharged within two days, Caesar ordered his own two legions to march first, the rest to follow close, so as to encamp at no great distance apart, and set the legate, Q. Fufius Calenus, in charge of this duty. In accordance with this instruction they marched from Spain to the River Varus, and there the rest of the army was disbanded.[49]

Here it was agreed that they should abandon Spain to Caesar, and that he should conduct them unharmed to the other side of the river Varus and allow them to proceed thence to Pompeius.[50]

Caesar kept each of his promises to them scrupulously. He did not put to death a single man captured in this war, in spite of the fact that his foes had once, during a truce, destroyed some of his own men who were caught off their guard; and he did not force them to fight against Pompeius, but released the most prominent and employed the rest as allies who were willing to serve for the gains and honours in prospect.[51]

Thus both Afranius and Petreius were freed to return to Pompeius, and what would have been a far from warm welcome, having failed in their efforts to detain Caesar in Spain until the following year. The date of the surrender is given as the second of August. One man kept prisoner by Caesar was L. Vibullius Rufus, the Pompeian legate sent by Pompeius to Spain with his orders. He was too useful as an emissary to Pompeius in Caesar's forthcoming campaigns (see Chapter Six).

Thus in just a few short months and without a major battle, Caesar had defeated the five legions of Afranius and Petreius. The decisive factors lay in the decision by the two Pompeian commanders to retreat from the stalemate at Ilerda, Caesar's bold decision to harry them and the ineptitude shown by the commanders during the retreat, with poor choices and indecision. Ultimately, we can only speculate about their reason for the decision to retreat, but we must wonder whether Pompeius' orders were hampering their natural instincts.

Caesar and The Third Commander (M. Terentius Varro)

Having defeated Afranius and Petreius, Caesar now had control of central and eastern Spain, but control of the whole of the two provinces of Spain was not yet his. There remained only one obstacle: the third of the Pompeian commanders, M. Terentius Varro. Varro held the south of Spain headquartered at Gades (modern Cadiz) and had used the intervening months to strengthen his position, both militarily and fiscally:

> *He held a levy throughout his province, and when he had made up two legions, he added about thirty auxiliary cohorts. He collected a great store of corn to be sent to the Massilians, some also to Afranius and Petreius. He ordered the Gaditanians to make ten ships of war and contracted for the building of many others at Hispalis. He bestowed in the town of Gades all the money and all the treasures from the temple of Hercules.*
>
> *He compelled the Roman citizens of the province, terrified by such proceedings, to promise him for the administration of public affairs 18,000,000 sesterces and 20,000 pounds of silver and 120,000 measures of wheat. On all the communities that he thought friendly to Caesar he proceeded to impose very heavy burdens, to move garrisons into them, and to deliver judgments against private persons who had uttered words or made speeches against the commonwealth; their property he confiscated for public purposes. He went on to compel his whole province to swear allegiance to himself and Pompeius.[52]*

Though outnumbered by Caesar in terms of land forces, by holding Cadiz, and with Pompeian naval superiority he held onto a vital Pompeian bridgehead in Spain, from which to challenge Caesar's dominance of the rest of the Spanish provinces and thus prolong the Spanish campaign, which again left Caesar with a dilemma. Though he had overcome Afranius and Petreius in just a few months, he too knew that the Spanish campaigns were a side show and that he needed to prepare for the main war with Pompeius in either Greece (Epirus) or Italy. He also knew that his control of Rome itself (and wider Italy) was superficial and could unravel if he were away too long. Certainly, he could leave a portion of his legions in Spain under a legate to continue the prosecution of the war against Varro, but he seemed eager to remain in the field himself.

To those ends, Caesar engaged in a two-prong strategy: military and political. In terms of the military aspect, he dispatched Q. Cassius Longinus into the province with two legions whilst he himself made for the city of Corduba (modern Cordoba) summoning all the local magistrates and tribal leaders to meet him there. With Caesar clearly on the ascendency in Spain and the Pompeian element reduced to just Varro, all of the main cities and tribes declared for Caesar and expelled their Pompeian garrisons, including the city of Gades itself (Varro and his legions not being present). Varro's situation deteriorated further when one of his two legions deserted his camp when they heard the news.

With his temporary headquarters lost, and with it access to the monies he had accumulated and the naval forces, Varro had no option but to send to Caesar and offer his surrender. Caesar dispatched a kinsman, Sex. Iulius Caesar to take control of Varro's one remaining Pompeian legion, whilst Varro went to surrender in person to Caesar in Corduba. Caesar made for Gades, to secure the Pompeian ships and the monies, and appointed Q. Cassius Longinus as the new Governor of Further Spain and left him four legions.

Caesar then made his way by sea to the north-eastern city of Tarraco (modern Tarragona), the provincial capital, where he received embassies from all the cities and tribes of Rome's two provinces, pledging their (superficial) allegiance to Caesar, as Rome's representative. Thus, having secured Spain, he set off by land to Massilia to oversee the surrender of the city (see above) and thence back to Rome for November/December 49 BC in time to organise the elections for the new year and pass emergency legislation to cement his (temporary) rule (see Chapter Five).

Summary

Thus, in just a few months, Caesar had overrun Pompeius' two Spanish provinces and eliminated the threat to his control of Gaul and Italy from the West, without becoming entangled in a drawn-out campaign that took him into the new year. Along with control of Sicily and Sardinia secured by his commanders (see Chapter Four), Caesar now (nominally) controlled the bulk of the Western Republic, with only North Africa in Pompeian hands. As would be demonstrated in the following years, Caesar's control of the provinces of Spain was as superficial as Pompeius' had been, as seen by the return of the civil war. Nevertheless, in the short-term, Caesar had achieved all his goals within the timescale he had set himself, freeing him to concentrate on planning the major campaign of the civil war: the invasion of Greece (Epirus) and the clash with Pompeius.

As we can see, this campaign highlighted some of Caesar's key traits which filtered into his leadership style; energy and an impatience which always caused him to take the initiative, combined with an unorthodox way of thinking. This was demonstrated when he defeated the armies of Afranius and Petreius by outmanoeuvring and outthinking them, rather than by force of arms. He also combined military prowess hand in hand with political strategy as seen by convincing the local tribes and cities to swap their (temporary) allegiance to him, an act which undermined both Afranius' and Varro's campaigns so much.

Nevertheless this desire to take the initiative nearly led to disaster at Ilerda, when he found his army trapped and it was only his unorthodox thinking that rescued them. Equally though Caesar's energy contrasted with the inertia of the Pompeian commanders, which was not entirely down to their own temperaments. Following his masterplan, Pompeius clearly wanted Caesar delayed in Spain but not defeated, and this must have impinged on Afranius and Petreius. Nevertheless, their caution spurned two good opportunities to defeat Caesar, first when they failed to destroy the two Fabian legions and secondly when they had Caesar trapped and opted to wait it out.

Overall however, despite Caesar's rapid victories in Spain, we would have to say that the result was a stalemate. Though not detained for as long as Pompeius wanted (into the new year), Spain did distract Caesar from disrupting Pompeius' preparations in the east, both in assembling his grand army and eliminating the Caesarian bridgehead in Illyria (see Chapter Four). Caesar's initial hopes (in January 49 BC) for a quick campaign had been lost and he found himself fighting in Spain and besieging Massilia rather than attacking across the Adriatic. Despite the rumours, Pompeius clearly entertained no illusion about rushing to Spain himself and happily sacrificed his commanders in Spain, by refusing to send reinforcements. His masterplan called for defeating Caesar in person and in front of the Senatorial elite in Greece at a time and on a battlefield of his own choosing. If anything, Caesar's victories in Spain, which enhanced his standing also enhanced the grave nature of the threat he posed, making the bulk of the oligarchy rely on Pompeius all the more.

Chapter Four

The Sicilian, African and Illyrian Campaigns (49 BC)

With Pompeius controlling Greece and Macedon and Caesar choosing to contest his control of Spain, attention shifted to the other provinces of the Western Republic, 'sandwiched' in the middle, namely the islands of Sardinia, Corsica and Sicily and Roman North Africa (see Map 3). Again, we encounter the problem of our lack of sources, with Caesar being the only detailed account for the African campaign and one which, as his commanders lost, is hardly an unbiased one.

Furthermore, perhaps the most significant campaign is the one which is almost completely missing from our surviving sources and receives little or no mention in Caesar, namely Illyria. This province, on the eastern side of the Adriatic was actually held by Caesar, thus providing him with a vital bridgehead in the Pompeian dominated Eastern Republic. Likewise for Pompeius this was a thorn in his side which needed to be eliminated as quickly as possible before Caesarian reinforcements arrived. Yet despite the loss of any detailed narrative for this campaign, it must not be overlooked.

Sardinia and Corsica

Nevertheless, we need to start with the minor campaigns, the three large islands off the coast of Italy. Of the two islands to the west of Italy, it was the island of Sardinia which was the strategic prize, dominating Italy's western coast and being an immediate source of grain for Italy. Yet Sardinia fell without a fight. Caesar himself tells us that he dispatched a legate (Q. Valerius Orca) with a legion to seize the island, following his capture of Brundisium.[1] The troops proved to be unnecessary as the Senatorial appointed Governor, M. Aurelius Cotta had been driven from the province by a native revolt, in favour of Caesar.

The people of Caralis [Cagliari], as soon as they heard that Valerius was being sent to them, before he had quitted Italy, of their own accord eject Cotta from the town. Terror-struck, because he gathered that the whole province was in accord with them, he flies from Sardinia to Africa.[2]

We must be careful to not to read this as evidence of a surge of support for Caesar, more the desire on behalf of the locals to ensure that they did not become battleground for a civil war conflict, with the resultant destruction and loss of life, that this would entail. Nevertheless, whatever the cause, the result was the loss of Sardinia from the Pompeian side, with Aurelius Cotta not choosing to fight his way onto the island, but withdrawing to Africa, leaving Caesar with his first prize. With Sardinia being occupied by Valerius Orca, we must assume that Corsica too fell without a fight.

Sicily

Whilst Sardinia was a small prize, the island of Sicily was a major one, in terms of its size, its strategic position, its food supplies and its role as a major naval base. Whilst Caesar had dispatched one legion to Sardinia after the fall of Brundisium, he seems to rightly place a greater importance on Sicily and dispatched troops there earlier in the campaign, after the fall of Corfinium (see Chapter Two), seemingly under the command of C. Asinius Pollio (later a noted civil war historian).[3] After the fall of Brundisium, Caesar dispatched his trusted lieutenant C. Scribonius Curio, along with two legions, with orders to capture Sicily and then move onto capture Africa.[4]

Facing Pollio and Curio was the Senatorial appointed Governor, none other than M. Porcius Cato, still a junior politician in age, but one with a fiercely Republican reputation, and latterly a reluctant supporter of Pompeius (see Chapter One), whom he seemed to view as the lesser of two evils. Cato had limited military experience, having annexed the island of Cyprus in 56 BC. We are not told how many troops he had with him though. Sicily had throughout its history been a battleground for various empires as best seen in the centuries-long wars between the Carthaginian and Syracusan Empires. Yet since the defeat of the Syracusans in the Second Punic War (211 BC) Sicily had been at peace (aside from two large slave rebellions). The island had avoided the worst bloodshed of the First Civil

War and only saw conflict during 81 BC when Pompeius seized it from the Cinnan leaders M. Perperna and C. Papirius Carbo without much of a fight. Again, it is Caesar himself who provides us with a description of Cato's activities, organising troops and ships for the Pompeian forces:

> *Cato in Sicily was repairing the old warships and requisitioning new ones from the communities, devoting much zeal to the performance of his task. Among the Lucani and Bruttii he was raising levies of Roman citizens through his legates and was exacting a fixed number of cavalry and infantry from the townships of Sicily.*[5]

It seems Cato was based in the regional capital of Syracuse, to the south, a city famous for its previous ability to resist a siege, whilst Pollio we are told occupied Messana, to the north, on the straits between Sicily and Italy.[6] It seems that when Pollio landed on the island, he met with Cato, from which the following story has been recorded by the sources:

> *When Cato asked him [Pollio] whether he had brought the order of the Senate, or that of the People, to take possession of a government that had been assigned to another, Pollio replied, 'The master of Italy has sent me on this business.'*[7]

It seems that there was a short period of standoff between the two forces, with Pollio in the north and Cato in the south. According to Plutarch's biography of Cato, it was Cato who had the larger army.[8] This standoff however was broken by the news that Scribonius Curio had been dispatched with two legions. It was at that point that Cato's nerve seems to have broken and, rather than defend this key strategic location, he withdrew from Sicily with the forces he had raised and retreated to Corcyra (Corfu). Several sources refer to Cato holding a meeting in Syracuse and claiming that he did not wish to see the island destroyed in a civil war,[9] whilst Caesar himself claimed that Cato gave a speech claiming that he had been betrayed by Pompeius.[10]

Whatever his motives, in the middle of civil war and unlike Cotta in Sardinia (who had not even reached his province), Cato withdrew from a defensible position and surrendered the strategic island of Sicily to Caesar's faction, enabling them to use it as both a staging post for military operations across the Mediterranean and opening up Italy from a blockade. This represented Caesar's first major success outside of Italy and inflicted a blow for the Pompeians. Having withdrawn from Corcyra to re-join Pompeius in Epirus, he was understandable side-lined from a further military command by Pompeius. Cicero provides the following contemporary commentary on Cato's actions:

> Cato, who might have held Sicily without any trouble – and, if he had held it, all loyalists would have joined him – sailed from Syracuse on the 23rd of April, as Curio has written to tell me. I only hope, as the phrase is, that Cotta may hold Sardinia; for there is rumour going about. Oh, if that were to be so, what a stigma on Cato![11]

North Africa

Though both Sardinia and Sicily had fallen to the Caesarian faction without a fight, it was in North Africa that this process was halted and then reversed. At first however, the Pompeian faction's control of North Africa got off to an inauspicious start. The Senatorially appointed Governor was L. Aelius Tubero, but he too was prevented from taking charge of his province. On this occasion however it was a fellow Pompeian commander who opposed him; none other than P. Attius Varus, one of the commanders who had lost their forces to Caesar in Italy (see Chapter Two). Varus however, having been outmanoeuvred by Caesar in Italy, seemingly had no wish to withdraw to Epirus to join Pompeius, but made for North Africa, a province he had formerly commanded (c.53 BC[12]) where he raised an army and prepared to fight Caesar on familiar territory:

> Tubero on reaching Africa finds Attius Varus in the province in military command; he, as we have explained above, after the loss of his cohorts at Auximum had immediately fled and gone to Africa and had on his own account seized on the vacant province. By raising a levy he had made up two legions, having by his knowledge of the people and the district and his familiarity with the province gained an opening for engaging in such undertakings, as he had held the province a few years previously after his Praetorship. He prevents Tubero on arrival at Utica with his ships from approaching the port and the town and does not allow him to land his son who was stricken with illness but compels him to weigh anchor and quit the district.[13]

Thus Tubero was forced to withdraw to join Pompeius in Greece, whilst Varus prepared to resist an invasion by Scribonius Curio and Asinius Pollio from the now Caesarian-controlled Sicily. The key difference with the defence of North Africa however lay in the role of the inhabitants and Roman allies in the region, and in particular the client kingdom of Numidia. Roman territory in North Africa was limited to the coastal region and some hinterland in the north roughly equivalent to modern Tunisia and the coastline of Libya (see Map 3). Further inland lay the kingdoms of Numidia and the Mauri, long term Roman allies.

Numidia had had and long and turbulent relationship with Rome, having been created in the aftermath of the Second Punic War as a counterweight to the defeated Carthage.[14] Nearly a century of friendship between the two powers ended with the First Romano-Numidian War (or Jugurthine War) 112–105 BC, which culminated in a Roman victory and Numidia's reduction in power. During the First Roman Civil War, Africa was twice used as a refuge for the Marian-Cinnan faction when they lost control of Rome, first by Marius himself in 88 BC and then by Cn. Domitius Ahenobarbus in 82–81 BC. On both occasions they were supported by the Numidians. This support was needed in 81 BC when Pompeius invaded and reconquered the country, bringing it back under the control of the Sullan-controlled Republic.

Once again, however Numidia decided to buck the trend for Roman allies to remain neutral in a civil war and their King Juba threw his weight behind the defending Pompeian forces. The reason behind this decisive action appears to stem from the year before (50 BC) where we learn from asides in the accounts of both Caesar and Dio of this campaign that a Tribune had proposed the annexation of the Kingdom of Numidia to Rome.[15] The Tribune in question was none other than C. Scribonius Curio, the Caesarian commander. Aside from the personal rancour and the suspicion that it had been Caesar who was behind the scheme, Juba would have realised that his very throne was under threat if he did nothing. On the other hand, if he swayed the campaign in favour of Pompeius and the exiled Senate then he could restore Numidia as a staunch Roman ally and avoid annexation. Thus, Juba determined to intervene in the Civil War, on the side of Pompeius though he avoided placing himself under the command of Varus and operated independently.

We are fortunate that we have excellent accounts of the campaign from Caesar himself and later accounts from both Dio and Appian. As had been seen throughout these opening campaigns, the Pompeian forces once again got off to a poor start. The most obvious first line of defence for North Africa against an invasion from Sicily was a naval force, and Caesar himself tells us that Varus had prepared a small fleet of ten warships, left over from Pompeius' pirate war in 67 BC and quickly refitted. Unfortunately, command of this fleet had been allotted to none other than L. Iulius Caesar, Caesar's kinsman, who had been Pompeius' emissary in Italy earlier in the year (see Chapter Two).

It seems however that the young Caesar had limited military experience and when sighting Curios' larger invasion fleet, off the coast of the city of Aspis, panicked and ordered his ship to beach at the nearest point after which he fled to the major port of Hadrumetum. Faced with the flight of their commander, the rest of the fleet was able to organise a more orderly withdrawal to Hadrumetum to await further orders. Thus, once again the poor quality of Pompeian commanders came to the fore and Curio won his first battle of the North African campaign without firing a shot.

The Siege of Utica

With the way open, Curio then landed his invasion force, of two legions (freshly raised in Italy, and composed of men originally levied by Pompeian commanders) and five hundred cavalry. He landed near to the main strategic asset of Roman North Africa, the provincial capital of Utica, where Varus and his army was encamped. This was a co-ordinated assault with his fleet moving towards the city and placing it under naval blockade.

Appian provides a story, found nowhere else, that Curio originally camped near the site of one of Scipio Africanus' old camps (from the Second Punic War) and that the natives anticipated this and poisoned the water supplies, but curiously not apparently with a fatal dose, merely enough to give Curios' army blurred eyesight, sleepiness, and vomiting. Apparently, realising his mistake Curio then moved the campsite closer to Utica.[16]

The first military clash came when Curio left his two legions in camp and went to reconnoitre Varus' camp, which was by the walls of Utica, at the head of the Caesarian cavalry (said to number five hundred).

Whilst examining Varus' camp Curio noticed a steady stream of civilians heading into the safety of Utica laiden down with their possessions and spying an easy target, Curio decided to attack them. Defending them however were a Numidian advance contingent whom Varus had charged with defending the civilians; some six hundred Numidian cavalry and four hundred infantry. Utilising the element of surprise and with the Numidians hampered by the presence of the civilians, Curio's cavalry were able to drive off the Numidians, who lost one hundred and twenty, and then presumably plunder the defenceless civilians. For the 'glorious' victory Curio was apparently proclaimed as 'imperator' when he returned to his legions.[17]

Curio then moved his legions to Utica, by the river Bagradas (modern Medjerda) and began to prepare siege works around the city. At this point Varus showed no signs of moving to engage him, buoyed by the knowledge that King Juba was sending reinforcements, which would soon ensure Curio was surrounded. Shortly afterwards Curio's scouts detected the arrival of another advance guard of Numidian cavalry and infantry, though Juba himself was in command of the main army, some days away. Showing a quick awareness, Curio ordered his own cavalry to attack the Numidians to buy time for his legions to form up (having been engaged in working on the siege lines). This quick thinking brought about another small victory as they seem to have caught the Numidians off guard, with the cavalry routed and a number of the infantry killed (though no exact numbers are given).

Though buoyed by the victory, a small contingent of Curio's men defected to Varus' camp, raising the hope in Varus, mind that the loyalty of Curio's legion was suspect. Here we have to bear in mind that Curio's legions were drawn from the men who had defected to Caesar at Corfinium, many of whose former officers were in Varius' army. Thus, to test the resolve of Curio's army, Varius deployed his legions into the field. There would also have been the need to buoy up the morale of his own forces, with them having seen the Numidian relief force routed. Thus the two Roman armies drew up facing each other, as Caesar states with '*only one small valley between them*'[18] though neither side committed to battle.

Of the two commanders, the pressure seemed to be felt most by Curio, who could not be assured of the loyalty of his legions, nor be assumed that fresh Numidian reinforcements would not arrive. Varus by contrast, whilst he may have worried about his own forces, could guarantee them that relief was on the way. Therefore he could afford to wait. Curio however, despite having satisfied himself as to the loyalty of his men,[19] still felt the pressure to give battle, clearly aware that he could soon be trapped between an advancing Numidians army and Varus' legions holding Utica, determined to force the issue and break the standoff.

The Battle of Utica (49 BC)

With the two armies arrayed on opposite sides of a small steep valley, it seems to have been Varus who committed his men first, sending his left wing down to cross the valley.

> Between the two lines there was, as explained above, a valley, not very large, but with a difficult and steep ascent. Each commander was waiting to see whether the enemy's forces would attempt to cross this, in order that he might join battle on more level ground. At the same time on the left wing the whole cavalry force of P. Attius and a number of light-armed troops placed among them were seen while descending into the valley. Against them Curio sends his cavalry and two cohorts of the Marrucini. The enemy's horse failed to withstand their first charge, and fled back at a gallop to their comrades. The light-armed men who had advanced with them, being abandoned by them were surrounded and slain by our men.[20]

Thus Varus' advance was beaten back, which turned into an (uphill) rout. Curio then pressed home his advantage and let the whole of his army down into the valley. Despite holding the high ground, the flight of their left wing seems to have taken the fight out of Varus' army, which broke and retreated (fled) back to their camp, but with Curios' army giving chase. Though they had the head start, many were overtaken by Curio's chasing forces, including Varus himself who was forced to defend himself, according to Caesar.[21] Nevertheless, the majority reached the safety of Varus' camp or the city:

> The gates of the camp are beset by this throng and turmoil of fugitives and the road blocked, and more perish in this spot without wounds than in the battle or the flight; they were indeed very near being driven even out of the camp, and some, without checking their course, hurried straight into the town. But not only did the nature of the ground and the defences of the

camp prohibit access, but also the fact that Curio's men, having marched out for a battle, lacked the appliances that were required for the siege of a camp.[22]

However, despite Curio having won the battle, Varus' losses were given as six hundred dead and one thousand wounded, out of what must have been two legions (roughly nine thousand men). According to Caesar's account (repeated in Appian), Curio only lost one man (who is named as Fabius, a centurion of Pelignian origin), killed in the attack on Varus.[23]

Nevertheless, despite his victory, Curio was still in the same position as before the battle, namely trapped between an advancing Numidian army and the city of Utica. Thus, with the field clear, Curio returned his men to creating siege lines around the city. However, shortly afterwards (the exact timeframe is not given), news reached both Varus and Curio that King Juba was approaching with the main Numidian army. Thus Curio took the sensible decision and abandoned the siege of Utica and took up a fresh defensive position, known as the Cornelian Camp.[24] He also sent word to Sicily for the other two legions which held the island to be ferried to him immediately.

The Battle of Bagradas River (49 BC)

However, having adopted a sensible defensive strategy, Curio threw it all away when he changed his mind, having received fresh 'intelligence':

When these arrangements had been made and his measures approved, he learns from some deserting townsmen that Juba, recalled by a neighbouring war and by quarrels with the people of Leptis, had stayed behind in his kingdom, and that his prefect Saburra, who had been sent on with a moderate force, was approaching Utica.[25]

Believing their story and sensing an opportunity to replicate his earlier victory, which had been brought about by a bold attack on Numidians before they were ready, Curio ordered his cavalry to leave their defensive position and launch a surprise night attack on the Numidians, camped by the river Bagradas. As Caesar details below, once again the attack was a success.

Urged on by such considerations, he [Curio] sends all his cavalry at nightfall to the enemy's camp at the River Bagradas. Saburra, of whom he had previously heard, was in command of this camp, but the king was following on with all his forces and had taken up a position at a distance of six miles from Saburra. The cavalry whom Curio sent complete their journey by night and attack the enemy taken off their guard and unawares. For the Numidians, according to some barbarous custom of their own, had taken up their position here and there and in no set order. Attacking them when overcome by sleep and dispersed, they kill a great number of them, many fly panic-stricken. Having achieved this, the cavalry returns to Curio and bring him back their captives.[26]

Having dispatched his cavalry, Curio then set off with the majority of his two legions, leaving five cohorts (roughly two and a half thousand men) and went to join up with his cavalry, whom he met on their return journey. Having met with them and discovered their success, Curio then made what was to be a fatal mistake. Rather than return to his defensive position, having disrupted what he believed to be the Numidian army, as he did so before, he decided to press home his (perceived) advantage and marched his army towards the 'defeated' Numidians, to 'finish them off'. Unfortunately for Curio, the main Numidian army was advancing towards him, alerted to the attack on Saburra:

Juba, having been informed by Saburra of the night battle, sends to his relief two thousand Spanish and Gallic cavalry which he had been wont to keep round his person as a bodyguard, and that part of the infantry on which he most relied, and himself follows more slowly with the rest of his forces and sixty elephants.[27]

Even more unfortunately for Curio, Saburra then laid a trap for Curio:

Saburra, suspecting that after sending forward the cavalry Curio would himself approach, draws up his forces, horse and foot, and orders them to feign fear and to give ground gradually and retire, saying that he himself would give the signal of battle when necessary and issue such orders as he might judge the situation to require. Curio, having the general opinion of the moment to confirm his former hopes, and thinking that the enemy was in flight, leads down his forces from the higher ground towards the plain.[28]

Thus, Curio's army found the awaiting Numidian force of Saburra, waiting to give battle:

> *Saburra gives his men the signal, draws up his line of battle, and starts going up and down the ranks and exhorting the men. But he uses his infantry merely to make a show a little way off and hurls his horse on the line. Curio is equal to the emergency and encourages his men, bidding them place all their hopes on valour. Nor did zeal for the fight or valour fail either the infantry, weary as they were, or the cavalry, though they were few and exhausted by toil. But these were only two hundred in number; the rest had stopped on the route.*[29]

What followed was the classic tactic of one army feigning retreat and drawing the attacking army out of position. What made this tactic so devastating on this occasion was that the defending army was being constantly reinforced by the larger army to its rear. Thus Curio was being both outmanoeuvred and outnumbered at the same time. Caesar describes the effects thus:

> [The Romans] *compelled the enemy to give way at whatever point they charged, but they could neither follow them when they fled to a distance nor urge their horses to more strenuous effort. But the enemy's cavalry begins to surround our force on either wing and to trample them down from the rear. Whenever cohorts left the main body and charged, the Numidians by their swiftness fled unscathed from the assault of our men and returning to their own ranks again, began to surround them and to cut them off from the main body.*

> *As the king sent up reinforcements the forces of the enemy were constantly increasing, while fatigue kept diminishing the strength of our men, and those who had received wounds could neither quit the line nor be carried to a safe place because the whole force was surrounded and closed in by the enemy's horse.*[30]

Seeing his army was being surrounded, though probably still unaware of the fresh Numidian army behind Saburra, Curio ordered a retreat to a defensive position in the nearby hills. However, the Roman forces had become so stretched that they were slaughtered by the advancing Numidian cavalry. Caesar tells us that Curio chose to go down fighting rather than flee and live with the defeat, though in reality he may have had little choice, as elements of his cavalry had already fled and the Numidians were not taking prisoners.[31] Here we see signs of Curio becoming a martyr to the Caesarian cause. The result was that the entire Roman army (one and half legions) was wiped out bar a handful of cavalry who managed to outrun the Numidian cavalry. Curio's corpse was identified, and his head removed and taken to King Juba. Amongst the survivors, according to Appian, was C. Asinius Pollio (later to become a noted civil war historian) whose role in the battle is omitted by Caesar, perhaps due to the circumstances around his retreat, which in Appian reads like him abandoning Curio at the first time of trouble:

> *Asinius Pollio, at the beginning of the trouble, had retreated with a small force to the camp at Utica lest Varus should make an attack upon it as soon as he should hear the news of the disaster at the river.*[32]

The Caesarian Retreat

When word reached Curio's camp that he had been killed and the army wiped out, it apparently fell to one of Curio's Quaestors, Marcius Rufus, to organise a retreat back to the fleet. However, given the scale of the disaster, the morale of the force broke, expecting a Numidian attack at any point and the evacuation became a rout.

> *And so, amid the universal panic, each took counsel for himself. Those who were in the fleet hastened to depart. Their flight instigated the captains of the merchant-ships; only a few boats gathered at the call of duty and the word of command. But on the closely packed shores so great was the struggle to be the first out of the multitude to embark that some of the boats were sunk by the weight of the crowd, and the rest in fear of this hesitated to approach nearer.*[33]

Appian reports that Asinius Pollio tried to salvage the situation, or be one of the first to flee, depending upon your point of view.

> *But Pollio rowed out in a small boat to the merchant ships that were lying at anchor nearby and besought them to come to the shore and take the army on board. Some of them did so by night, but the soldiers came aboard in such crowds that some of the small boats were sunk.*[34]

Thus, very few of the five remaining cohorts managed to evacuate North Africa, the others surrendered, with most being executed. Notable amongst the survivors was Asinius Pollio himself.

> *Thus it fell out that only a few soldiers and fathers of families, who prevailed either by influence or by exciting compassion, or who could swim to the ships, were received on board and reached Sicily in safety.*
>
> *The rest of the forces sent centurions by night to Varus in the capacity of ambassadors and surrendered themselves to him. And Juba, seeing the men of these cohorts next day in front of the town, declaring that they were his booty, ordered a great part of them to be slain and sent back a few picked men to his kingdom, Varus the while complaining that his own honour was being injured by Juba, but not venturing to resist.*[35]

Thus, the Caesarian forces suffered their first major defeat in the civil war campaigns, with their invasion force wiped out, nearly to a man, with the loss of two legions. As we can see, their defeat did not come at the hands of the Pompeian forces but at the hands of the Numidians, showing the vital role that allied forces could play in this civil war. King Juba himself seems to have left no doubt as to who ruled North Africa.

> *Juba, himself riding into the town with an escort of several Senators, among them Ser. Sulpicius and Licinius Damasippus, briefly arranged and ordered what he wanted to be done at Utica, and a few days afterwards withdrew with all his forces to his own kingdom.*[36]

Nevertheless, by acting so decisively in the civil war, Juba received different receptions from the two Senates (Epirus and Rome); acclamation from one and condemnation from the other, thus tying his fate inexorably with that of Pompeius and his faction:

> *Juba received honours at the hands of Pompeius and the senators who were in Macedonia and was saluted as king; but by Caesar and those in the city he was called to account and declared an enemy, while Bocchus and Bogud were named kings, because they were hostile to him.*[37]

Thus, thanks to the Numidians, the majority of North Africa and its manpower and food supplies, remained in Pompeian hands, under the nominal command of P. Attius Varus. The only Caesarian foothold was with the Kingdom of the Mauri (to west of Numidia), whose rulers had declared for Caesar, yet could offer little practical help at this point.

Illyria and the Adriatic

In many respects however, the campaign in Africa was a side show, compared to the lesser known one in Illyria. The province of Illyria (see Map 1) represented something different, as it was already held by Caesarian forces. As is often overlooked, as well as holding commands in the two Gallic provinces (Cisalpine and Transalpine) Caesar also held command of Illyria.[38] This immediately gave him forces on the eastern shores of the Adriatic and the ability to harass the Pompeian forces in Epirus. Thus, for Pompeius the main focus for his campaign in 49 BC was to eliminate those Caesarian forces before Caesar could swing back from Spain and reinforce them. Naturally, for the Caesarians, they needed to harass Pompeian forces before they secure full control of Greece and ensure they secured control of Illyria as a bridgehead for a Caesarian invasion once Caesar had been able to assemble a fleet in the Adriatic.

Command in Illyria fell to C. Antonius (brother of the Tribune), as a legate of Caesar, with P. Cornelius Dolabella in command of Illyria's small fleet. Despite the importance of this campaign, given the outcome, unsurprisingly we do not find an account of it in Caesar's own commentary of the wars. Whilst he devoted a number of chapters to the 'heroic' defeat Curio suffered in North Africa at the hands of a 'perfidious' foreign ally, Caesar is silent on the Illyrian campaign. This means we have to fall back on other sources, all of whom seem to have fewer details of this campaign, seemingly a legacy of Caesar's own reticence about it.

Nevertheless, we can piece together the basics. Whilst Caesar had forces stationed in Illyria (at least three legions, according to Orosius[39]) and a fleet, they were dwarfed by the size of the Pompeian forces and more importantly the Pompeian fleet which effectively controlled the Adriatic. Command of the Adriatic fleet fell to L. Scribonius Libo, who had been driven from Italy by M. Antonius, and M. Octavius. Florus preserves the best account of the campaign for Illyria and control of the Adriatic.

> *For when Dolabella and Antonius, who had been ordered to hold the entrance to the Adriatic, had encamped, the former on the Illyrian coast and the latter on the shore near Curicta, at a time when Pompeius enjoyed a wide command of the sea, the latter's lieutenant-general Octavius [Scribonius]* Libo *suddenly surrounded both of them with large forces*

from the fleet. Famine compelled Antonius to surrender. Some rafts sent to his assistance by Basilus, as good a substitute as he could make for the lack of ships, were captured, as in a net, by means of ropes drawn along under the water, a new device on the part of some Cilicians in Pompeius' service. The tide, however, floated two of them off; but one of them, which carried troops from Opitergium, went aground on the shallows and provided an incident worthy of record in history. A band of barely 1,000 men withstood for a whole day the weapons of an army which had completely surrounded them, and when their valour procured no way of escape, at last, at the exhortation of the tribune Vulteius, in order that they might not be forced to surrender, they fell upon one another and died by the blows of their fellows.[40]

Marcus Octavius and Lucius Scribonius Libo, with the aid of Pompeius' fleet drove out of Dalmatia Publius Cornelius Dolabella, who was there attending to Caesar's interests. After this they shut up Caius Antonius, who had been desirous of aiding him, on a small island, and there, after he had been abandoned by the natives and was oppressed by hunger, they captured him with all his troops save a few; for some had escaped in season to the mainland, and others, who were sailing across on rafts and were overtaken, made away with themselves.[41]

Orosius adds some additional details, including the size of Antonius' force and the actions of the future historian Sallust:

On the other hand, Dolabella, Caesar's supporter in Illyricum, was defeated by Octavius and Libo lost his troops and fled to Antonius. Basillus and Sallustius, each in command of a single legion, Antonius, who likewise had one legion, and Hortensius, who came to join them from the Inner sea [Adriatic] all marched together on Octavius and Libo but were defeated by them.

Antonius and his 15 cohorts surrendered to Octavius and these were all taken to Pompeius by Libo.[42]

Thus we can see there were two key phases of the campaign. The Pompeian fleet of Libo and Octavius engaged with the Caesarian fleet of Cornelius Dolabella and defeated them, killing, or capturing Dolabella's whole force. Appian reports that Pompeius seized forty ships of Caesar's Adriatic fleet.[43] The remaining Caesarian commanders, L. Minucius

Basilus and C. Sallustius Crispus then combined their forces with those of C. Antonius, creating an army of three legions. However Antonius managed to become trapped with his army on an island and was starved into submission, with his troops all being transferred to Pompeius' army. Antonius was captured but Sallustius and Basilus seem to have escaped.

Despite the scant details available to us, this Illyrian campaign was a major defeat for Caesar and a victory for Pompeius. In Africa, Caesar lost two newly formed legions, but in a strategically insignificant part of the world. Here he lost at least three legions, probably established ones, and more importantly lost the only bridgehead he had on the eastern side of the Adriatic and his Adriatic fleet. Control of all land east of the Adriatic now fell to Pompeius as did control of the Adriatic itself, bottling Caesar up in the western half of the Republic and meaning that Pompeius controlled access to the east.

The Eastern Mediterranean

Whilst civil war raged throughout the Western Republic, by contrast the Eastern provinces and client kingdoms were mostly peaceful. The bulk of Rome's provinces in Asia Minor and the Near East had fallen to Rome in the last twenty-five years, during the 70s and 60s BC, in the war against the Pontic and Armenian Empires whose final commander was none other than Pompeius himself.[44] Thus the richest parts of Rome's empire all had close ties to Pompeius and could therefore be used to fund his war effort.

This recruitment and funding was overseen by Pompeius' second in command (and his father-in-law), Q. Caecilius Metellus Scipio, scion of two of Rome's most noble families. Metellus had been appointed as Proconsul of Syria, Rome's most easterly province (the rump of what had been the Seleucid Empire). Yet Syria itself was recovering from the aftermath of the First Romano-Parthian War, which had seen M. Licinius Crassus, and his seven legions destroyed at the Battle of Carrhae (53 BC)[45] and Syria itself invaded by the Parthians (52 BC). As discussed (see Chapter One), Crassus' death was one of the factors that precipitated this Third Civil War.

Syria had been commanded by M. Calpurnius Bibulus, a long-time enemy of Caesar. The expectation was that the Romano-Parthian War was still underway and that a Parthian invasion was imminent. These fears were heightened by Rome's collapse into civil war, giving the Parthians a further inducement. Despite this however, Metellus withdrew the Roman legions stationed to defend Syria, again prioritising civil war over external war. Though the Parthian Empire had successfully defeated the Roman invasion of 53 BC and launched punitive raids into Syria, they too were recovering from their own decades-long civil war and were ruled by a monarch (Orodes II) who was seemingly more worried about threats to his throne than expanding his empire.[46]

Nevertheless, Pompeius felt it necessary to send a personal envoy (C. Lucilius Hirrus) to the Parthian court, to ensure that they were made aware that Pompeius had not forgotten the region and perhaps offering inducements to stay neutral. In any event, a range of factors from Pompeius' inducements to Orodes' natural caution meant that the Parthians did not exploit the opportunity afforded them by the Roman Civil War until a decade later (in 40 BC).[47] Aside from stripping the region of its military resources, Metellus also ensured that the 'riches of the east' flowed into the Pompeian campaign coffers:

> Meanwhile sums of money, requisitioned with the utmost harshness, were being exacted throughout the province. Many kinds of extortion, moreover, were specially devised to glut their avarice. A tribute was imposed on every head of slaves and children; pillar-taxes, door-taxes, corn, soldiers, arms, rowers, freightage, were requisitioned; any mode of exaction, provided a name could be found for it, was deemed a sufficient excuse for compelling contributions.[48]

Another example of the Roman civil war interfering with the politics of the native client kingdom comes from the example of Judea. Towards the end of Rome's great Eastern War, the Kingdom of Judea had collapsed into civil war and Rome had intervened, eventually occupying it militarily and placing their chosen candidate (Hyrcanus II) on the throne. The defeated rival and brother of the king, Aristobulus II was taken to Rome as a royal hostage and was still there when Caesar took the city in 49 BC (see Chapter Two). Though only there a few days, one of Caesar's acts was to release Aristobulus and send him back to Judea, to stir up trouble in the kingdom and possibly retake it, as a Caesarian client king.

Unfortunately for him, Pompeius or Metellus got wind of this plot and arranged to have him poisoned before he could reach Judea. Metellus went further and, apparently on Pompeius' 'orders' had one of the king's sons and heir (Alexander) beheaded at Antioch. Another son (Antigonus II) evaded capture and went on to lead another rebellion against Rome, eventually becoming King of Judea, as a Parthian client and the last of the Hasmonean dynasty.

Aside from collecting men and money from the eastern provinces and kingdoms, Scipio even found time to fight a military action in the region of Mount Amanus in the Roman province of Cilicia, though no other details are given.[49] Having accomplished all this, he wintered in Pergammum, with his forces, waiting to cross back into Greece to re-join Pompeius for the campaigns of 48 BC.

Summary

Of the four theatres of conflict, we can see that in three of them the Pompeian faction made a poor showing, with Sardinia (and Corsica) and then Sicily falling to the Caesarian faction without a fight. North Africa too, would have fallen to the Caesarians too, were it not for the Numidians choosing to intervene and destroying the Caesarian army. The significance of North Africa being held by the Pompeian faction would not have been immediately obvious but would be critical to the continuation of the war, when again it acted as a refuge for the defeated faction.[50]

Yet all three of these regions had one thing in common: none of them seemed to fit into Pompeius' masterplan and none of them received any reinforcements from Pompeius himself, who seems to have considered them incidental. It was only in Illyria, which Pompeius rightly deemed to be of key strategic significance to his overall strategy, that Pompeian forces were deployed and then to overwhelming effect.

By the same token, with Caesar adding Spain to Gaul and Italy, these campaigns only brought the islands of Sardinia, Corsica, and Sicily under Caesarian control, none of which directly benefited Caesar's strategic aims. If he were to bring the war to a conclusion then he needed a bridgehead on the eastern shores of the Adriatic and to be able to have enough control of the Adriatic to cross it at a time of his choosing.

Thus, by the end of 49 BC, Caesar had control of the Western Republic and Pompeius the Eastern one. Yet for all of Caesar's victories – notably breaking the Pompeian pincer strategy by taking Spain – the overall strategy of this civil war was still following the pattern and tempo that Pompeius dictated. It seemed that the war would not be over quickly, and that the decisive battles would be fought at a time and a place of Pompeius' choosing. If Caesar wanted to avoid these outcomes then he needed to once again seize the initiative and force Pompeius' timescales.

Possible bust of C. Marius.

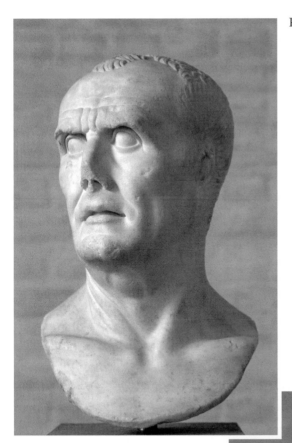

Bust of L. Cornelius Sulla.

Bust of Cn. Pompeius Magnus.

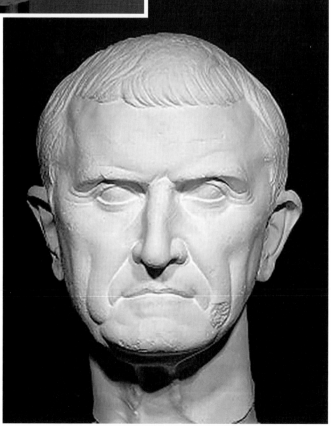

Possible bust of M. Licinius Crassus.

Bust of C. Iulius Caesar.

Bust of M. Tullius Cicero.

Bust of M. Antonius.

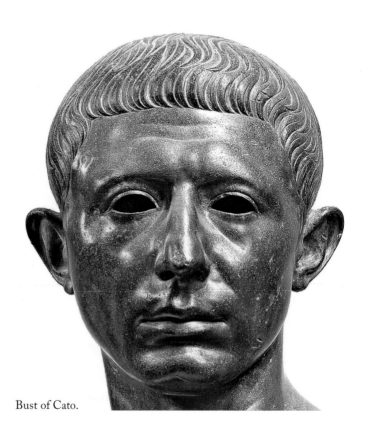

Bust of Cato.

Bust of Sextus Pompeius.

Coin of Metellus Scipio.

Bust of Juba I.

Illyrian coastline.

Ruins of Amphitheatre of Dyrrhachium. (*Adobe Stock*)

Roman ruins of Apollonia. (*Pudelek via Wiki Commons*)

Corcyran coast.

Modern harbour of Massilia. (*Adobe Stock*)

Chapter Five

Between the Campaigns:
The First Citizen and the Dictator

As we have seen, aside from the siege of Brundisium in March 49 BC, the two main protagonists of the war did not meet in battle for the rest of the year but fought a series of proxy wars. As we have also seen, the most obvious factor in these proxy wars was the difference of approach taken by these two leading men. Whilst Caesar attacked and overran Italy followed soon after by Spain, Pompeius is nowhere to be seen in the narrative of these events. This absence is not down to the loss of surviving sources or the bias in those that do survive towards the Caesarian side. This absence reflects a fundamental difference in the approach the two men took to this civil war, which seems to have reflected a wider difference in their respective political and military styles, which can crudely be reflected as the 'tortoise and the hare'.

Whilst Caesar launched an immediate invasion of Italy hoping to finish the war within three months, Pompeius wanted it to be a drawn-out affair and would only fight on his own terms. With Caesar then rushing off to Spain, to prevent a Pompeian flanking manoeuvre, Pompeius again refused to be equally rushed, with no counter invasion of Italy, but stuck to his methodical plan and timetable. For Pompeius there would be no active conflict between the main protagonists until he was sure he was ready. Thus Pompeius stayed in Greece throughout 49 BC, building up his forces and only committing them to clear strategic aims that fitted into his wider masterplan, such as securing control of Illyria.

This difference in the styles between the two men can also be seen in the various political dealings they had, with Caesar, ever the impatient politician, ruling by diktat (as Dictator) whilst Pompeius adopted a subtler approach, ruling by stealth and manipulating his, sometimes temporary, supporters to appoint him as the first amongst equals (a Princeps).

Waiting For Pompeius

The contrast between Caesar's and Pompeius' tactics and approach could not have been greater in 49 BC and seems to reflect their personalities and approach. Caesar, ever restless, forever on campaign versus Pompeius, methodical, measured and calculating, a classic conflict between the hare and the tortoise. Whilst Caesar spread his forces and attention across the Western Republic, and a multitude of battlefields, Pompeius chose to focus on the bigger picture. It can be argued that, to Pompeius, Spain and Africa were side shows, nothing more than distractions, from the main event. From Crassus' death in 53 BC, through to 49 BC, Pompeius seems to have been working to a masterplan for sole dominance over the Republic. His last opponent was his greatest one, a threat to the Republic so grave that his victory would ensure the Senate acquiesced to his permanent role as Guardian of the Republic or Princeps. In reality, the threat was so grave because it had made it so, with Pompeius manipulating events so that Caesar would be forced to attack Rome and be shaped as the new villain of the Republic.

The period between April and December of 49 BC was a study in tactical patience for Pompeius. With Caesar campaigning in Spain, he could have used his mastery of the Adriatic to launch an invasion of Italy, much as Sulla had done in 83 BC, a campaign that Pompeius was heavily involved in. Yet re-securing Rome before Caesar had been defeated would have actually worked against his aims, both political and military.

In political terms, he had now created a new Republican government in exile, with the majority of the Senate and the established political families. This exacerbated the sense of crisis and the gravity of the situation. In the political narrative he had weaved, Rome had fallen to a tyrant and could not be recovered until that tyrant had been defeated. Had Rome been recovered then this sense of crisis would have dissipated, with many of his temporary supporters looking for a negotiated settlement. For Pompeius to maintain his role, he needed the crisis.[1]

In military terms, throughout his career he had only ever fought on his own terms and now, facing the definitive campaign of his career, more than ever he needed to stick to these principles. Thus, he would choose his battlefield and he would dictate the timing and only when he was ready would he give battle. Spain, Sicily, Africa: none of those fitted into this masterplan, only the campaign in Illyria and the Adriatic did and the Pompeian forces efficiently removed the only Caesarian presence on the eastern coast of the Adriatic and secured his control of the seas and controlled Caesar's ability to cross it, thus seizing control of the military narrative and the direction of the war.

Nor do we find Pompeius rushing about, with hastily assembled armies. For this final campaign of his career, he wanted to ensure that he had the most forces available. Hence his supporters and legates were sent throughout the Eastern Republic and all the Roman allies, gathering up a new army and a new navy, to emulate the two campaigns which had cemented his position as one of Rome's' greatest generals' – the Pirate War and the Eastern War.[2] Caesar himself provides us with an admiring description of Pompeius' preparations:

> *Pompeius, availing himself for the purpose of collecting forces of a whole year which had been free from war and without disturbance from an enemy, had gathered a large fleet from Asia and the Cyclades islands, from Corcyra, Athens, Pontus, Bithynia, Syria, Cilicia, Phoenice, Egypt; had contracted for the building of a large fleet wherever possible; had requisitioned a large sum of money from Asia, Syria, and all the kings, potentates, and tetrarchs, and from the free communities of Achaia; and had compelled the tax-farming associations of the provinces of which he was himself in control to pay over large sums.*[3]

> *He had made up nine legions of Roman citizens: five from Italy, which he had conveyed across the sea; one of veterans from Cilicia, which, being formed out of two legions, he styled the Twin Legion; one from Crete and Macedonia out of veteran troops which, when disbanded by their former commanders, had settled in those provinces; two from Asia, for the levying of which the Consul Lentulus had arranged.*

> *Besides, he had distributed among the legions by way of supplement a large number of men from Thessaly, Boeotia, Achaia, and Epirus. With these he had mixed men who had served under Antonius. Besides these he was expecting two legions with Scipio from Syria. He had archers from Crete and Lacedaemon, from Pontus and Syria and the other states to the number of three thousand; also two cohorts, six hundred strong, of slingers, and seven thousand horsemen. Of these Deiotarus had brought six hundred Gauls, and Ariobarzanes five hundred from Cappadocia;*

Cotys had provided the same number from Thrace and had sent his son Sadala; from Macedonia there were two hundred under the command of Rhascypolis, a man of marked valour.

The young Pompeius had brought with his fleet five hundred of the Gabinian troops from Alexandria, Gauls and Germans, whom A. Gabinius had left there with King Ptolomaeus on garrison duty. He had collected eight hundred from his own slaves and from his list of herdsmen. Tarcondarius Castor and Domnilaus had provided three hundred from Gallograecia; of these the one had come with his men, the other had sent his son. From Syria two hundred had been sent by Antiochus of Commagene, on whom Pompeius bestowed large rewards, and among them many mounted archers. To these Pompeius had added Dardani and Bessi, partly mercenaries, partly secured by his authority or influence, also Macedonians, Thessalians, and men of other nations and states, and had thus filled up the number stated above.[4]

Appian's account provides an even higher estimate for Pompeius' forces:

Caesar at that time had ten legions of infantry and 10,000 Gallic horse. Pompeius had five legions from Italy, with which he had crossed the Adriatic, and the cavalry belonging to them; also the two surviving legions that had served with Crassus in the Parthian War and a certain part of those who had made the incursion into Egypt with Gabinius, making altogether eleven legions of Italian troops and about 7,000 horse. He had auxiliaries also from Ionia, Macedonia, Peloponnesus, and Boeotia, Cretan archers, Thracian slingers, and Pontic javelin-throwers. He had also some Gallic horse and others from eastern Galatia, together with Commageneans sent by Antiochus, Cilicians, Cappadocians, and Pisidians.[5]

Plutarch adds further detail:

His navy was simply irresistible, since he had five hundred ships of war, while the number of his light galleys and fast cruisers was immense; his cavalry numbered seven thousand, the flower of Rome and Italy, pre-eminent in lineage, wealth, and courage; and his infantry, which was a mixed multitude and in need of training, he exercised at Beroea, not sitting idly by, but taking part in their exercises himself, as if he had been in the flower of his age.[6]

Nor had Pompeius neglected to adequately provision his new army:

> *He had collected a very large quantity of corn from Thessaly, Asia, Egypt, Crete, Cyrene, and other districts.*[7]

Thus Pompeius had built up a new army, of eleven legions, including two of battle-hardened veterans from the Romano-Parthian War, along with seven thousand cavalry and a large number of auxiliaries. Yet this compared to Caesar's ten legions and ten thousand cavalry, meaning that Pompeius had the larger army in numerical terms. He had also had the rest of 49 BC to train and integrate the various elements. There were however two obvious downsides; the first being that many of his legions were newly assembled and, aside from the Illyrian campaign, most of them had not seen combat, unlike Caesar's legions. Secondly, aside from the eleven legions of Roman citizens there was a huge multinational element in terms of auxiliaries, from a range of kingdoms, and with a vast range of languages and fighting styles.

Nevertheless, in the short term, Pompeius' strategy had paid off militarily, allowing him time to assemble what he hoped would be an overwhelming military machine with a vast army and navy, allowing him to take to the field in 48 BC. Politically his strategy had paid off as well, as can be seen from the support he received from his Senate in exile. As is common, Appian presents us with what purports to be the words from a speech Pompeius gave to his assembled forces and Senate, which, if accurate, shows us his strategy of abandoning Rome, with historic parallels to the Persian Wars and the Gallic Sack, thus making Caesar the new 'bogey man', akin to the Persian Emperor Xerxes or the Gallic Tribes who burnt Rome:

> *Fellow-soldiers, the Athenians, too, abandoned their city for the sake of liberty when they were fighting against invasion, because they believed that it was not houses that made a city, but men; and after they had done so they presently recovered it and made it more renowned than even before. So, too, our own ancestors abandoned the city when the Gauls invaded it, and Camillus hastened from Ardea and recovered it. All men of sound mind think that their country is wherever they can preserve their liberty.*[8]

Appian also provides the following description:

When Pompeius had thus spoken the whole army, including the Senators and a great many of the nobility who were with him, applauded him vociferously and told him to lead them to whatsoever task he would.[9]

Whilst Plutarch adds:

When their Senate convened and a decree was passed, on motion of Cato, that no Roman should be killed except on a field of battle, and that no city subject to Rome should be plundered, the party of Pompeius was held in still greater favour.[10]

Thus we can see that, despite being in exile for the best part of a year, Pompeius had only cemented his position as '*primus inter pares*' or first amongst equals, and the Princeps (First Citizen) of the Eastern Republic.

With control of the Adriatic, Pompeius distributed his fleet to protect the eastern Adriatic ports and prevent a crossing, dangerous enough in winter times. With that protection, he was able to disperse his land forces into winter quarters throughout Thessaly and Macedonia, whilst he remained in his new temporary capital of Dyrrhachium. Again, Pompeius had been able to dictate the overall pace of this Third Civil War, stretching it from Caesar's preferred short campaign, into a long drawn-out affair. The inevitable clash between the two men would come in 48 BC and would be fought at the time of and in the location of Pompeius' choosing.

The one key question remains about Pompeius' strategy: namely the intended location of this final campaign. Was it to be Greece or Italy? As we have seen he had already spurned the chance to invade Italy in 49 BC in Caesar's absence, but did this mean that he would continue to do so once his army was ready? Clearly, he would have assumed that in 48 BC Caesar would attempt to retake the initiative and attack him in Greece (it being Caesar's nature) and thus his control of the Adriatic would hopefully guard against this. Yet once Pompeius had judged his army ready to fight would he have launched an invasion of Italy and challenged Caesar there or would he have removed the Adriatic fleet and allowed Caesar to cross and face him?

Here, there were both political and military considerations, as Pompeius did not just have to beat Caesar but he had to be seen to beat Caesar, and this raises questions about his audience. Did he want to be seen as the man who followed Sulla's example and invaded Italy from the East, like a foreign invader, especially with such a large contingent of non-Roman forces, and risk the devastation which the eighteen-month long Sullan campaign had inflicted upon the country (82–81 BC)? On the other hand, did he want to defeat Caesar under the eyes of the Senate (which was in Greece) and then return to Italy (and Rome) as the 'liberator'?

In military terms there was also the consideration of shipping such a large army across the Adriatic and re-assembling them in Italy without Caesarian interference. Italy was also held by Caesar and Pompeius would need to recapture the ports, notably Brundisium beforehand, allowing Caesar time to assemble a counter offensive. Crossing the Adriatic would also stretch his supply lines, forcing his army to live off the land and thus increase the chance of devastating the Italian countryside and population.

Thus, it seems the most likely that Pompeius intended to fight in Greece, his new powerbase rather than risk an invasion of Italy. The clear theoretical risk would be that Caesar would refuse and sit back, taking the impetus out of the crisis, and allowing third parties the chance to negotiate. Yet in practice we must assume that Pompeius viewed this possibility as remote, given Caesar's character and record.

Caesar's Return to Italy – The Mutiny at Placentia

Caesar's return to Italy, late in 49 BC, was marked by two notable events: a mutiny by elements of his legions and his elevation to (temporary) supreme power in Rome as Dictator. Unsurprisingly we find no mention of the mutiny in Caesar's own account of the war, but the other surviving sources provide coverage of the incident, including a long account in Dio.[11] The mutiny of an unknown number of legions took place at the Roman colony of Placentia (Piacenza) in the Po Valley and broke out whilst Caesar was still at Massilia. Naturally enough the matter was so serious that Caesar immediately went to Placentia with additional forces to quell the mutiny before it spread. Dio and Appian present the following as the reasons behind the mutiny:

At Placentia, some soldiers mutinied and refused to accompany Caesar longer, on the pretext that they were exhausted, but really because he did not allow them to plunder the country nor to do all the other things on which their minds were set; for their hope was to obtain from him anything and everything, as he stood in so great a need of them.[12]

and another army of Caesar mutinied at Placentia, crying out against their officers for prolonging the war and not paying them the five minae that Caesar had promised them as a donative while they were still at Brundisium.[13]

Thus it seems that, as is commonly the case, it was money (or the lack of it) that lay at the root of the mutiny. This does highlight an issue which faced civil war armies and their commanders. In a normal campaign a typically victorious army could expect to supplement their meagre pay by plunder, but a civil war commander, and one trying to shake an image of being a bloodthirsty tyrant at the head of a barbarian horde, could not allow his armies to plunder Italy or the provinces that had not opposed him.

This also seems to highlight another issue that Caesar was facing, namely a lack of money. Though he had ransacked the Temple treasuries in Rome, he still only had command of the agriculturally rich but poorer Western Republic, whilst the richer eastern provinces, whose tax monies usually flowed into Rome's coffers, were now under Pompeius' control and funding his armies. This just emphasised the imbalance between the resources of the two men and the urgency with which Caesar needed to confront Pompeius. As had been shown by Caesar's invasion of Italy (see Chapter Two), aside from his original forces, Roman armies in civil wars tended to follow the commander who would bring them the most success. Whilst Caesar had accomplished military glory, it was Pompeius who had the wealth at his disposal.

Nevertheless, in the short term, Caesar's characteristic swift action in confronting the mutinying army, no doubt suitably defended personally, seems to have taken the steam out of the mutiny. The fate of Caesar's first father-in-law, L. Cornelius Cinna, who effectively ruled Rome between 87 and 84 BC during the First Civil War, cannot have been far from his mind, as Cinna was killed during a mutiny by his troops in Italy in 84 BC. Dio presents what purports to have been Caesar's speech to the assembled army[14] which aside from the flowing rhetoric about serving his country in its hour of need, promised to pay the monies that were owed and only to execute a handful of ring leaders. Faced with such promises, the majority of the legions stood down and fell back into line. Nevertheless, it was a sign that Caesar's newly raised armies were growing restless and that their loyalty could not automatically be taken for granted but needed to be paid for.

Caesar the Dictator

When Caesar first took Rome, in April of 49 BC (see Chapter Two), he only stayed for a few days, showing his customary impatience, and despite speeches to the remaining Senate and the People, managed to outstay his welcome with another customary blunt show of force, threatening to murder a Tribune who was blocking his ransacking of the State treasury for his own ends. Clearly Caesar would have much rather been on campaign than stay in Rome and deal with the political situation there, even a Rome purged of his obvious enemies. As stated before (Chapter One) Caesar had spent nearly a decade in the field, first in the Gallic Wars and now the Civil War and seemed to have the classic general's impatience with the subtitles and delays of political life. Even before his departure to Gaul, Caesar's later political career showed little of the earlier promise, with his Praetorship becoming entangled with the Second Civil War and the aftermath of the attempted coup in Rome (62 BC) and his Consulship only coming about as an agent of Pompeius and Crassus.

Clearly however, with the Republic temporarily at peace, albeit split in two (once again), Caesar had to engage with the constitutional niceties and cover his military control of the Western Republic in a veil of legality. Despite having (somewhat miraculously) lived through the Dictatorship of Sulla during 83–82 BC, when his very heritage (Marian) and marriage (Cinnan) should have condemned him to proscription, Caesar again chose the direct route and organised his election as Dictator of Rome.

As has often been stressed, originally the office of Dictator had none of the connotations that it does today of arbitrary and, usually, bloody rule. It was an emergency office of state, only to be used in times of military crisis when the Romans needed one clear commander, not the usual two equal Consuls. Yet the office had not been used in that capacity since the Second Punic War (202 BC being the last time), after which Republican Italy was seldom under direct threat. The only other time it could have been used in that capacity was during the Northern Wars (113–101 BC) when migrating northern tribes destroyed Roman armies and threatened to invade Italy itself. Yet it was Caesar's maternal uncle, C. Marius who was chosen as Rome's sole commander to face this threat yet did so by the mechanism of repeated Consulships and the ability to select his own running mate. The same method had been used by Caesar's father-in-law, L. Cornelius Cinna to rule Rome following Marius' death. It was only under their rival and Marius' former protege (and Pompeius' former father-in-law), L. Cornelius Sulla, that the office of Dictator was revived and began to be associated with bloody political sole rule.

Yet, having grown up in Rome during this period and narrowly avoiding becoming one of its many victims, Caesar choose to revive the Dictatorship. Here again, the contrast with Pompeius is clear. In 52 BC when Rome fell into bloody political chaos (see Chapter One), the Senate turned to Pompeius and some proposed reviving the Dictatorship. Pompeius, ironically and hypocritically, having no wish to be associated with such a barbed political comparison (Sulla's Dictatorship) wisely chose to publicly turn down such a request and chose the 'Marian' route of utilising the Consulship, albeit initially as sole Consul and then being able to nominate his own colleague (none other than his father-in-law, L. Caecilius Metellus Scipio).

Thus Caesar could, and in fact did, utilise this option and ensure he was elected as Consul for 48 BC alongside a compliant partner. This being late November/early December 49 BC, he would only need to wait for another month to six weeks before he could wield formal political power. Caesar also had a further option at his disposal, namely using the Praetors and Tribunes to pass legislation through the Assemblies. Given the flight of his outright opponents and the threats issued to Metellus earlier in the year, he could be certain that any token opposition could be overcome. Again, as we see below, Caesar did utilise this option.

A third option was also available, namely the election of an Interrex, a temporary official who was appointed to oversee the elections for 48 BC when the Consuls were not available, as was the case at the time. Yet, despite these three options being available to him, Caesar clearly felt the need for more direct and immediate power and thus organised (via the Praetor M. Aemilius Lepidus, another son of a First Civil War general) to propose his election as Dictator to a cowed Assembly. Again here we can see Caesar's direct and military approach to Roman politics; taking the most practical approach regardless of the message it sent, not only to his opponents but more importantly to the worried neutrals. Thus Caesar assumed the office of Dictator, last used by the 'bloody tyrant' Sulla, tarring himself with the same brush and fulfilling the propaganda of his opponents and the fears of the many neutrals.

Having been appointed Dictator, he then oversaw the elections for 48 BC, which unsurprisingly saw him elected as one of the Consuls, P. Servilius Isauricus being the other. Naturally, his key supporters were selected to command the provinces of the Western Republic he controlled, and he tried to ensure that all domestic officials could be relied on to keep Roman politics quiet whilst he was on campaign, with varying levels of success.

Aside from the election, Caesar passed some measures on debt relief, though refused a petition to abolish debts outright, and distributed free corn to the poorest of the city. He also possibly passed a measure restoring the rights to the children of those men proscribed by Sulla, which was a campaign he had championed as a young politician in the 60s BC and allowed him to again try to distance himself from any comparisons to Sulla.[15] In terms of overturning more recent prohibitions, he allowed the Praetor and Tribunes to overturn the exiling of those men convicted under the lex Pompeia of 52 BC (see Chapter One), allowing them to return to Rome.

On the one hand this sent a clear message that he was distancing himself from Pompeius and that these men would therefore owe some loyalty to him. On the other hand however, although many were enemies of Pompeius, many had been the very elements that had participated in the bloody chaos of the late 50s BC and therefore Caesar was importing those troublemakers back into Rome, a Rome that he, and any central authority figure, would be absent from. One notable exception was T. Annius Milo, the Pompeian gang leader who had organised the murder of Clodius. Naturally enough this prohibition did not stop Milo, who promptly used Caesar's absence in Greece during 48 BC, to return to Rome and stir up revolt (see Chapter Six).

Finally he organised the Latin Festival, an ancient religious ceremony, usually organised by the Consuls. Then after just eleven days, he quit his Dictatorship, having apparently achieved all he wanted and promptly left

Rome to winter in Brundisium with his army, planning the invasion of the Pompeian-held eastern Adriatic coast. Once again, we see Caesar's impatience with political life, wanting to spend as little time as possible on domestic matters and preferring to leave it to subordinates whilst he concentrated on military matters. It was an attitude that continued to be demonstrated throughout the civil war years and ultimately led to his infamous murder in 44 BC.

Nevertheless, in the short term, he ended 49 BC back at Brundisium, where he had been nine months earlier, still facing the same fundamental issue of how to bring Pompeius to battle, without control of the Adriatic. Again, the surviving sources bear out Caesar's frustration and impatience at not being able to instantly go on campaign, an impatience which Pompeius was clearly relying on.

Section III

The Dyrrhachium Campaign (48 BC)

Chapter Six

The Road to Dyrrhachium (48 BC)

As we have seen, the year 49 BC proved to be something of an anti-climax in terms of the Third Civil War, especially after it opened in such an explosive manner with Caesar's invasion of Italy. This anti-climax was down to the actions and policies of one man: Cn. Pompeius 'Magnus', who having engineered the whole crisis that preceded Caesar's invasion had no wish to indulge his opponent by meeting his characteristic rush into battle. In both the military and political fields, Pompeius needed time, both to raise and train a grand army and allow the crisis to worsen to ensure that the bulk of the non-aligned oligarchy turned to him to save them from Caesar: Rome's new 'bogeyman'.

Thus Italy, Rome and even Spain were sacrificed on the altar of Pompeius' policy, with the contrast between the two men hardly being starker. On the one hand was Caesar, a ball of energy, invading Italy with one legion, chasing Pompeius across the Peninsula, then rushing back to Rome, staying for only a few days before rushing off to Spain and then back to Italy before year end. On the other hand, we have Pompeius, conducting an orderly withdrawal to Greece (Epirus), and then drawing on the resources of the Eastern Republic and its allies to patiently build up a large army and only committing military resources to eliminating the Caesarian bridgehead in Illyria.

Thus, a year that had started with Caesar seizing the initiative (perhaps as his opponent had intended him to) had ended in stalemate, with Caesar on one side of the Adriatic and Pompeius on the other. Overall, both men had had their triumphs and defeats. Pompeian Spain had fallen more quickly than Pompeius would have liked, meaning Caesar was ready to attack Epirus at the start of 48 BC rather than later in the year. Yet Caesarian Illyria too had fallen, denying Caesar the bridgehead he needed on the eastern shore of the Adriatic. North Africa too had remained Pompeian with the destruction of Caesar's invasion force; the significance of which was only to become clearer as the civil war progressed.

Aims & Tactics – Caesar

As we have seen, Caesar's main military tactic was one of always taking the initiative and acting at speed, sometimes recklessly so. He would have been well aware that for all his successes in Italy and Spain he was still dancing to Pompeius' tune, with Pompeius playing for the time he needed to assemble his army. He would have been equally aware that he needed to act before Pompeius finished his preparations and would no doubt have been kept informed by agents and sympathisers of the military build-up taking place in Greece. Equally, however, he would also have been aware that by not becoming entangled in a long campaign in Spain he had disrupted Pompeius' timetable. As we will see, whilst Pompeius had assembled a large army in Greece, a large contingent of his forces were still in Asia Minor under the command of Q. Caecilius Metellus Scipio, who was wintering there.

Thus, by both inclination and military necessity, Caesar's clear tactic was to invade Epirus quickly and establish a bridgehead there, taking advantage of the dispersal of Pompeius' forces throughout Greece for winter and before Metellus Scipio arrived from the east. The two major problems he faced were that firstly, Pompeius' fleet had naval superiority in the Adriatic and secondly, crossing the Adriatic itself in the depths of winter was no easy proposition, given the foul weather and rough seas.

Aims & Tactics – Pompeius

As we have said above, Pompeius represented the opposite of Caesar; a patient and calculating commander who never rushed headlong into a campaign without ensuring that his preparations were satisfactory. Whilst on the whole, this civil war was playing out according to his grand strategy, Caesar had certainly disrupted his timescales. More than willing to sacrifice Spain, he would have been delighted when Caesar took the bait and, ignoring him in Greece, invaded Spain. He would have been far from delighted however when news reached him that Spain had fallen in a few months and Caesar would be back in Italy before year end.

Again, as we have stated above, although Pompeius was in the process of assembling a vast army from all corners of the Eastern Republic, a significant portion of this force was wintering in Asia under the command of Metellus Scipio. Furthermore, his army in Greece was scattered at their winter quarters through Greece and Epirus. Pompeius would have clearly seen his own weakness here and would have known that Caesar would too. Not only knowing Caesar personally, but having seen his campaigns of the previous year, Pompeius would have been all too aware that Caesar would be eager to cross the Adriatic and would not wait until spring (the normal time to start crossing troops over the Adriatic).

Thus Pompeius would have to rely on his naval control of the Adriatic to prevent a crossing, which given the stormy nature of the seas was a double-edged sword. Whilst the bad weather and rough seas would make it difficult for an enemy to attempt to force a crossing, it would also hamper his navy's attempts to provide an effective blockade. Yet equally there also lay an opportunity here for Pompeius. He could guess with some certainty that it would be Caesar himself who would lead the initial foray across the Adriatic. Thus, if Caesar did make it across the Adriatic and Pompeius could cut him off, then Caesar would be trapped, much like he was at Ilerda, on the wrong side of a body of water (albeit much magnified). However, given that Caesar had not only escaped the trap in Spain but had turned it into a victory, this tactic had its clear risks.

The Pompeian Republic

Dio provides us with some detail of the Republican government in exile, or the Pompeian Republic, which was based in the city of Thessalonica (modern Thessaloniki), the provincial capital of the Roman province of Macedonia, and connected to Dyrrhachium by the Via Egnatia:

> *Those in Thessalonica had made no such appointments, although they had by some accounts about two hundred of the Senate and also the Consuls with them and had appropriated a small piece of land for the auguries, in order that these might seem to take place under some form of law, so that they regarded the people and the whole city as present there. They had not appointed new magistrates for the reason that the Consuls had not proposed the lex curiata; but instead they employed the same officials as before, merely changing their names and calling some proconsuls, others Propraetors, and others Proquaestors.*[1]

Thus Pompeius wintered in the new capital of the Eastern Roman Republic, holding on to his Proconsular command, but effectively the first citizen (Princeps) of the Eastern Republic.

The Caesarian Invasion of Epirus (48 BC)

As Appian himself details, unsurprisingly Caesar was restless whilst having to wait at Brundisium for suitable weather to cross and was beaten back in his initial efforts.[2] Yet on 4 January Caesar was able to cross the Adriatic, evade the Pompeian fleet commanded by his old enemy, M. Calpurnius Bibulus, and land on the eastern shores of the Adriatic.[3] We are told that Caesar had twelve warships and more than thirty transports, but Caesar himself informs us that he was able to transport seven legions across the Adriatic, whilst Appian adds six hundred cavalry.[4]

Yet whilst this tactic had all the hallmarks of Caesar, being bold in its inception and in its attempt to seize the initiative, it also bore the other hallmarks of a Caesarian move, in that it was incredibly risky. A small fleet could evade the many Pompeian patrols and land on an undefended coastline, but the minute his forces were detected on land, in such an act as trying to seize a port to act as a bridgehead, then he had betrayed his position to the Pompeian fleet, who would know where to focus their efforts. Thus, again Caesar needed to rely on speed and surprise and seize as many ports as he could and hold them, long enough for the main bulk of his army to cross, before they were intercepted by the Pompeian fleets.

As we have Caesar's detailed account of this campaign, we know the route he took, avoiding the shortest route, straight across from Brundisium to Apollonia or further north to Dyrrhachium, to avoid the Pompeian fleets. Instead he went further south and landed on the undefended and uninhabited coastline to the south of Oricum (north of the main Pompeian fleet at Corcyra), by the Ceraunian Mountains (modern Albania), at Palaeste (see Map 5).

The nearest port to Caesar's landing was that of Oricum, which lay to the north and which had a Pompeian fleet of eighteen ships, commanded by Q. Lucretius Vespillo and a Minucius Rufus. Whilst they were too late to prevent Caesar from landing further up the coast, they were able to send a message to Bibulus and the main Pompeian fleet (one hundred and ten ships) anchored at Corcyra (modern Corfu). Wasting no time and not able to pinpoint exactly where Caesar intended to cross, Bibulus deployed the Pompeian fleet and was able to catch a portion of the empty transports as they returned to Italy, destroying over thirty of them. Bibulus then was able to deploy his fleet in blockade of that portion of the coast to prevent any further crossing, cutting Caesar off in Epirus.

Thus Caesar had achieved his initial objective and was able to land an advance guard of his army in Epirus, but at the cost of betraying his position to the Pompeian fleet. Having now lost the element of surprise, Caesar chose to send an envoy to Pompeius: L. Vibullius Rufus, the Pompeian officer sent to Spain with Pompeius' orders and who had been captured there (for the second time, having been captured and released by Caesar in Italy, earlier in 49 BC).

Vibullius, who was seemingly a friend of Pompeius, was dispatched to Corcyra to report Caesar's long-standing offer that both participants should disband their armies and seek arbitration of the Senate and People. Given the state of the war there was absolutely no chance that either side would agree to those terms, but it allowed Caesar to try to counter the Pompeian propaganda that Caesar was a new Sulla (which in itself was always ironic given the respective and opposing roles that Caesar and Pompeius played in the First Civil War).

Nonetheless, as Vibullius disembarked at Corcyra he immediately made for Pompeius who was already returning to Epirus from Thessalonica in Macedonia and thus was able to give him a first-hand briefing on Caesar's preparations and invasion. Clearly realising the danger, but also the opportunity (Caesar trapped in Epirus), Pompeius immediately made for the Epirote coast and his winter headquarters of Dyrrhachium, using the Via Egnatia (the Roman military road which ran the length of Macedonia to the Hellespont), the two sides now in a race to secure the coastal cities of Epirus (see Map 5).

As was so often the case, the first blood went to Caesar, who, marching northwards along the coast, was able to secure the nearest coastal city, that of Oricum, which was commanded by a Pompeian officer: L. Manlius Torquatus. The town was garrisoned, not with Roman forces, but with men from the surrounding Illyrian tribe: the Parthini. Unfortunately for Torquatus, when Caesar's army approached, neither the Parthini nor the townspeople wanted to endure a siege at Roman hands, and thus declared their neutrality in the civil war. Faced with no alternative, Torquatus had to surrender both himself and the town to Caesar, though he was soon released back to Pompeius, much to Caesar's eventual cost.

Having thus secured his first port, and with Pompeius yet to reach the coast, Caesar continued his northern march and set out for the larger target of the coastal city of Apollonia (see Map. 5). Apollonia was commanded by a junior Pompeian officer: L. Staberius. Again however, when faced with an advancing Roman army and not wishing to be on the losing side of a civil war, the inhabitants of Apollonia also refused to follow Staberius in defending the city and Apollonia too fell without a fight, with Staberius escaping the city.

Clearly Pompeius' strategy was beginning to unravel, and Caesar had established himself a secure bridgehead in Epirus, controlling both sides of the Gulf of Oricum, the territory opposite Brundisium, and thus the shortest route across the Adriatic. Furthermore, as Caesar himself boasts, following this latest defection, the surrounding tribes of the Byllidenses and the Amantini also defected to Caesar, offering him their (wafer-thin) support.[5] Nevertheless, although he had secured a bridgehead, the real prize lay further to the north, the city of Dyrrhachium itself, the largest and most important military port in the eastern Adriatic, and start of the Via Egnatia, and which was also Pompeius' main headquarters.

Clearing realising the danger and learning that neither Oricum nor Apollonia had slowed Caesar down, Pompeius marched his army night and day and reached Dyrrhachium first, thus checking Caesar's progress and forcing him to halt at the River Apsus (the modern Seman river). Having secured Dyrrhachium, Pompeius then led his force south to the Apsus and camped on the opposite bank. For the first time since Brundisium in 49 BC, Pompeius and Caesar came face to face with each other.

Stalemate at Apsus

Yet what this situation (which must have been late January or early February 48 BC) represented was a stalemate. Caesar had secured a bridgehead on the Adriatic coast, which effectively was surrounded by Pompeian forces on all sides. To the north lay Pompeius and his army. To the south lay the Pompeian naval base of Corcyra, home of the Pompeian fleet. To the east lay Pompeian controlled Macedonia and the advancing army of

Metellus Scipio and most importantly to the west lay the Adriatic, which cut Caesar off from Italy and the rest of his army at Brundisium.

Though Pompeius and Caesar faced off each other with only a river separating them, here again we have an interesting divergence of accounts as to the course of the stalemate. Caesar states that no clashes took place between the two sides and in fact that he and Pompeius held regular meetings, though, interestingly, does not record what they talked about.[6] Appian's account has a standoff, but with cavalry clashes between the two:

> By crossing the stream they had occasional cavalry skirmishes with each other, but the armies did not come to a general engagement, for Pompeius was still exercising his new levies and Caesar waited for the forces left at Brundisium.[7]

It seems that of the two armies, Pompeius had the greater number, though we are not told how many legions he had with him, only that it was more than Caesar's seven. The sources are naturally concerned with answering the question as to why no battle took place here. Interestingly both Appian and Dio have Pompeius eager for battle:

> Pompeius, in order to anticipate Caesar's reinforcements, made haste and led his army forward prepared for battle. While two of his soldiers were searching in midstream for the best place to cross the river, one of Caesar's men attacked and killed them both, whereupon Pompeius drew back, as he considered this event inauspicious. All of his friends blamed him for missing this capital opportunity.[8]

> Caesar advanced to meet him [Pompeius] as far as the river, thinking that even as he was, he would prove a match for the troops then approaching; but when he learned that he was inferior in numbers, he halted. And in order that it might not be thought either that he was halting through fear or that he was making the first move in the war, he submitted some conciliatory proposals to the other side and delayed on this pretext. Pompeius, perceiving his motive, wished to try conclusions with him as soon as possible and for this reason undertook to cross the river. But the bridge broke down under the weight and some of the advance guard, thus isolated, perished. Then he desisted, discouraged because he had failed in the first action of the war.[9]

Thus, both accounts have Pompeius attempting to attack Caesar but giving up when losing men in a river crossing, either to Caesar's forces or the river itself. Yet neither reason stands up to scrutiny. The loss of two men or a bridge would not stop a general of the calibre of Pompeius. Caesar himself takes pains to refer to a peace conference held between envoys of the two commanders, again wanting to be portrayed as the peacemaker forced into war.[10] P. Vatinius spoke for Caesar, whilst Caesar's old lieutenant, T. Labienus represented Pompeius. Yet the parlay was interrupted:

> From among this concourse Titus Labienus comes forward, who begins to talk and dispute with Vatinius, but says nothing about peace. A sudden shower of missiles from every quarter breaks off their discourse; protected by the arms of the soldiers, he avoided them, but many are wounded, among them Cornelius Balbus, M. Plotius, L. Tiburtius, and some centurions and soldiers. Then Labienus exclaimed: 'Cease then to talk about a settlement, for there can be no peace for us till Caesar's head is brought in!'[11]

Regardless of the stories in Appian and Dio, about bridges and inauspicious events, it is clear that if Pompeius really wanted to attack Caesar then he would have done so. The obvious reason that he did not is that it did not suit his overall strategy. Though he had the superior number of troops, they were freshly levied and faced an army composed of Gallic veterans.

Furthermore, we are not told by what number Pompeius outnumbered Caesar and it may not have been by enough to be confident of victory (as discussed below, it may have been in the region of nine to ten legions). Furthermore, the situation favoured Pompeius, with Caesar cut off from reinforcements, whilst his own reinforcements were crossing Greece. Thus Pompeius was happy to sit back and contain Caesar until the situation swung decisively in his favour.

Caesar by contrast for once had to curb his natural boldness. The bulk of his army lay on the other side of the Adriatic and facing him was Pompeius Magnus himself, with a larger number of troops and with a secure supply line to his base at Dyrrhachium. Though Caesar, for once, choose a cautious approach, presumably as even he must have realised that he was outnumbered, he would also have realised (as would Pompeius) that time was not on his side. Pompeius had scrambled his forces from their winter quarters to counter Caesar's thrust and every day more would have been converging on Dyrrhachium.

Furthermore, it was now a race against time to see which set of reinforcements could reach their commander first. The nearest (geographically) was the Caesarian army, commanded by Fufius Calenus, yet they lay separated by the Adriatic and the Pompeian fleet, who now had a clear target. Those furthest away were the Pompeian army of Metellus Scipio, who had crossed from Asia, and were marching across Thessaly and Macedonia, presumably along the Via Egnatia. For Caesar, receiving his reinforcements was a necessity, for Pompeius a luxury. Thus, with both sides locked in stalemate at the River Apsus, the focus of the war shifted once again to the Adriatic. If the Pompeian fleet could hold the Caesarian army at Brundisium, then Caesar would be cut off in Epirus, forcing him to attack Pompeius or retreat before the army of Metellus Scipio arrived.

The Adriatic Campaign – Stalemate

Though Caesar had secured the ports of Oricum and Apollonia, he only controlled the physical cities themselves; he did not control the waters off their coast. It seems that M. Calpurnius Bibulus (Caesar's former Consular colleague) had moved his fleet swiftly from Corcyra and put the two cities under naval blockade. Once again, though Caesar had seized the initiative with his bold landing and swift capture of the two ports, Pompeian forces had countered and disrupted Caesar's strategy. Just as Pompeius had cut Caesar off from Dyrrhachium on land, so Bibulus cut Caesar off from Brundisium by sea. Caesar himself informs us that his fleet, under the command of Q. Fufius Calenus had actually left Brundisium, bound for Oricum or Apollonia, when he received a communication from Caesar himself that the ports were under blockade, forcing him to turn back. One ship did not obey the order and paid the price:

> One of these, which kept on its way and did not attend to the command of Calenus, because it was without soldiers and was under private command, was carried to Oricum and attacked and taken by Bibulus, who inflicted punishment on slaves and freemen, even down to beardless boys, and killed them all without exception.[12]

According to Dio, from this point onwards Bibulus kept Brundisium under close blockade, preventing the Caesarian fleet from leaving.[13] Nevertheless, Bibulus himself however was having difficulties in maintaining the blockade, with Caesarian forces patrolling the lands on the Italian side of the Adriatic, making foraging for food and fresh water difficult. Thus he needed to be re-supplied by sea, from his base on Corcyra, making him more reliant on that island.

With the situation locked in stalemate, Caesar's natural restlessness came to the fore once more, and leaving his army facing Pompeius at the River Apsus, he took one legion and marched southwards seemingly with two aims in mind. The first was to try to secure fresh food supplies for his army, which was now cut off in Epirus. The second was made apparent in his move towards the island of Corcyra itself, perhaps hoping to see if he could capture Pompeius' main naval base in the Adriatic. As Caesar himself reports, he reached as far as the town of Buthrotum, a town on the mainland parallel to Corcyra. Given Caesar's history of bold campaign moves, he perhaps wanted to see whether he could take the island itself by a surprise attack. Ultimately however the move came to nought.

With both Bibulus' and Caesar's forces locked in a stalemate and with both sides suffering from supply issues, it is perhaps not surprising that talk of truce broke out amongst the officers on both sides. On receiving the proposal, Caesar left his legion at Buthrotum and returned to Oricum to meet the Pompeian commanders. The Pompeian fleet was represented by L. Scribonius Libo, with Bibulus both ill and being a decade-long personal enemy of Caesar. As with the case with all such attempts at negotiation, they ultimately came to nought and the stalemate continued. One notable event however was the subsequent death of the Pompeian fleet commander: M. Calpurnius Bibulus, who died at sea after a short illness. Command of the fleet fell to Scribonius Libo, who embarked on a fresh campaign to break the stalemate in the mid-Adriatic. Taking fifty ships from the blockade, he set out to attack Brundisium itself.

The Battle of Brundisium (March 48 BC)

Scribonius' tactic was an equally bold one. If Brundisium could be captured, or at least if Caesar's fleet could be destroyed in harbour, then

Caesar himself would be trapped in Epirus with no reinforcements and no escape back to Italy, forcing him to change his campaign strategy. Scribonius' strategy initially met with success and he seemed to catch the Caesarian forces off guard:

> *Approaching suddenly, he found some merchantmen; these he burned, and one loaded with corn he towed off, filling our men with great terror. Then landing by night some soldiers and archers, he dislodged the cavalry outpost and made such good use of the opportunities of his position that he sent a dispatch to Pompeius saying that, if he liked, he might order the rest of his ships to be beached and repaired, and that with his own fleet he would keep off Caesar's reinforcements.*[14]

Command of Brundisium seems to have fallen to M. Antonius, who, realising the danger, took counter measures. Again, he realised that any naval blockade would require supplies of fresh water from the mainland, so he dispatched the Caesarian cavalry along the coastline in both direction to prevent the Pompeian fleet from sending men ashore. He also calculated that Scribonius would be wanting a quick victory in this attack, so as not to suffer the supply issues which Bibulus had at Oricum and Apollonia. To those ends Antonius set a trap, hoping that Scribonius would take the bait:

> *He protected with fascines and screens about sixty row-boats belonging to his large ships, and, putting picked men on board, stationed them singly at various places along the coast, and gave orders that two triremes which he had caused to be built at Brundisium should go out to the mouth of the harbour under the pretence of exercising the rowers. When Libo saw them advance so boldly he sent five quadriremes against them, hoping that they could be intercepted. On their approaching our ships, our veteran crews began to retreat to the harbour, while the foe, impelled by their zeal, incautiously followed. Then suddenly, the signal being given, the Antonian rowboats threw themselves on the foe from every side, and at the first onset captured one of these quadriremes with its rowers and fighting men and compelled the rest to a discreditable flight.*[15]

Thus the first attack by Scribonius had failed, but only with the loss of one warship and damage to another four. Yet however, this loss and the lack of fresh water seemed to overwhelm Libo, who abandoned the attack on Brundisium and took some of the pressure off Caesar by returning to the blockade of only the eastern side of the Adriatic.

Civil War in Italy – A Pompeian Second Front?

Whilst this stalemate was ongoing in both Epirus and the Adriatic during the early months of 48 bc, Caesar's grip on the capital and desire to ensure peaceful Roman political discourse faced a major challenge. At the centre of this political chaos lay two men. One was M. Caelius Rufus, who held the office of Praetor Peregrinus (one of the two Praetors who traditionally stayed in Rome and helped administer justice). Freshly elected, we must presume he was a Caesarian supporter who had been approved by Caesar, even though he had Pompeian political connections (see below).

The other man was none other than T. Annius Milo, the notorious former Tribune (57 bc) and gang leader who had played such a leading role in the bloody chaos of the 50s bc. Originally a Pompeian agent, he had been exiled in 52 bc following the murder of Clodius (see Chapter One). Milo was the only man not to be recalled by Caesar when he took Rome in 49 bc, presumably due to his bloody reputation and former Pompeian sympathises.

The issue that drove these two men together and which brought Rome and Italy back into bloody political chaos was the long standing and thorny issue of debt. At the best of times, the level of debt amongst the citizen body was always a tricky political issue, but during a civil war, even one that brought limited fighting within Italy, the situation was exacerbated. As we have seen (Chapter Five), Caesar had been called upon to address the issue politically, but refused to waste time on the matter, other than pass a law allowing for arbitration on the valuation of the debt and repayment rates.

The men charged with discharging this task were the Urban and Peregrine Praetors (C. Trebonius[16] and M. Caelius Rufus). Yet, as expected, this measure was more style over substance and had no impact on debt levels or the level of popular discontent within Rome. It was at this point that Caelius chose to break ranks with the Caesarian faction's policy of not inflaming any political tensions by proposing a new law abolishing interest on debt owed. Several sources comment on why Caelius broke ranks. For Velleius it was due to the fact that, ironically, Caelius was himself heavily in debt.[17] For Dio, it was the fact that Caesar was looking like he would be defeated in Epirus.[18] As is often the case it may very well have been the case that both these factors were at play. What is clear however is that, with the absence of both Caesar and Pompeius, there was no strong central control over political life in Rome, even with the bulk of the oligarchy in exile in Greece.

Naturally, the remaining Consul, P. Servilius Isauricus, attempted to block the law, not wishing to stir up political violence in Rome, in Caesar's absence. At first Caelius acceded to his wishes and withdrew the law, but shortly afterwards at a public meeting, proposed two more radical replacements: one allowing tenants to have a year's rent free and another cancelling all debts. Naturally enough his colleague (Trebonius) tried to oppose him but was attacked by a mob of citizens and driven from the Rostrum.

Clearly fearing a return to mob violence in Rome, Servilius sent for a detachment of Caesarian troops bound for Gaul and used them to guard the Senate. However, whatever measures Servilius was intending were blocked by an unknown number of anonymous Tribunes, who used their power of veto (*ius intercessionis*), despite the presence of the military (an act which is totally absent from Caesar's own account[19]). Nevertheless, Servilius ordered his officials to remove the two laws which had been published on tablets, which naturally led to another riot, with Caelius' supporters attacking the officials in question and the Consul himself. Servilius then reconvened the Senate and passed a motion stripping Caelius of his office, barring him from the Senate and removing him from the Rostrum when he stood (using the troops at his command). It is not recorded whether the Tribunes again vetoed these measures, were prevented, or were simply ignored.

With Servilius controlling Rome using the military, and seemingly overriding normal political custom, Caelius sought permission from Servilius to withdraw from Rome, on the pretext of travelling to see Caesar and state his case in person. Despite the sheer implausibility of this excuse and the fact that Caesar was under blockade, Servilius agreed and even sent an anonymous Tribune to accompany him (again only recorded in Dio[20]), despite Tribunes having to remain in the city. Naturally Caelius had no intention of journeying to see Caesar, but instead set out to meet his old political ally: T. Annius Milo.

It is here that again we must question Caesar's vetting policy. In 52 BC, Caelius was one of the Tribunes who supported Milo, yet Caesar still allowed him to be elected as the Peregrine Praetor (one of two Praetors who held power in Rome). So, whilst he may have prevented Milo from returning from exile, he allowed one of his colleagues to hold power in Rome, in his absence. Though still barred from returning to Italy, with Caesar trapped in Epirus for several months, Milo saw his chance and returned from exile. Caesar himself records that Milo claimed he was acting on the orders of his 'former' patron Pompeius:

> Meanwhile Milo after sending dispatches round the municipal towns to the effect that in what he was doing he was acting by the order and authority of Pompeius, on instructions conveyed to him through Vibullius, began to stir up those whom he supposed to be oppressed by debt.[21]

We have no way of knowing whether Caesar's claims were true, but it would fit in with Pompeius' strategy to have an agent to raise rebellion in Italy and undermine Caesar's control of the region and hopefully tie up some of his forces in suppressing it. Milo again went straight to exploiting the issue of debt. Yet Milo it seems met with little initial success. His early efforts were focussed on Campania and in particular on Capua (site of the Spartacan slave revolt) and also Naples. Yet the local magistrates were able to stamp out any dissension and there seems to have been little popular support to rebel, particularly with so many legions active in Italy. Thus Milo turned north towards Etruria and the city of Cosa.

Servilius meanwhile had not been idle and once word of Milo's attempts had reached Rome, dispatched one of the Praetors (Q. Pedius), with a Caesarian legion to crush Milo's rebellion. Milo by this time had raised a force of freed slaves, to accompany his retinue of gladiators, and for some reason (not given in the sources) was attacking the town of Cosa. It was here that he was confronted by Pedius. The only account of the clash is to be found in Caesar who only notes the following:

> [Milo] began to besiege Cosa, in the Thurine district. There, meeting with the Praetor Q. Pedius at the head of a legion, he was struck by a stone from the wall and perished.[22]

Thus, Milo's attempted rebellion was crushed by Caesarian forces, failing in its aims of disputing Caesarian control of Italy or tying up Caesarian forces. Caelius meanwhile was still in Rome, having been placed under closer scrutiny by Servilius. Nevertheless, he was able to slip his restrictions and left Rome to join Milo but diverted further south when he heard the news of Milo's defeat and death. He journeyed to the port of Thurii (on the southern Italian coast) where he attempted to suborn the Caesarian garrison, which would have made it an attractive target for the Pompeian forces. Again, there is a brief note in Caesar covering his lack of success:

> *And Caelius, setting forth, as he gave out, to Caesar, reached Thurii. There, on trying to tamper with certain inhabitants of the municipality and promising money to Caesar's Gallic and Spanish horsemen who had been sent there on garrison duty, he was killed by them.*[23]

Thus, both Caelius' and Milo's attempts at rebellion were crushed easily. With Italy under Caesarian military occupation, any rebellions could swiftly be put down and the mere presence of Caesarian legions was likely to deter any potential rebels. Nevertheless, the incident does show the fragile grip the Caesarian faction held on Roman politics and that even military occupation did not deter political opportunism or resistance.

The Adriatic Campaign – The Breakthrough (Late March / Early April 48 BC)

Scribonius' failure to either take Brundisium or place it under an effective blockade meant that not only had he passed up an opportunity to ratchet the pressure up on Caesar, but he had effectively given the Caesarians a free hand to break the blockade on the eastern Adriatic. The various sources have a number of Caesarian commanders at Brundisium, either Q. Fufius Calenus, A. Gabinius or M. Antonius. Appian seems to imply that Gabinius was the most senior, followed by Antonius and then Fufius Calenus. Interestingly we do not find a mention of Gabinius in Caesar's own account, only Antonius and Fufius. Even more interestingly, we find in Appian's account that Gabinius ignored Caesar's orders to send reinforcements across the Adriatic and instead chose to march a portion of the army (we are not told the size) around the Adriatic by land:

> *Gabinius did not obey the order but led those who were willing to go with him by way of Illyria by forced marches. Almost all of them were destroyed*

by the Illyrians and Caesar was obliged to endure the outrage as he could not spare time for vengeance.[24]

This incident can also be also found in Plutarch's biography of Antonius:

But Gabinius was afraid to make the voyage, which was difficult in the wintertime, and started to lead his army a long way round by land.[25]

Interestingly we can find no mention of this incident in Caesar's own account. However, as we have seen earlier, Caesar did have a marked tendency not to mention his forces' defeats. Furthermore, it is also possible that Appian and Plutarch (or a common source) were confusing a later campaign fought by Gabinius (later in 48 BC) against the Illyrian tribes, in which he was also defeated.

Nevertheless, it seems that the bulk of the Caesarian army was still at Brundisium and commanded by M. Antonius, who was determined to follow Caesar's orders and force a crossing of the Adriatic. Caesar, who could still break the blockade and send messages to Brundisium apparently, realised that once again, he had the initiative. By taking the coastal cities of Oricum and Apollonia, they had drawn in the bulk of the Pompeian fleet, who had to maintain a blockade of those ports and patrol those crossing routes. This meant that potentially their attention was diverted from other crossing points. By now several months had passed and it was spring (late March, early April), meaning the weather and seas in the Adriatic were more conducive to crossing.

Thus whilst Caesar had sailed his fleet to the south, Antonius and Fufius opted to wait until the weather would take them further to the north and to the other side of Dyrrhachium, avoiding Pompeius. In what seems to have been early April, the Caesarian fleet left an unblockaded Brundisium and sailed north past Dyrrhachium, evading the Pompeian patrols. It does not seem that the Pompeian fleet had any ships anchored off Brundisium to inform them that the Caesarian fleet was on the move. In fact, it seems that the first they became away of this invasion fleet was when it passed Dyrrhachium itself.

The commander of the Pompeian fleet at Dyrrhachium was a C. Coponius (Pr. 49 BC) who, upon being notified, scrambled the Pompeian fleet, and gave chase. However, the winds favoured the Caesarian fleet and they were able to enter a safe harbour just north of Lissus (three miles) known as Nymphaeum (see Map 5). To compound matters, the chasing Pompeian fleet sailed into a storm, which the Caesarian fleet narrowly avoided by sheltering in the bay, and lost sixteen ships. This meant that they were unable to interrupt the Caesarian fleet from landing the army.

Slightly further to the south, the Pompeian garrison of Lissus, commanded by Otacilius Crassus were alerted to the landing by the mooring of two stragglers from the Caesarian fleet off their harbour. He sent forces in rowing boats to intercept them. One craft manned by new recruits surrendered and were promptly slaughtered on Crassus' orders. The other, manned by veterans, fought off the Pompeian forces and beached their ship and then apparently fought off four hundred cavalry (roughly twice their number) which Crassus had dispatched to guard the nearby coastline.

However, more importantly, Crassus clearly did not have the forces to prevent Antonius and his army from disembarking, some three miles to the north of Lissus. Thus, four more Caesarian legions (three veteran and one newly formed), and eight hundred cavalry, were able to land north of Lissus and march on the city. Antonius then dispatched the bulk of his fleet back to Brundisium to collect further forces, whilst leaving a pontoon harbour where he landed to facilitate any further landings or re-embarkation. He then marched on Lissus itself, which promptly followed its fellow coastal cities (of Oricum and Apollonia) and surrendered without a fight. Otacilius Crassus fled the city to take the news to Pompeius.

Thus, the Caesarian forces emerged victorious from the Adriatic campaign, breaking through the Pompeian blockade, and landing the additional forces in Illyria. The key to the failure of the Pompeian campaign was their inability to blockade Brundisium and prevent the Caesarian fleet from leaving port. Their strategy of blockading the few ports Caesar held in Epirus and hoping to intercept any Caesarian fleet was proved to be flawed and ultimately handed the initiative to Antonius, and thus Caesar. The landing of the Caesarian reinforcements before the arrival of Pompeius' effectively broke the stalemate. Not only did Caesar have another four legions on the Illyrian/Epirote coast, but they were to the north of Pompeius at Dyrrhachium, whilst he was to the south, trapping Pompeius between them.

The Race to Antonius

It must be acknowledged that the total size of the reinforcements is not clear. Although four legions are clearly attested in the first wave of landings, there is no mention of how many came in any second wave, though Antonius is recorded as sending his ships back for them. Nevertheless, the arrival of Antonius, and the additional legions he brought with him, did not only break the stalemate, but switched the advantage from Pompeius to Caesar. Not only did Caesar have sufficient forces to challenge Pompeius but he now had him trapped between two Caesarian armies, (to the North and South) with his own reinforcements still making their way across Greece, to the East (see below). Dio clearly states that it was Caesar who now had the largest army:

> [Caesar] *encouraged by the fact that, with the reinforcements that had arrived, he was superior to the adversary in the number of troops then at his disposal.*[26]

Caesar thus now had at least eleven legions in Epirus/Illyria, providing us with an estimate of the size of Pompeius' army at this point (around nine to ten legions). Both Pompeius and Caesar were camped to the south of Dyrrhachium on opposite banks of the River Aspis. Both commanders received word of the landings from their respective sides at roughly the same time and both realised that the balance of the campaign was swinging away from Pompeius. As it was, both commanders reacted in the same fashion, but for different reasons.

For Pompeius, it was clear that he now had a Caesarian army to his rear (the north) which could trap him between two Caesarian forces. Therefore, he abandoned his usual cautious approach, and took immediate action, determined to disengage himself from the site at Apsus and head north to fight Antonius, using his greater numbers to destroy Caesar's reinforcements before they could be brought to bear. Thus Pompeius ordered his army to withdraw from their position at Apsus during the night and headed north by means of a forced march.

Caesar too had determined to march north to meet up with Antonius and take command of his reinforcements but seems to have been caught off-guard by Pompeius' night-time withdrawal. Thus his army only broke camp the next day, increasing Pompeius' head start. Pompeius meanwhile, having marched northwards, seemed reluctant to attack Antonius' forces openly, possibly due to the presence of Caesar's army to his rear and thus set an ambush, hoping to catch Antonius' army on the march, a ploy which ultimately failed:

> [Pompeius] *hastened by forced marches towards Antonius, and on learning of his approach, finding a suitable spot, stationed his forces there and kept all his men in camp, forbidding fires to be lighted that his arrival might be kept more secret. These facts are immediately reported to Antonius through some Greeks. He sent messengers to Caesar and kept his men one day in camp; on the next day Caesar reached him.*[27]

Thus, Antonius' scouts spotted the ambush and Antonius pitched camp, forcing Pompeius to make the decision to attack him openly, whilst in a defended position, and with Caesar's army approaching from the south. Though Pompeius still had the superior numbers (to Antonius), he again refused to fight on the ground chosen by his opponents and facing the prospect of being trapped between the two Caesarian armies. Thus Pompeius chose to return to a more cautious approach and withdrew, allowing the two Caesarian armies to unify. He withdrew to the nearby town of Asparagium, close to Dyrrhachium itself, whilst he awaited the arrival of his own reinforcements under Metellus Scipio.

Expanding the Campaign

Despite having bolstered his army with the four legions of Antonius, Caesar too seemed reluctant to march on Pompeius and force a battle, with neither commander believing that they had a strong enough position. Caesar also had three other priorities. The first was to secure his position in Epirus and Illyria by securing supplies from the surrounding neighbourhoods, especially given the Pompeian control of the Adriatic. The second was to spread his influence and widen the campaign throughout the region, not just the narrow strip of Epirote/Illyrian coastline it had previously been confined to. The third priority was to stop or more likely slow down the arrival of Metellus Scipio. Thus Caesar, having just unified his army, now started to spread it out once more:

> [Caesar] *sent into Thessaly L. Cassius Longinus with the legion of recruits, called the Twenty-seventh, and two hundred horse; into Aetolia, C. Calvisius Sabinus with five cohorts and a few horsemen; and he gave*

them special instructions, as the districts were close at hand, to provide for the corn supply. He ordered Cn. Domitius Calvinus to go into Macedonia with two legions, the Eleventh and Twelfth, and five hundred horsemen.[28]

Thus Caesar dispatched some three legions from his force to spread into Thessaly, Aetolia, and Macedon. This also meant that he went from having the largest army in Epirus to once again having a smaller army than Pompeius. Nonetheless, Calvisius was dispatched into Greece proper to try to secure some of the city states held by the Pompeian forces, and with it supplies for the main army, as well as possibly opening up new naval routes to Italy. Cassius was sent into Thessaly, again to secure territory and supplies and also possibly to support Domitius in his campaign against Metellus Scipio. Domitius was sent with two legions to try to slow or stop Metellus Scipio. Each commander met with contrasting fortunes. Of the three it was Calvisius Sabinus that had the most success, even though his force was the smallest. The only details we have for his campaign come from one line of Caesar:

Of these officers Calvisius was received on his arrival with the utmost goodwill of all the Aetolians and having expelled the garrisons of the foe from Calydon and Naupactus gained possession of the whole of Aetolia.[29]

Thus, Calvisius was apparently able to expel the Pompeian garrisons, who again proved unable to hold towns that had no wish to be drawn into a Roman civil war, and gained (a cursory) control of the whole region of Aetolia, including the strategic port of Naupactus. Cassius we are told initially met with a mixed reception in Thessaly.

The War in Macedonia and Thessaly – Metellus Scipio & Faustus Sulla

The campaigns which followed, both in Macedon and Thessaly, are hampered by a lack of detail in the other surviving sources and some notable omissions in Caesar's own account. As we have noted before (see Chapter Four), Caesar had a marked tendency to omit defeats by subordinates, unless they fitted his narrative, the best exception of this being of Scribonius Curio in Africa in 49 BC, at the hands of 'perfidious natives'.

Thus, we have to reconstruct the campaigns from the scraps in other sources and reading between the lines in Caesar's own account. The two other accounts we have are a short excerpt from Appian and a slightly more detailed one from Dio:

> *The same winter Scipio, Pompeius' father-in-law, advanced with another army from Syria. Caesar's general, Caius Calvisius, had an engagement with him in Macedonia, was beaten, and lost a whole legion except 800 men.*[30]

> *Lucius Cassius Longinus and Cnaeus Domitius Calvinus had been sent by him into Macedonia and Thessaly. Longinus had been disastrously defeated in Thessaly by Scipio and by Sadalus, a Thracian; and Calvinus had been repulsed from Macedonia by Faustus, but on receiving accessions from the Locrians and Aetolians had invaded Thessaly with these troops, and after being ambushed had afterwards set ambuscades himself and conquered Scipio in battle, thereby winning over a few cities.*[31]

The first matter to clarify is the defeat of Cassius Longinus in Thessaly. In Caesar's account Metellus does march his army in pursuit of Cassius but breaks off when his own rearguard is threatened by the arrival of Domitius. Caesar even goes as far as to say the following: '*Thus the energy of Domitius brought safety to Cassius.*'[32] Yet the later sources (using material that no longer survives) paint a totally different picture; namely that Cassius' army was destroyed by that of Metellus. As we are told, Cassius only had one legion with him as opposed to an unknown number of legions with Metellus and was heavily outnumbered. Appian, clearly confusing Cassius with Calvisius, states that his legion was destroyed (with the exception of eight hundred men) whilst Dio refers to a 'disastrous defeat.'[33] Thus, Caesar's Thessalian army seems to have been destroyed and Thessaly remained Pompeian.

Whilst Metellus was dispatching the Caesarian legion in Thessaly, it seems that Domitius was also encountering stiff resistance from the Pompeian forces in Macedon itself. Whilst Caesar is all too eager to demonstrate how easily Aetolia fell, again he mentions nothing of Pompeian resistance in Macedon, led as it was by none other than Faustus Cornelius Sulla, son and heir of the late Dictator and Pompeius' son in law.[34] We have no other detail, other than the brief mention in Dio that Faustus was able to drive Domitius out of Macedonia.[35]

Though we are not told what losses Domitius suffered, Dio does state that it was only with additional allied Locrian and Aetolian forces that Domitius was able to take to the field once more, again a crucial detail omitted from Caesar. Caesar does provide a detailed narrative of the subsequent clash between Domitius and Metellus, though again we must exercise our caution here given Caesar's previous omissions and apparent twisting of the actual events to fit his narrative of inevitable success.

The two armies met at the River Aliacmon (modern Haliacmon), which separated Macedonia from Thessaly, though exactly where is not recorded. Caesar records that Metellus crossed the river hoping to force a battle, but the terrain was not suitable and so he withdrew again, leaving behind a detachment of cavalry to ambush Domitius' foragers. A subsequent smaller clash is recorded between the two smaller forces, with the Caesarians (according to Caesar) emerging victorious, killing eighty of the Pompeians, for losses of two (again if we are to believe Caesar).[36]

A second larger clash is also recorded by Caesar, with Domitius attempting to lure Metellus into an ambush, which does tie in with Dio's account. Domitius broke camp in some haste and lured Metellus into following him, having set his army in an ambush. However Metellus' advance guard spotted the ambush, and the majority of Metellus' army was able to escape. Caesar records that two Metellan detachments were cut off and destroyed.

Thus, despite the two earlier Caesarian defeats, the war in Thessaly/Macedonia seemed to settle into another stalemate, between the forces of Domitius and those of Metellus, which overall was therefore a victory for Caesar, as it prevented Pompeius from receiving his reinforcements from the east.

The Road to Dyrrhachium – The Adriatic Counterattack

With another stalemate in Greece, attention swung back to Epirus, where the armies of Caesar and Pompeius remained in deadlock. Of the two commanders it was Caesar who now had the upper hand, having received his reinforcements, and having blocked Pompeius from receiving his. Of the two commanders, as we have repeatedly seen, Caesar was the more adventurous, Pompeius the more cautious, and their next actions again reflected this contrast. Despite Antonius having successfully broken the

Pompeian naval blockade of the Adriatic, to land Caesar's reinforcements, the blockade itself remained in place and the Pompeian forces still maintained a successful blockade of the Adriatic. The Caesarian faction now controlled three ports on the eastern Adriatic coast: Oricum, Apollonia and Lissus. Whilst Caesar held these ports there was always the option of further Caesarian incursions across the Adriatic, either to bring fresh forces or supplies.

Whilst Caesar's forces had now expanded throughout Greece and held Aetolia, and had progressed in Thessaly and Macedonia, Pompeius seems to have returned to his fundamental strategy of severing the link between Caesar and Italy and trapping him in Epirus. To those ends, the Pompeian Adriatic forces turned their attention to the Caesarian fleet and the ports of the eastern Adriatic shore. Having been, quite frankly, let down by the previous commander of the Adriatic forces (Scribonius Libo) Pompeius put the Adriatic fleet under the command of someone he could rely on, namely his younger son Sex. Pompeius, who throughout his career showed an unusual (for a Roman) flair for naval warfare.[37]

Pompeius' first target was the port of Oricum, whose defences Caesar had been forced to weaken when he withdrew the legion that was stationed there to support his push into the wider theatres of Greece, Macedonia and Thessaly. In their place were three Caesarian cohorts (less than a third of a legion), command of which fell to a Caesarian legate, M. Acilius Caninus. Acilius (and Caesar) clearly realised the danger and Acilius took the following precautions to defend the port:

> *He withdrew our ships into the inner port behind the town, moored them to the shore, and sank a merchant-ship to block the mouth of the port and attached to it another ship, on which he constructed a tower, setting it just opposite the entrance of the harbour. This he filled with soldiers and gave it them to hold against all unforeseen risks.*[38]

Sex. Pompeius chose Oricum as the first port of his campaign and attacked the city by land and sea. As Caesar himself details, although Pompeius was apparently unable to take the port, he did secure its harbour and burn the Caesarian ships there.[39] Having thus neutralised the strategic usefulness of Oricum, he left D. Laelius in charge of the siege. Whilst Caesar does not state whether the port eventually fell, Appian does.[40] Nevertheless Pompeius turned his attention to the recently acquired Caesarian port of Lissus. Again, Sex. Pompeius attacked the port and destroyed the Caesarian fleet there (thirty ships), but was unable to take the city itself.

In what seems to be a lightning campaign, Sex. Pompeius had neutralised the Caesarian ports of Oricum and Lissus and destroyed a significant portion of Caesar's transport fleet. More importantly he had swung the balance of the Adriatic campaign back in favour of the Pompeians, actively contesting the control of the ports they occupied, unlike his predecessor, and also showed the native cities that had defected to avoid a Caesarian siege, that they could expect a Pompeian one in return.

The Road to Dyrrhachium – Stalemate at Asparagium

Whilst Pompeius chose to attack Caesar indirectly, Caesar naturally chose the opposite and seemed determined that the time had come to force Pompeius into battle. Having failed to destroy the Caesarian forces commanded by Antonius in an ambush (see above) and having no wish to be trapped between the two Caesarian forces, Pompeius had withdrawn to a fortified position by the town of Asparagium. The town lay close to Dyrrhachium on the River Genusus (modern Shkumbin)[41] and was presumably on the Via Egnatia, allowing Pompeius swift movement either to Dyrrhachium itself or further into Macedonia.

Thus Caesar marched his army to Asparagium and arrayed his army in battle formation. No details are given as to Pompeius' disposition or defences, but it seems that his position was too well fortified for Caesar to consider an attack. For the second time in the campaign, the armies of Caesar and Pompeius faced each other. Yet again however, there was no battle between the two. On the first occasion neither commander considered himself to be in a position to offer battle. On this occasion, Caesar (with his reinforcements) was eager, Pompeius (without his reinforcements) was not. Thus another stalemate broke out.

On this occasion however, Caesar was eager to bring the matter to a head, before Metellus Scipio could fight his way through the Caesarian forces and link up with Pompeius. Caesar himself does not mention Metellus, but he must have been in constant communication with his own commander, Domitius, who would have been informing him of Metellus' progress (or the lack thereof). Nevertheless, Caesar needed to force Pompeius to give battle sooner or later and, as we have seen, was a notoriously impatient commander.

Stalemate at Dyrrhachium

Therefore Caesar once again determined on a fresh course of action; namely making an attack on the city of Dyrrhachium itself, which would force Pompeius to either come to the city's aid, and thus leave his position at Asparagium, or allow his eastern capital, and his nearest supply depot, to fall into Caesar's hands, providing him with his biggest port on the Adriatic. Naturally enough, Caesar had no wish to tip his hand to Pompeius and so set off by a circuitous route. Inevitably, Pompeius' scouts soon determined that Caesar was making for Dyrrhachium, which forced Pompeius to break camp and try to intercept the Caesarian army, and at least bar their path, if not force them into battle. Thus once again, it became, a race between the two armies to see who could reach Dyrrhachium first. On this occasion it was Caesar's which arrived at the city first, apparently with Pompeius' army in sight. Having won the race, however, and having forced Pompeius to move from his position at Asparagium, Caesar inevitably faced the question of what next? With Pompeius' army behind him, he could not lay siege to the city, without becoming surrounded, nor would the city fall without a fight due to the presence of a large Pompeian garrison. In fact, his whole strategy was to force Pompeius into battle.

Yet equally Pompeius too realised this and, having moved his army to stop Caesar having an uncontested attack on Dyrrhachium, was under no pressure to give battle. Furthermore, if anything, coming second in the race to the city seemed to confer more benefits than coming first. Had Pompeius' army reached the city first, then Caesar would have again been forced into another strategy and marched off. Now Caesar had placed himself between Pompeius' city and Pompeius' army. Whilst Pompeius still had no wish to give battle and would have allowed his opponent to move off unmolested, he deployed a new tactic, and one which suited his campaigning style rather than Caesar's. Thus Pompeius set about fortifying his position and occupied the high ground near the coastline of the bay, at a place known as Petra (see Map 7), which allowed him access to the sea and thus to be supplied by his navy.

Thus the tables were turned on Caesar again, who found that, once more, Pompeius was unwilling to give battle. Caesar faced a choice: withdraw or become entangled in a drawn-out face off. If he withdrew, Caesar did have a range of options available to him. To the south lay Pompeius and his fortified position and to the east lay the Adriatic. This effectively left the north and Illyria, which was of no strategic significance or march to the west and push further into Macedonia, where his advance forces were holding the Pompeian army of Metellus Scipio. Yet uncharacteristically, Caesar chose to remain at Dyrrhachium and even became drawn into what can only be seen as the ancient world's version of trench warfare.

Caesar himself later stated that he was worried that this would become a drawn-out prolonged campaign, for which he did not have the resources, with the Pompeian fleet controlling the coast.[42] Yet not only did he commit to this situation but found himself fighting on Pompeius' terms, slow and grinding, rather than his own. Caesar himself provides no explanation for what was to be such a near disastrous decision but it must have been borne out of frustration with his opponent's refusal to give battle. Thus both sides settled down for what was effectively to become a war of attrition.

Summary – A Game of Cat and Mouse

Thus we can see that after the drama of 49 BC, the Caesarian invasion of Italy and the subsequent conquest of Spain, the campaigns of 48 BC had so far been anticlimactic, with the highly anticipated clash between Rome's two greatest living commanders becoming a series of stalemates, with move and counter move. Caesar inevitably seized the initiative with his early invasion of Epirus, but Pompeius seized it back by his Adriatic blockade, which came close to ending Caesar's campaign. Caesar was able to restore the initiative again thanks to Antonius' breach of the blockade, and in preventing Metellus Scipio from reaching Pompeius quickly. Yet again however, Pompeius then regained the initiative by not playing into Caesar's hands by giving battle and thus took the energy out of Caesar's campaign. Now the two armies faced each other, for the third time in as many months, in sight of the city of Dyrrhachium. On this occasion however the two sides seemed determined to force the matter, though not through open battle.

Chapter Seven

The Battle of Dyrrhachium –
The Early Manoeuvres

When examining the campaign that followed, the one point that must be noted is the absence of a timescale. Though we have a full account of the battles in Caesar, we do not know how long they took, and this must be borne in mind throughout any analysis.

Aims & Tactics

The situation the two commanders found themselves in at Dyrrhachium was, to say the least, an unusual one. Thanks to the various manoeuvrings of the two armies during the previous months Pompeius and Caesar now found themselves locked in an unusual siege situation. It is unusual as it was far from clear who had the upper hand. On the one hand, Caesar seemed to have Pompeius trapped in the Bay of Dyrrhachium with the sea to his rear and cut off from the city which was his military capital. Yet on the other hand, Pompeius had Caesar pinned between the city and his army, with his control of the Adriatic meaning he was not surrounded but had his entire western flank open. It must further be noted that whilst, at one point, Caesar had superior numbers in terms of soldiers in the campaign, having dispatched various legions throughout Greece, including those under Domitius to face Metellus Scipio, Caesar now seemed to have the smaller army at Dyrrhachium, a point he himself makes on several occasions.

Of the two commanders, Pompeius was probably the happiest with his strategic situation; he had checked Caesar's momentum, denying him the city of Dyrrhachium as a base and forcing him to fight a slow and grinding campaign of attrition, rather than a lightning campaign with set piece battles (his forté). Furthermore, although Caesar had the larger army overall, and had successfully landed his reinforcements from Italy, he had not been able to make these additional forces count. Added to this was the fact that Caesar now had no more additional forces to call on, but Pompeius was still awaiting significant reinforcements from the army of Metellus Scipio, making its way across Greece. Thus, in many ways, Pompeius now had Caesar where he wanted him, bogged down in a drawn-out siege and potentially trapped between Pompeius, the city of Dyrrhachium and eventually the Pompeian army approaching from the east.

Thus, the tactics and objectives of the two commanders were clear and were in fact the same as they had been throughout this whole campaign. For Caesar it was to bring Pompeius to battle, where he could use his superior forces and defeat him cleanly. Failing that he needed to avoid becoming tied down in a protracted siege and regain the momentum in the campaign. He also needed his subordinates to keep Metellus Scipio and the second Pompeian army restricted in Greece and unable to reinforce Pompeius.

Again, though technically trapped in the Bay of Dyrrhachium, Pompeius' tactics remained the same, namely, not to fight Caesar in open battle until his reinforcements arrived and he was able to choose the time and battlefield that suited him. An additional aim would be to keep Caesar contained at Dyrrhachium until Metellus Scipio arrived. Thus both commanders settled down for a siege with Caesar trying to bring Pompeius to battle and Pompeius trying to avoid just that.

The absence of Metellus Scipio seems to figure largely in both commanders' thoughts, yet the surviving sources do not detail his progress to any great degree. As already discussed (Chapter Six), we know that Caesar had dispatched a portion of his forces to engage with Metellus and slow him down, with some measure of success. Both sides must have been aware of Metellus' progress, thanks to reports from either Metellus' or Caesar's forces, yet we are not privy to this information nor how it shaped their thinking. Certainly, as Metellus showed up in the immediate aftermath of the battle (mid-July on a modern calendar), he must have been making steady progress across Greece.

Both commanders also shared another problem, namely access to food and resources. Caesar, though he had Pompeius' army tied down, was operating in hostile territory with no clear supply lines to Italy. Pompeius, though pinned down, with control of the Adriatic, could be re-supplied from the sea though this would be a logistical challenge to keep landing that much food, water, and fodder. Furthermore, he had a plentiful supply of cavalry with which to bring in as many supplies as they could before Caesar encircled them. Caesar himself sums up the respective issues they faced:

> *Pompeius, being cut off from Dyrrhachium, on failing to gain his purpose adopts the next best plan and entrenches a camp on a lofty spot called Petra, which allows a moderately good approach for ships and protects them from certain winds. He gives orders for some of his warships to meet there, and for corn and stores to be brought in from Asia and from all the districts that he held.*
>
> *Caesar thinking that the war was going to be unduly prolonged, and despairing of his supplies from Italy, because all the shores were being held with such vigilance by the Pompeians, and his own fleets which he had constructed in the winter in Sicily, Gaul, and Italy were slow in coming, sent Q. Tillius and the legate L. Canuleius into Epirus in order to get provisions, and because these districts were some distance off he established granaries in certain places and apportioned to the neighbouring communities their respective shares in the carriage of corn. He also gave orders that all the corn that there was should be sought and collected at Lissus, among the Parthini, and in all the fortified posts. This was of very small amount, partly from the nature of the land, because the district is rugged and hilly and the people generally use imported corn, and also because Pompeius had foreseen this and had at an earlier date treated the Parthini as spoils of war, and, hunting for all their corn by ransacking and digging up their houses, had carried it off by means of his horsemen to Petra.*[1]

Drawing the Battlelines

As we have seen it was Pompeius who was able to choose his ground first, occupying and securing an elevated position with access to the sea, known as Petra. This became the centre of Pompeius' position. By doing so, he threw down the challenge to Caesar, either withdraw or attempt to force Pompeius into battle. It was perhaps a measure of Caesar's desperation that he chose the latter and attempted to besiege an army holding a fortified position and with secure access to the coast. Caesar's most famous siege had of course been the Battle of Alesia in Gaul (52 BC), one of his most famous victories, but then the circumstances of this siege were much different including the Pompeian access to, and control of, the Adriatic.

Nevertheless, Caesar had limited options at this point. Pompeius was clearly not intending to give battle until Metellus Scipio arrived and if Caesar had moved his army away and targeted other cities or perhaps launched an attack on Metellus himself he would have found himself shadowed by Pompeius' army, alert for any opportunity to trap Caesar. Furthermore, as we have stated, Caesar was operating in hostile territory that had been under Pompeian control for over a year and the further he moved into the interior of Greece or Macedon the worse this problem became.

Thus, Caesar chose to accept Pompeius' challenge and began to lay siege to the Pompeian army. A major challenge for any siege was the very territory itself. Again, the circumstances were as far from Alesia as could be found. As can be seen from the map (Map 7), the Bay of Dyrrhachium was not a flat one but was mountainous (evident from the photographs in Veith's work[2]), thus Caesar's siege lines would need to secure the various hilltops that surrounded Pompeius' army, a difficult task at the best of times, never mind one being contested by the opposing force. Caesar himself provides a description of the task he faced:

> On learning of these things, Caesar forms a plan to suit the nature of the ground. Around Pompeius' camp there were very many lofty and rugged hills. These he first occupied with garrisons and erected strong forts on them. Then, according to the indications afforded by the nature of each locality, by drawing a line of works from fort to fort he proceeded to invest Pompeius, with these objects in view: first, that as he had a scanty supply of provisions and Pompeius had a large preponderance of cavalry, he might be able to bring in for his army corn and stores from any direction at less risk; and also that he might prevent Pompeius from foraging and might make his cavalry useless for active operations.[3]

Thus Caesar attempted to create a network of fortifications which stretched some seventeen miles long to encircle Pompeius' army,[4] and either starve him out and force the collapse of his army's morale and cause mass defections, the latter of which was the more likely, given Pompeius' supply lines from the Adriatic. On the face of it, Pompeius had two options, attempt to flee the encirclement, or fight it (fight or flight). Whilst he wanted to avoid a set piece battle, he could focus his forces on disrupting the building of the hilltop forts.

Furthermore he could have withdrawn his forces to the south east of the bay. Yet, as we discussed above, Pompeius had no intention of ceding the initiative to Caesar once again and wanted him tied down and unable to besiege his military capital of Dyrrhachium.

Thus Pompeius doubled down, perhaps with one eye on keeping the whole of his army occupied, thus not giving them time to brood on their position, and set about building his own line of fortifications, as described by Caesar:

> *The only remaining course was to adopt a desperate method of warfare by occupying as many hills as possible, by holding with garrisons the widest extent of land possible, and by keeping Caesar's forces as far extended as he could; and this was done. By making twenty-four redoubts he embraced a circuit of fifteen miles, and within this he foraged; and in this district there were a number of hand-sown crops with which he could meanwhile feed his animals. And just as our men by a continuous line of fortifications took measures to prevent the Pompeians from breaking out anywhere and attacking us in the rear, so the enemy made an unbroken line of defence in the interior of the space so that our men should not be able to enter any part of it and surround them from the rear. They, however, outstripped us in the work, being superior in numbers and having a shorter interior circuit to complete.[5]*

Thus both sides threw up lines of fortifications around the Bay of Dyrrhachium (see Map 7) though we are not told how long this took. In the meantime, Pompeius did commit to disrupting Caesar's men building their fortifications, by harrying them with distance weapons, though no casualty figures are given:

> *Whenever Caesar had to occupy any spot, although Pompeius had decided not to try to prevent it with his whole armed force and fight a pitched battle, yet he kept sending up, in suitable positions, archers and slingers, of whom he had a great number, and many of our men were wounded.*

A great dread of the arrows fell on them, and to avoid the missiles nearly all the soldiers had made themselves jerkins or other protections out of felt, quilt, or hide.[6]

Thus both armies committed to building rival series of fortifications and engaged in a race against each other to build them the quicker and to occupy the most favourable strategic positions:

In occupying positions each strove with the utmost energy: Caesar to confine Pompeius within the narrowest limits, Pompeius to occupy as many hills as he could in the widest possible circuit.[7]

Caesar himself comments on the uniqueness of the situation:

The method of warfare was new and unprecedented both on account of the large number of redoubts, the wide space covered, the great defensive works, and the whole system of blockade, as well as in other respects. For whenever one army has attempted to blockade another, it is when they have attacked a discomfited and weakened foe, overcome in battle or demoralised by some reverse, and have thus hemmed them in, being themselves superior in number of horse and foot, while the motive of the blockade has usually been to prevent the foe from getting supplies. However on this occasion Caesar with an inferior number of men was hemming in fresh and uninjured forces, the enemy having an abundant supply of all necessaries.[8]

The Initial Skirmishes

Caesar's account again presents a brief insight into the fighting that occurred during the construction of the two lines of fortifications, which highlights the nature of these initial skirmishes:

In one of these [clashes], when Caesar's Ninth Legion had occupied a certain post and had begun to fortify it, Pompeius occupied a hill near and opposite to it and began to hinder our men in their work; and since on one side Caesar's position admitted of an almost level approach, he first of all threw round a force of archers and slingers, and then, sending up a great multitude of light-armed men and putting forward his engines, he began to hinder the works; nor was it easy for our men at one and the same time to stand on the defensive and to fortify. Caesar, on seeing that in every direction his men were being wounded, ordered them to retire and to quit the position. The way of retreat lay down a slope. The enemy, however, pressed on all the more keenly, and did not allow our men to retire, because they appeared to be abandoning the position under the influence of fear.

Caesar, fearing for the retreat of his men, ordered hurdles to be carried to the furthest point of the hill and to be set up fronting the foe to bar their way, and within these a ditch of moderate width to be drawn to thwart their path, the men being under cover, and the place to be made as difficult as possible in every direction. He himself drew up his slingers in suitable places to serve as a protection to our men in their retreat. When these arrangements were finished, he ordered the legion to be withdrawn. The Pompeians then began with all the more insolence and audacity to press and close in on our men, and in order to cross the ditches overthrew the hurdles that had been set up as a defence against them. And Caesar, on observing this, fearing lest his men should appear to have been flung back rather than withdrawn and a more serious loss should be incurred, exhorted his men about midway down the slope, by the mouth of Antonius, who was in command of that legion, and ordered the signal to be given with the clarion and the enemy to be charged.

The men of the Ninth with prompt and unanimous resolution hurled their pikes and, breaking into a run from the lower ground and charging up the hill, drove the Pompeians headlong and compelled them to turn their backs in flight; the overturned hurdles and the uprights planted in their way and the ditches that had been drawn across proved a great hindrance to them in their retreat. But our men, who considered it sufficient to depart without disaster, when several of the enemy had been killed and five in all of their own comrades lost, retired with the utmost quietness and, halting a little on this side of that spot, included in their lines some other hills and completed their defensive works.[9]

Thus, both sides were committing to an almost daily series of skirmishes on the other, which would not have inflicted heavy casualties in terms of the dead but would certainly have resulted in an increasing number of injuries.[10] Nevertheless, despite this low-level warfare, both the Pompeian and Caesarian lines of fortification were completed, though how long they took is not recorded, and both sides settled down for a siege.

Supply Issues

As previously stated, both sides suffered from supply issues in this unique situation. Caesar's forces, although they controlled access to wider Epirus and Greece, were themselves camped in a hostile country and had no clear supply lines to Caesarian-controlled territory or control of the seas. Pompeius' forces had access to the Adriatic and were being resupplied by sea but were limited as to what could be brought in. Caesar's own commentary speaks of a constant stream of ships resupplying Pompeius' army, whilst his own army starved (and here we must be careful of dramatic license).[11] Yet Caesar's forces had dammed up all the streams that fed into the Bay, meaning that Pompeius' army had limited access to fresh water other than that which arrived by ship and were forced to dig temporary wells on the territory they controlled. According to Caesar, this meant that although Pompeius' cavalry survived, the other pack animals perished. Overall though, whilst both armies suffered from privations, both were able to endure their respective sieges and thus the stalemate would not be broken by a lack of food and water.

The Attack on Dyrrhachium

At some point, hoping to break the stalemate, Caesar seemed to have switched his attention back to the city of Dyrrhachium itself, hoping to take it by a surprise attack and with the aid of sympathisers within the city itself. There is no account of this attack in Caesar other than reference to battles at Dyrrhachium and this may be down to an unfortunate gap in the surviving manuscripts which means that a portion of the text is lost to us. It is also equally possible that even if we had a complete text, we would find no detailed description of the attack, due to it being a failure and apparently one that nearly cost Caesar his own life. As we have seen throughout this period, Caesar did not like to dwell on defeats in his own campaign histories, especially ones in which he was personally involved. All we do have is an account by Dio:

> *Upon Dyrrhachium itself Caesar made an attempt by night, between the marshes and the sea, in the expectation that it would be betrayed by its defenders. He got inside the narrows, but at that point was attacked both in front and in the rear by large forces which had been conveyed along the shore in boats and very nearly perished himself.*[12]

Thus it seems that Caesar walked into an ambush and was nearly killed. The Pompeian forces were waiting for him and had him pinned down between the marshes and the sea on a narrow strip of land. Although this is just a brief account in Dio, the implications are that Caesar clearly had contact with supposed sympathisers within the city who would open the city gates and allow the Caesarian forces in at night. Caesar had already taken the cities of Apollonia and Oricum by betrayal from within rather than siege and clearly, he hoped to emulate this tactic here.

However, what is clear is that on this occasion that tactic backfired and these 'sympathisers' betrayed his plan to Pompeius who rowed in additional forces to be stationed outside of the city by the marshes to trap Caesar at night. We are not told how many men Caesar lost or how he managed to escape, though Caesar does refer to three battles at Dyrrhachium on the same day,[13] but it clearly gave a victory to Pompeius, even if Caesar chose not to acknowledge it for posterity.

The Battle of the Redoubts

Having foreknowledge of Caesar walking into a trap, Pompeius seems to have planned an offensive campaign on the Caesarian fortifications to accompany it. With the two lines of fortifications complete, the situation is vaguely reminiscent of the trench warfare in the First World War, with two opposing lines of fortification and a no-man's land between them. This analogy is a helpful one, more so than that of traditional siege, as Pompeius forces were not trying to break out and escape. Thus, rather than punch a hole in the fortifications where they were weakest, Pompeius chose to focus on what he saw as the key to the whole Caesarian defensive line: namely the redoubts that anchored the defences.

Each redoubt was garrisoned (though we do not know by how many men), but the key to this strategy lay in a surprise attack by Pompeian forces on key redoubts, and overwhelming them, before reinforcements could arrive from the main Caesarian army. We are told by Caesar that Pompeius chose three redoubts to attack, though not their locations.

Here we do suffer from the gap in Caesar's accounts, which covers the main Pompeian attack. It seems that, inevitably the redoubt in question, which seems to have been to the north of Caesar's defensive line and near to his main camp, was being overwhelmed and Caesar's men on the point of defeat: '*In one of these fights in front of a redoubt Caesar's men were worsted*'[14]

Clearly Pompeius had hoped that with Caesar trapped in an ambush at Dyrrhachium itself, and possibly dead, then his main army would be in no position to counter-attack his thrust. Unfortunately for Pompeius, the portion of the forces left at the main Caesarian camp were commanded by P. Cornelius Sulla (Cos. 65 BC), the nephew of the Dictator, who had chosen to follow Caesar in the civil war. Caesar's own account resumes at this point:

> *Meanwhile P. Sulla, whom Caesar at his departure had put in charge of his camp, being informed of this came to the support of the cohort with two legions; and by his arrival the Pompeians were easily repulsed. In fact, they could not endure the sight or the onset of our men, and when the first of them had been overthrown the rest turned to flight and abandoned the position. But when our men followed, Sulla recalled them lest they should go too far in pursuit.*
>
> *Many people, however, think that if he had chosen to pursue more vigorously the war might have been finished that day. But his policy does not seem deserving of censure. For the duties of a legate and of a commander are different: the one ought to do everything under direction, the other should take measures freely in the general interest. Sulla, having been left by Caesar in charge of the camp, was contented with the liberation of his men, and did not choose to fight a pitched battle, a course which in any case admitted possibly of some reverse, in order that he might not be thought to have taken on himself the duties of a commander.*
>
> *As to the Pompeians, their situation caused them great difficulty in retreating; for, having advanced from unfavourable ground, they had halted on the top: if they were to withdraw by the slope, they feared the pursuit of our men from the higher ground, nor was there much time left before sunset, since in the hope of finishing the business they had prolonged the action almost till nightfall. So Pompeius, of necessity and adapting his plans to the emergency, occupied a certain hill which was so far removed from our fort that a missile discharged from a catapult could not reach it. In this place he sat down and entrenched it and kept all his forces confined there.*[15]

Thus, the main Pompeian attack, led by Pompeius himself, was repulsed by Sulla and his two legions. We are not given the figure for Pompeius' forces, though the casualties detailed by Caesar show it was probably more than a legion. Caesar's account also details the other two Pompeian attacks:

> At the same time there was fighting in two other places besides, for Pompeius had made attempts on several redoubts with the object of keeping our force equally scattered, so that succour might not be brought from the nearest garrisons. In one place Volcatius Tullus sustained with three cohorts the attack of a legion and drove it from its position; in the other the Germans went out of our lines, and after killing a number of men retired in safety to their comrades.[16]

Thus all three Pompeian attacks were beaten off, with Caesar giving casualty figures for the two sides (which must again be taken with a pinch of salt).

> Thus six battles having taken place in one day, three at Dyrrhachium and three at the outworks, when account was taken of them all we found that about two thousand in number of the Pompeians had fallen, and very many reservists and centurions; among them was Valerius Flaccus, son of the Lucius who had governed Asia as Praetor; and that six military standards had been brought in. Of our men not more than twenty were lost in all the battles.[17]

Dio however paints a different picture:

> After this occurrence [the failed attack on Dyrrhachium] Pompeius took courage and planned a night assault upon the enclosing wall; and attacking it unexpectedly, he captured a portion of it by storm and caused great slaughter among the men encamped near it.[18]

Overall, the battles of this day (the date is not recorded) failed to produce a breakthrough and again left both armies in stalemate. Both commanders had been involved in the fighting and both could claim victories; Pompeius at Dyrrhachium and Caesar at his defensive line – ironically, both being the battles that the two commanders were not involved in; Sulla defeating Pompeius and an unknown Pompeian commander defeating Caesar. Caesar failed to take Dyrrhachium and Pompeius failed to destroy Caesar's fortifications.

Of the two men however it would probably have been Pompeius that would have been the more pleased, as his plan was to keep the status quo and deny Caesar the initiative, whilst waiting for Metellus Scipio. Caesar's attack on Dyrrhachium had been betrayed and failed and seemingly nearly cost him his life and it was only due to the actions of P. Cornelius Sulla that Pompeius had not broken through his defensive lines and marched on his main camp. Caesar reports that after fending off these attacks, he moved his army out of camp (into the no-man's land) and offered battle, perhaps showing his desperation.[19] In return Pompeius marched his army out of his camp in an equal show of martial strength (and to maintain morale) but, as ever, refused to give battle.

The Campaigns in Greece

It is at this point, with stalemate restored at Dyrrhachium, that Caesar's narrative breaks off to provide further information about the wider campaigns. Before reaching Dyrrhachium Caesar had sent a portion of his army (three legions) into Greece and Macedonia, both to challenge Pompeian control of the region and to slow Metellus Scipio down. As we have seen (Chapter Six), Caesar dispatched three commanders into Greece proper, Cn. Domitius Calvinus (Cos. 53 and 40 BC), L. Cassius Longinus and C. Calvisius Sabinus. As we have also seen the three men met with mixed success, with Domitius being defeated by Metellus, but Cassius and Calvisius meeting with more success (depending on which source you read).

With Domitius tied down in Macedonia with Metellus Scipio (see below) Calvisius and Cassius were operating in Greece proper. Here again we are hampered by not knowing how many garrisons Pompeius had in Greece, but the similar pattern emerged of the native cities without garrisons welcoming whichever army was the nearest. Thus according to Caesar, Cassius and Calvisius were able to secure the territories to the south of Epirus (Aetolia and Acarnania) but only due to Pompeian forces not really contesting them. The key to the Pompeian control of the region lay on the island of Corcyra, home to the Pompeian fleet and any ports that the Caesarian commanders could secure would be rendered ineffective by the Pompeian control of the Adriatic.

Caesar it seems sent further reinforcements to these regions under another commander Q. Fufius Calenus (Cos. 47 BC) to extend this territory under their control across the Gulf of Corinth and into Achaea.

Unfortunately for the Caesarian commanders, the Pompeian commander of the region P. Rutilius Lupus (Pr. 49 BC) seems to have fallen back in the face of their advance and retreated to the Isthmus of Corinth itself which he held as a defensive position. Presumably backed by a Pompeian fleet in the Gulf itself this was sufficient to prevent the Caesarians from crossing, thus Achaea remained under Pompeian control with Greece north of the Isthmus being uncontested and thus falling to Caesarian forces (however temporarily). The main Pompeian capital of Thessalonica, containing the Pompeian Senate, was presumably home to a large Pompeian garrison and seems to have remained untouched.

The Campaigns in Macedonia – Caesar's Dilemma

If there were limited Pompeian forces in Greece, the same was not true of Macedonia, hosting the large eastern army of Metellus Scipio, which had been transported from Asia Minor. Though the clashes with Domitius Calvinus had slowed him down, Metellus was still progressing across Macedonia towards Dyrrhachium. Here Caesar faced perhaps his most important challenge. Domitius had certainly slowed Metellus down, but nowhere near enough for Caesar's plans and Caesar himself would have realised that if he remained at Dyrrhachium much longer then he would become trapped between the two Pompeian armies. Furthermore, such a fate would similarly befall him if he broke off from Dyrrhachium and moved to attack Metellus himself, with Pompeius bound to march his army in Caesar's rear and shadow his movements but not give battle until Metellus arrived.

Thus the only two options that were open to Caesar were to break off the standoff at Dyrrhachium and retreat, either to the north (Illyria), the south (Greece proper) or to the west (back across the Adriatic) or to remain at Dyrrhachium and defeat Pompeius before Metellus arrived. Given that Caesar always preferred taking the initiative in his campaigns and perhaps worried over the effect on the morale of his army if he did break off and retreat, he chose to remain at Dyrrhachium and persist with the 'siege'.

It also appears that Caesar ruled out sending any further reinforcements to Domitius, given both his need for them at Dyrrhachium and in Greece and the fact that he would need to send a sizeable proportion of his forces to have any hope of defeating Metellus; anything less would be a waste of men. All Caesar did send was another envoy, a certain A. Clodius, who, according to Caesar, was a friend of Metellus. Clodius was sent with a letter from Caesar to Metellus trying to break him away from his alliance with Pompeius (his son-in-law) and become a neutral third power. Whilst given a friendly reception, Clodius was sent back to Caesar with Metellus unchanged in his resolve to crush Caesar, and again become the second most powerful person in the Republic. Thus Metellus' army continued its westward advance through Macedonia towards Epirus and Dyrrhachium.

Summary – Waiting for Metellus?

Thus after what was probably several months (May and June) of the two armies fighting at Dyrrhachium, the stalemate continued and the civil war itself seemed to become becalmed, waiting for an outcome at Dyrrhachium. Caesar remained in control of Spain, Italy and Sicily, Pompeius in Africa, and the Eastern Republic, with Illyria, Greece and Macedonia contested between the two. Again, of the two commanders, it would have been Pompeius who would have been the happier, having stymied Caesar's bold incursion across the Adriatic and tied him down at Dyrrhachium for several months.

One gets the sense that both sides were expecting the arrival of Metellus and the second Pompeian army to bring matters to a head and finally have the set piece battle between Pompeius and Caesar that had been anticipated since the start of the civil war in 49 bc. As it turned out, by what is estimated to be late June 48 bc, the stalemate at Dyrrhachium was about to be broken without outside intervention and the first full blooded clash between Pompeius and Caesar was about to occur.

Chapter Eight

The Battle of Dyrrhachium – The Decisive Clash

Feeling the Pressure

When dealing with the details of the final and decisive clashes of the Battle of Dyrrhachium we inevitably encounter the issue that the most detailed account is the one written by the loser. If anything, Caesar's account begins to signal to the reader that a defeat is coming when he shifts the focus onto a story narrating the treachery of 'perfidious foreigners' again.[1]

On this occasion it was two Gallic chieftains, named Roucillus and Egus (from the Allobroges tribe[2]) amongst his army who defected to Pompeius and then apparently betrayed the best location to attack. Thus in Caesar's mind it was this foreign treachery that cost him the battle and not Pompeius' tactical acumen in spotting a weak link in Caesar's fortifications, nor could there be the possibility that the fault lay in Caesar's own tactical ability.

Naturally, Caesar chose to labour the point that Pompeius' army was the one feeling the pressure of the deadlock, again stressing the supply issues he was facing, in this case a shortage of fodder for his cavalry and that his army was suffering from defections to Caesar's army, but that (prior to the Allobroges brothers) there were apparently no defections from Caesar's army.[3] Again, naturally, Caesar's account choses to dwell on the individual failings of the two Gallic chiefs, who apparently suffered from arrogance and avarice and were embezzlers. Caesar's character assassination continues:

The occurrence, however, brought on them great obloquy and contempt in the sight of all, and they understood that this was so not merely from the reproaches of others but also from the judgment of their intimates and from their own conscience. Influenced by this sense of shame and thinking, perhaps, that they were being reserved for punishment on a future occasion rather than let off free, they determined to quit us.[4]

Thus we have a wonderful double standard here; when Pompeius' men defect to Caesar it is perfectly natural as his army was under pressure, but when Caesar's men defect to Pompeius, it can't be because Caesar's army is under pressure and they believe he may lose; no, it has to be due to their personal moral defects. Cutting through this arrogance, the fact is that a large contingent of Caesar's Gallic allies abandoned his cause and defected to Pompeius. We are not given the size of this force, but Caesar himself admits that they left with *'a great retinue and many animals'*[5] and a considerable sum of money. Thus it seems that after several months of deadlock at Dyrrhachium, the pressure was being felt on both armies and both sides were suffering from defections.

The Pompeian Breakout

Though the stalemate and delay were more acceptable to Pompeius' overall strategy than Caesar's, it seems that Pompeius again chose to take the initiative and planned a large scale attack on Caesar's fortifications. Though he was still awaiting the arrival of Metellus, his army was suffering from supply issues and would inevitably be suffering from a morale problem, having been pinned in the Bay of Dyrrhachium for several months and were perhaps becoming dubious about the arrival of Metellus. The high-profile defections of a portion of Caesar's Gallic allies would definitely have been a morale boost to Pompeius and may well have been the decisive factor in the timing of his assault; this was proof positive that morale in Caesar's army was just as fragile.

Having been repulsed in his attack on Caesar's redoubts, Pompeius chose a fresh target and highlighted where he believed Caesar's line to be weakest, namely where the fortifications met the sea to the south and thus furthest away from Caesar's main camp and on the opposite side of the bay to the city of Dyrrhachium (see Map 7). Here Pompeius was playing to his strengths and building on the success he had from the 'day of six battles'; his only success coming when he used his fleet to carry his troops to the marshes which surrounded the city of Dyrrhachium, ambushing Caesar.

Here again, Pompeius chose to utilise his naval superiority to ferry his troops from his camp to the Caesarian side of their fortifications and attack them in the rear. The attack was timed for dawn and Pompeius had – if we are to believe Caesar – sixty cohorts, or thirty thousand men, more than likely a serious exaggeration. The spot he chose had naturally been identified by Caesar as a weak point and was in the process of being reinforced, which may well have spurred Pompeius decision to attack before it was completed:

> At these entrenchments Caesar had his Quaestor Lentulus Marcellinus posted with the Ninth Legion, and as he was in unsatisfactory health, he had sent up Fulvius Postumus to assist him.
>
> There was in that place a ditch fifteen feet wide and a rampart ten feet high facing the enemy, and the earthwork of this rampart was also ten feet in breadth. And at an interval of six hundred feet from this there was a second stockade facing in the other direction with a rampart of rather lower elevation. For on the preceding days Caesar, fearing lest our men should be hemmed in by the fleet, had constructed a double stockade in this spot, so that in case of an attack on both sides it might be possible to hold out. But the magnitude of the works and the continuous toil of every day, since he had taken in entrenchments of seventeen miles circuit, did not allow opportunity of completion. And so he had not yet completed the cross stockade facing the sea to join these two lines.[6]

Thus, Pompeius launched an overwhelming dawn attack on the Caesarian defences, from both the land and the sea, with only two cohorts of the Ninth Legion (less than a thousand men) defending the seaward approach. Caesar himself details the attack:

> For two cohorts of the Ninth Legion being on sentry duty by the sea, the Pompeians suddenly approached at early dawn; at the same time soldiers conveyed round on shipboard began to hurl javelins at the outer stockade, the ditches were being filled up with earth, the Pompeian legionaries, having brought up ladders, were terrifying the defenders of the inner line with engines of every kind and missiles, and a great multitude of archers were being thrown around them on every side. But the osier coverings placed on their helmets protected them to a great extent from the blows of stones, which were the only weapon our men had. And so when our men

were being hard pressed in every way and with difficulty holding their ground, the defect, mentioned above, of the line of entrenchment became observable and between the two stockades, where the work was not yet finished, the Pompeians, disembarking, took our men in the rear on both sides and dislodging them from each line, compelled them to take to flight.[7]

Thus Pompeius landed with overwhelming force at dawn taking the defenders by surprise and punched his way through a weak point in the Caesarian defences. On the previous occasion when Pompeians had broken through the Caesarian defences they were repelled by reinforcements from the nearest Caesarian camp. On this occasion Lentulus Marcellinus, the Caesarian commander of the Ninth also dispatched additional forces to try to force the Pompeians back, but these were overwhelmed, due to a combination of the sheer weight of Pompeian numbers (who on this occasion were attacking on flat ground) and the flight of the Caesarian defenders, making a sustained stand impossible. Having poured through the breach, the Pompeians made for the nearest Caesarian camp, that of Marcellinus and the Ninth.

A complete collapse of the Caesarian position was prevented however, by the arrival of M. Antonius, who was the nearest Caesarian commander to the Ninth Legion, along with twelve cohorts (just under six thousand men). He was supported by the arrival of Caesar himself and additional reinforcements, having been alerted by pre-arranged smoke signals that a breach had occurred.

Again it seems that no pitched battle occurred, with the Pompeians happy to consolidate their newly-won position, allowing Pompeius to build a fresh camp next to the sea and improve his supply lines. Likewise Caesar seemed to accept that he did not have sufficient forces to counterattack and reclaim his former defensive position, given the number of the Pompeian forces and their naval support. Caesar chose not to provide the numbers of his forces lost in the engagement, a sure sign that they were of note, merely saying that there was a great slaughter of his men. He does provide an example however: *'all the centurions of the first cohort were slain except the senior centurion of the second maniple.'*[8]

With Pompeius having broken through the Caesarian lines and improved his access to the sea, not to mention having gained a morale-improving victory, Caesar was faced with two choices; either to dislodge

Pompeius or abandon the whole Dyrrhachium campaign. Naturally enough, and with few other options he chose to continue with the campaign and made plans to try to dislodge Pompeius from his newly won territory. This would need to be done quickly before Pompeius was able to consolidate his control of the newly won coastal area and improve his supply lines and undermine Caesar's whole 'trench warfare'/siege tactics.

The Caesarian Counterattack

Towards these ends, Caesar created a new forward base close to the Pompeian army and waited for an opportunity to counter-attack. The opportunity came within a matter of days when Caesar's scouts reported that the Pompeians were creating a new forward base, by enlarging a previously-built smaller camp, but only manned by one legion at that moment. Caesar determined on a surprise attack before the new camp could be finished and quietly amassed a force of thirty-three cohorts (just under sixteen thousand men, assuming they were full strength). Caesar himself chose to lead the attack and provides a first-hand description:

> *Caesar, hoping to be able to crush this* [Pompeian] *legion and anxious to repair the loss of that day, left two cohorts at the work* [in his new camp] *to give an appearance of fortifying. Himself taking a divergent route in the utmost secrecy, he led out in double line towards Pompeius' legion and the smaller camp the remaining cohorts, numbering thirty-three, among which was the Ninth Legion, which had suffered the loss of many centurions and a diminution of the rank and file. Nor did his original idea fail him. For he arrived before Pompeius could be aware of it, and though the defences of the camp were large yet by attacking quickly with the left wing, where he himself was, he drove the Pompeians from the rampart. Beams studded with spikes barred the gates. Here there was fighting for a while, our men attempting to break in, the others defending their camp, Titus Pulio, by whose aid we have said that the army of C. Antonius was betrayed, leading the fighting with the utmost bravery at that spot. Nevertheless our men won by their endurance and cutting down the beams burst first into the larger camp, then also into the fort which was included within the larger camp, whither the legion when routed had retired for shelter. There they slew a few men who continued the struggle.*

Thus on the face of it, Caesar's strategy had succeeded, leading a characteristically bold surprise attack on the Pompeian forward camp, and disrupting Pompeius' plans. Yet, as was often the case, Caesar's boldness had left him exposed. Certainly, he had fifteen thousand men and possession of the half-built Pompeian forward camp, but though pinned down and heavily outnumbered, the Pompeian legion continued to fight and contest possession of the camp. Thus Caesar was now effectively in no man's land between his main army and Pompeius' and had not yet secured full control of his newly won possession, though without Pompeian reinforcements, it was clearly a matter of time.

The Decisive Clash

When news of this attack reached Pompeius and the fact that his legion still fought on, Pompeius clearly realised that this represented an opportunity. If he did nothing then his legion would be destroyed and put to flight and he would lose his forward base, which would effectively reverse the gains he had recently made. Furthermore, he would have realised that this was one of Caesar's bold moves and that he did not have his full army present.

Thus Pompeius acted with uncharacteristic boldness and went on the counterattack, advancing on Caesar's position with five legions and cavalry (thus outnumbering Caesar by at least ten thousand men). Even if his defending legion had been overwhelmed then there was every chance that Caesar was still exposed in advance of his main army and had not yet had time to secure the forward base from counterattack. Thus Pompeius found Caesar with fewer numbers and bottled up in the Pompeian camp rather than in the open field. Caesar himself describes the events that followed:

> Meanwhile, a fairly long interval of time had elapsed, and the news having reached Pompeius, he withdrew five legions from their work and led them to the relief of his men; and at the same time his cavalry approached our horsemen, and his serried ranks came into the view of our men who had occupied the camp.
>
> At once everything was changed. The Pompeian legion, encouraged by the hope of speedy succour, attempted resistance by the decuman gate, and

taking the initiative began to attack our men. Caesar's cavalry, fearing for its retreat, as it was mounting by a narrow track over the earthworks, began to flee.

The right wing, cut off from the left, observing the panic among the cavalry, to avoid being overwhelmed within the defences began to withdraw by the part of the rampart which it had levelled; and many of these men, fearing that they might get involved in the cramped space, flung themselves from the ten-foot rampart into the fosses, and when the first were crushed the rest tried to attain safety and a way of escape over their bodies.

On the left wing the soldiers, seeing from the rampart the approach of Pompeius and the flight of their own men, fearing that they might be cut off in the narrow space, as they had the enemy both inside and outside the camp, took counsel for themselves, retreating by the way by which they had come; and every place was full of disorder, panic, and flight, so much so that when Caesar grasped the standards of the fugitives and bade them halt, some without slackening speed fled at full gallop, others in their fear even let go their colours, nor did a single one of them halt.[9]

Thus Pompeius' counterattack succeeded and the Caesarian army collapsed into a rout. Outnumbered and trapped in the Pompeian camp and with the surviving Pompeian legion counterattacking, they were denied the freedom of movement on the battlefield that they were so successful at utilising. Fearful of being bottled up and overwhelmed, the morale of Caesar's legion collapsed; the forces routed to escape back to the safety of Caesar's lines.

As Caesar himself states the only reason his entire army was not destroyed is that Pompeius did not commit to a full pursuit of the fleeing Caesarian soldiers, and his cavalry was hindered by the same defence of the camp that had hindered Caesar's attack.

The only relief that came to mitigate these great disasters, preventing the destruction of the whole army, was the fact that Pompeius, fearing, I suppose, an ambuscade, since these events had happened contrary to his expectation, for a little while before he had seen his men fleeing from the camp, did not venture for a long time to approach the lines, and his horsemen were hindered in their pursuit by the narrowness of the passages, especially as they were occupied by Caesar's troops. So have small events

often turned the scale of fortune for good or evil. For the lines which were
drawn from the camp to the river interrupted the victory of Caesar, which
when once Pompeius' camp had been stormed was all but assured, and the
same circumstance by checking the speed of the pursuers brought safety to
our men.[10]

Thus Caesar and the bulk of his forces were able to reach the safety of the
Caesarian lines. Nevertheless, it was clear that Caesar had been defeated
and his army routed, and unlike the defeat during the night attack on
the city of Dyrrhachium, this one was in the full sight of both armies.
Caesar himself provides casualty figures for the defeat, which once again
we must treat with cation, and he admits to losing nearly a thousand men
and thirty-two military standards:

In these two battles in one day Caesar lost nine hundred and sixty men and
some well-known Roman knights, Tuticanus the Gaul, son of a Senator,
G. Fleginas of Placentia, A. Granius of Puteoli, M. Sacrativir of Capua,
and thirty-two military tribunes and centurions; but the majority of these
were overwhelmed at the ditches and lines of investment and river-banks
in the panic and flight of their comrades and perished without any wound;
and thirty-two military standards were lost. In this battle Pompeius
received the appellation of Imperator.[11]

Caesar also comments on an unknown number of his men being taken
prisoner, who were then promptly, and publicly, executed by T. Labienus,
Caesar's former lieutenant:

But Labienus, having induced Pompeius to order the captives to be handed
over to him, brought them all out, apparently for the sake of display, to
increase his own credit as a traitor, and, styling them 'comrades' and
asking them with much insolence of language whether veterans were in
the habit of running away, killed them in the sight of all.[12]

Naturally, Caesar presents his own summation of the defeat, where he
acknowledges (with faint praise) that Pompeius believed he had won a
victory:

By these successes, the Pompeians gained so much confidence and spirit that
instead of forming a plan of campaign they regarded themselves as having
already conquered.[13]

He then goes on to further downplay the defeat and diminish the loss by pointing out that it was not a 'proper' battle and that it was misfortune rather than Pompeius' skill that led to the rout. Thus we have a clear example of the (ultimate) winner writing the history books and starting to erase his losses:

> *They did not reflect that the cause of their success had been the small number of our troops, the unfavourable conditions of the site and the narrow space, when they had forestalled us in the occupation of the camp; the twofold panic, within and without the fortifications; the severance of the army into two parts, one being unable to bear aid to the other.*
>
> *They did not consider further that they had not fought in a sharp encounter or in a pitched battle, and that our men had brought a greater loss upon themselves by their numbers and the confined space than they had suffered from the enemy.*
>
> *Finally, they did not recollect the common chances of warfare, how often trifling causes, originating in a false suspicion, a sudden alarm, or a religious scruple, have entailed great disasters, whensoever a mistake has been made in an army through the incapacity of a general or the fault of a tribune; but just as if their victory were due to their valour and no change of fortune could occur, by reports and dispatches they proceeded to celebrate throughout the world the victory of that day.*[14]

The Appianic Version – A Greater Defeat?

As is often the case, Appian's account (written centuries later) contains some significant, and possibly illuminating, differences from Caesar's own. Appian (or whoever his source was) mostly glosses over the detail of the original battle and focusses on the rout, which continued far beyond that recorded by Caesar. In Caesar's account, he is defeated in Pompeius' camp and his army routs, but seemingly is not pursued and makes it safely back to his own lines with minimal casualties. However, in Appian's account, not only does Caesar's force from the camp fail to recover their morale and make a stand, but that reinforcements drawn from the rest of Caesar's army also lost their discipline and refused to defend Caesar's camp from the advancing Pompeian army.

Nevertheless, they fought one great battle in which Pompeius defeated Caesar in the most brilliant manner and pursued his men in headlong flight to his camp and took many of his standards. The eagle (the standard held in highest honour by the Romans) was saved with difficulty, the bearer having just time to throw it over the palisade to those within.

After this remarkable defeat Caesar brought up other troops from another quarter, but these also fell into a panic even when they beheld Pompeius still far distant. Although they were already close to the gates, they would neither make a stand, nor enter in good order, nor obey the commands given to them, but all fled pell-mell without shame, without orders, without reason. Caesar ran among them and with reproaches showed them that Pompeius was still far distant, yet under his very eye some threw down their standards and fled, while others bent their gaze upon the ground in shame and did nothing; so great consternation had befallen them.

One of the standard bearers, with his standard reversed, dared to thrust the end of it at Caesar himself, but the bodyguard cut him down. When the soldiers entered the camp, they did not station any guards. All precautions were neglected, and the fortification was left unprotected, so that it is probable that Pompeius might then have captured it and brought the war to an end by that one engagement had not Labienus, in some heaven-sent lunacy, persuaded him to pursue the fugitives instead. Moreover Pompeius himself hesitated, either because he suspected a stratagem when he saw the gates unguarded or because he contemptuously supposed the war already decided by this battle. So he turned against those outside of the camp and made a heavy slaughter and took twenty-eight standards in the two engagements of the day, but he here missed his second opportunity to give the finishing stroke to the war. It is reported that Caesar said, 'The war would have been ended today in the enemy's favour if they had had a commander who knew how to make use of victory.'[15]

Thus Caesar's reinforcements refused to make a stand and seemingly the whole army in that sector fled, allowing Pompeius to advance unopposed. The second key point in Appian's account is that this continued lack of resistance led to a 'great slaughter' of Caesar's forces, far more than the thousand Caesar himself reports. Though Appian's account was written several hundred years later, he would have been using earlier (and possibly contemporary[16]) sources, and certainly ones not written from the Caesarian point of view. Whilst Appian frequently presents odd variant versions of battles found in other accounts, on this occasion, he is describing events that are noticeably absent from Caesar's own version.

Caesar details the defeat and rout (he has no alternative given the number of witnesses and eyewitness accounts and Pompeius' own dispatches [see below]), but naturally plays down the impact. Thus, his own attack on Pompeius' camp was defeated, but the wider effects were limited. Yet in the Appianic version, defeat in Pompeius' camp turns into a general rout of his whole army (at least in the southern sector) and his men leave his camp undefended.

The supposed quote from Caesar is interesting and as with most quotes in later sources, is open to questions of its authenticity. The value of Pompeius storming Caesar's undefended camp depends entirely on what was within it. Crucially, in Appian's account it is not clear where Caesar himself was. This is repeated in the other accounts (see below). If Caesar was not in the camp and the majority of his army had fled, then there may well have been little of military value left in the camp. If that was the case, then Labienus probably had the right idea to focus on slaughtering as many of Caesar's forces as possible and increasing the scale of the defeat.

The question of where Caesar was in this rout is not answered either, in any of the accounts. The most likely explanation is that, given his army in the south of the Bay had disintegrated, Caesar retreated further to the north of his line of fortifications to the nearest army base and consolidated his position. Again the Appianic version has a much greater description of the aftermath of the defeat on Caesar's army than Caesar does himself. In Caesar' account, aside from a section on the reasons for the defeat and why it was not a serious one (see above), there is no further discussion concerning the state of his forces. Appian however devotes a section to the recriminations within Caesar's legions for their flight from battle.[17]

Appian also details that Caesar did not institute widespread sanctions such as decimation but '*he reluctantly punished a few*'.[18] Furthermore, Appian also presents what purports to be a verbatim discussion between Caesar and his officers about the wisdom of a subsequent attack on Pompeius, who now controlled the south of the Bay, and that his campaign at Dyrrhachium was a mistake; naturally not one found in Caesar's own works:

He privately admonished his friends that it was necessary first for the soldiers to recover from the very great alarm of their recent defeat, and for the enemy to lose something of their present high confidence. He confessed also that he had made a mistake in encamping before Dyrrhachium where Pompeius had abundance of supplies, whereas he ought to have drawn him to some place where he would be subject to the same scarcity as themselves.[19]

The Other Sources – Additional Details and Variant Traditions

Aside from Appian, our other main source for this period is Dio, in whose account this battle is noted by its absence. As we have seen earlier, Dio has a description of Caesar's failed attack on Dyrrhachium, but seems to combine Pompeius' subsequent night attack on the walls with the final battle:

After this occurrence Pompeius took courage and planned a night assault upon the enclosing wall; and attacking it unexpectedly, he captured a portion of it by storm and caused great slaughter among the men encamped near it.

Caesar, in view of this occurrence and because his grain had failed, inasmuch as the whole sea and land in the vicinity were hostile, and because for this reason some had actually deserted, feared that he might either be defeated while watching his adversary or be abandoned by his other followers.[20]

Plutarch's account of Pompeius does mention the battle and has the same quote as Appian:

In these skirmishes Caesar was for the most part victorious and carried the day; but once he narrowly escaped being utterly crushed and losing his army, for Pompeius made a brilliant fight and at last routed Caesar's whole force and killed two thousand of them. He did not, however, force his way into their camp with the fugitives, either because he could not, or because he feared to do so, and this led Caesar to say to his friends: 'Today victory would have been with the enemy if they had had a victor in command.'[21]

Thus we can see that Plutarch and Appian both seemed to have shared the same source for this information. Again we find an expanded version of this clash in Plutarch's biography of Caesar:

There was constant skirmishing about the fortifications of Pompeius, and in all of them Caesar got the better except one, where there was a great rout of his men and he was in danger of losing his camp. For when Pompeius attacked not one of Caesar's men stood his ground, but the moats were filled with the slain, and others were falling at their own ramparts and walls, whither they had been driven in headlong flight.

And though Caesar met the fugitives and tried to turn them back, he availed nothing, and when he tried to lay hold of the standards the bearers threw them away, so that the enemy captured thirty-two of them.[22]

Furthermore, Plutarch adds further detail to the rout with a story on how close Caesar himself came to being killed, naturally not found in Caesar's own account:

Caesar himself, too, narrowly escaped being killed. For as a tall and sturdy man was running away past him, he laid his hand upon him and bade him stay and face about upon the enemy; and the fellow, full of panic at the threatening danger, raised his sword to smite Caesar, but before he could do so Caesar's shield-bearer lopped off his arm at the shoulder.[23]

Again Plutarch uses the famous quote about Pompeius not taking Caesar's camp, though on this occasion he adds detail that there were men within:

So completely had Caesar given up his cause for lost that, when Pompeius, either from excessive caution or by some chance, did not follow up his great success, but withdrew after he had shut up the fugitives within their entrenchments, Caesar said to his friends as he left them: 'Today victory had been with the enemy, if they had had a victor in command.'[24]

Plutarch's account also has Caesar ruminating on the decisions he had made in this campaign:

Then going by himself to his tent and lying down, he spent that most distressful of all nights in vain reflections, convinced that he had shown bad generalship. For while a fertile country lay waiting for him, and the prosperous cities of Macedonia and Thessaly, he had neglected to carry the war thither, and had posted himself here by the sea, which his enemies controlled with their fleets, being thus held in siege by lack of provisions rather than besieging with his arms. Thus his despondent thoughts of the difficulty and perplexity of his situation kept him tossing upon his couch, and in the morning, he broke camp.[25]

As always, we must lament the loss of Livy and his narrative for these events. Nevertheless, we do have Orosius, a much later source but one believed to have been based on Livy:

> *Meanwhile at Dyrrhachium, a large number of Oriental Kings came bringing support for Pompeius. When Caesar arrived, he besieged Pompeius in vain, for although he dug a ditch fifteen miles long, the seas lay open to Pompeius. Pompeius destroyed a strongpoint by the sea guarded by Marcellinus and killed Caesar's garrison posted there. Caesar set out to take Torquatus and his single legion by storm. Pompeius, realising his allies' danger, concentrated his forces where, upon which Caesar abandoned his siege and immediately marched against him. Torquatus then sallied forth and attacked his rearguard. This led to Caesar's troops panicking at their sudden danger and they fled, while Caesar vainly tried to rally them. Pompeius, whom Caesar admits was the victor, then recalled his army. 4,000 of Caesars' troops, 22 centurions, and a good number of Roman knights were killed in this battle.*[26]

As is usually found with Orosius, we have additional details not found in other accounts. Whilst we have the key attack by Pompeius on the coastal fort, guarded by P. Cornelius Lentulus Marcellinus, we have additional details for the subsequent battle. Orosius seems to confirm that the Pompeian legion, which was holding the forward base, was commanded by L. Manlius Torquatus. More importantly Orosius preserves a crucial difference to the account of the subsequent battle found in Caesar. Here it is Caesar who broke off the siege of the base and marched on Pompeius, rather than Pompeius' forces attacking Caesar whilst he was still in the base. Here Caesar was undone by Torquatus attacking his forces from the rear whilst he was confronting Pompeius, and it was this that caused his army to panic and rout. Thus, in this tradition, it was Caesar's decision to break off the siege and confront Pompeius that was responsible for the defeat, not his army being caught in unfavourable topography.

Orosius, who does have a good reputation for reporting accurate losses (thanks to the sources he used), has the highest figure for numbers killed amongst the Caesarian forces, at four thousand plus. Thus, once again, we can see a variant tradition at play amongst the histories written of this period that has Caesar clearly defeated. The final source is a more unusual one, Lucan and his famous poetical work, the Pharsalia:

So swift Torquatus saw, and prompt to wage
The war more closely, he withdrew his men
Within a narrower wall.
Now past the trench
Were Caesar's companies, when from the hills
Pompeius hurled his host upon their ranks
Shut in and hampered. Not so much overwhelmed
As Caesar's soldiers is the hind who dwells
Writhing beneath his load spouts o'er the plains
A blazing torrent. Blinded by the dust,
Encircled, vanquished, ere the fight, they fled
In cloud of terror on their rearward foe,
So rushing on their fates. Thus had the war
Shed its last drop of blood and peace ensued,
But Magnus suffered not, and held his troops
Back from the battle.[27]

Thus Lucan too repeats the main tradition that Caesar's forces were shut up in the fort when Pompeius attacked and fled, though he does add the detail that Manlius Torquatus fell back when Caesar attacked the camp into a narrower line of defence to prevent his single legion from being overwhelmed.

Again, as with Orosius' account, the role of L. Manlius Torquatus is brought to prominence. Torquatus was a Patrician who had been a pro-Pompeian Praetor of 49 BC. His father had been Consul in 65 BC, one of the replacements for the deposed Consuls Elect of P. Cornelius Sulla and P. Autronius Paetus; whose deposition was part of an anti-Sullan faction backlash which contributed to the outbreak of the Second Civil War (see Chapter One). As a young man Torquatus himself was involved in the accusation that led to the pair being stripped of office. As we have seen, Torquatus was the officer commanding the city of Oricum, which was betrayed to Caesar, and he himself was captured (see Chapter Six). As was so often the case, in a public display of his clemency, and to show that he was not the 'bloodthirsty monster' that he was being portrayed as, Caesar released Torquatus, an act which seems to have backfired on him spectacularly.

Both Orosius and Lucan have a Torquatus (which we must assume is him) commanding the Pompeian legion which had been sent to guard the bridgehead Pompeius' attack had created. In Lucan it was Torquatus who was responsible for withdrawing his men into a more defensible position to prevent them being overwhelmed by Caesar's forces when they attacked the forward camp. In Orosius, it was Torquatus who led this legion in an attack on Caesar's rearguard when he went to confront Pompeius, thus trapping Caesar's forces between them. In either respect, a good deal of the credit for Pompeius' victory seems to belong to L. Manlius Torquatus. The only other sources to note are Velleius and Florus:

> Conflicts followed, with shifting fortunes. One of these battles was much more favourable to the Pompeians, and Caesar's troops were severely repulsed.[28]

> At one time he blockaded Pompeius' camp, which he had surrounded with a rampart sixteen miles in circumference; but what harm could a siege do to an army which, from its command of the sea, could obtain supplies of every kind in abundance? At another time he made an attack on Dyrrhachium, but in vain, since its very site alone rendered it impregnable.[29]

The Impact of the Battle

Naturally, analysing the impact of this battle depends to an extent on which account you choose to follow, from the minor defeat in Caesar to the major defeat in Appian. What is clear, is that in either case, Caesar's strategy of besieging Pompeius in the Bay of Dyrrhachium had failed. Pompeius had broken through Caesar's siege lines to the south of the bay, by the sea and established a forward base which had then been secured, having driven off Caesar's counterattack. If we follow the Appianic tradition then Caesar's entire army in that region had been driven off, leading to the total collapse of Caesar's siege lines in the south of the bay. Thus, we either have Pompeius securing a bridgehead through Caesar's lines or we have Pompeius driving a massive hole through them. In either event Pompeius' army would now have a clear route though to open countryside beyond the bay, rendering Caesar's attempts at a siege null and void.

The critical issue would be 'what next?' for the two armies, both of which had endured several months of siege warfare, and the privations that this brought. It would have been clear to everyone there that Pompeius was the victor; as Caesar himself begrudgingly admits:

In this battle Pompeius received the title of Imperator. To this title he adhered and afterwards allowed himself to be saluted as such, but he was never wont to use the ascription in his dispatches, nor did he display the insignia of the laurel on his fasces.[30]

Interestingly the sources are conflicted over the manner in which Pompeius announced his success to the wider Roman and non-Roman world. In both Appian's and Plutarch's account Pompeius seemingly wastes no time in publicising his victory at Dyrrhachium:

Pompeius sent letters to all the kings and cities magnifying his victory.[31]

Pompeius, however, although he wrote to distant kings and generals and cities in the tone of a victor.[32]

Yet in Dio we find that Pompeius apparently sent no word to the Senate or People in Rome about his victory:

Hence he made no attempt on Italy, nor even sent to the government any despatch about his successes.[33]

Naturally, it is difficult to reconcile these two accounts and it would seem especially puzzling that Pompeius would not want to claim the propaganda coup that his victory had brought, especially as it smashed the myth of Caesar's invincibility. Even though he may have sent no official dispatch to the rival Senate in Rome, we must assume that he ensured that everyone in Rome knew of the victory, which again would have been as magnified in his own account as it was downplayed in Caesar's eventual account. Caesar himself tells us the following:

At the same time, letters having been sent by Pompeius through all the provinces and communities after the battle at Dyrrhachium, couched in a more exaggerated and inflated style than the facts warranted, a report had spread abroad that Caesar had been beaten and was in flight with the loss of nearly all his forces.[34]

Yet ultimately, whilst the victory at Dyrrhachium was a bonus, it did not change Pompeius' overall strategy, which still called for awaiting the arrival of his eastern army, commanded by Metellus Scipio and only then facing Caesar in a set piece battle to give him the clear victory he needed over the 'enemy of the Republic' and cement his place as its saviour.

Nevertheless, Dyrrhachium must have greatly heartened him and convinced him that his strategy was a sound one. In the course of the Dyrrhachium campaign Caesar had been defeated twice, firstly during the ambush at Dyrrhachium itself and then in the battle for the southern camp. On both occasions Caesar's boldness had cost him the victory and nearly his life. This would have just emphasised in Pompeius' mind that he could exploit Caesar's boldness in a way that his subordinate commanders had failed to do in Spain and that if he continued his policy of 'giving Caesar enough rope' then he would surely hang himself. Furthermore, Pompeius had now seen first-hand that Caesar's army had broken and fled, something which he would surely factor into any future encounters.

Plutarch also reveals that the 'Pompeian' Senate assembled after Dyrrhachium to discuss the future of the campaign where a number of the Senators, seemingly led by L. Afranius, advocated an invasion of Italy, just across the Adriatic from the Pompeian position. Though Italy, and Rome, did stand underdefended, with the bulk of Caesar's legions in Greece, this clearly did not fit in with the Pompeian masterplan and thus was ignored by Pompeius.

Naturally, the majority of the sources focus on Caesar in the aftermath of the battle, but again Pompeius would have re-established his supply lines by land and then sat and awaited the next move by Caesar, confident that time, and now the momentum, was on his side.

Naturally enough the opposite was true for Caesar. His immediate priority would have been to regroup his army and calm the legions that had not been present at the battle (which represented the majority of his army). Once that had been achieved then, clearly, he needed to rethink his whole strategy.

Dyrrhachium had not merely been a defeat on the battlefield but had seen his whole strategy of a lightning attack across the Adriatic and an early battle with Pompeius (before Metellus arrived) collapse into a several-month-long siege which ended with a portion of his army being very publicly routed. In short, he had been drawn into playing out Pompeius' strategy rather than his own. His forces in Greece had met with some success, but mostly due to the Pompeians falling back, and his efforts to slow Metellus had also met with some success, but his arrival was now considered to be sooner rather than later.

Thus Caesar was stuck holding onto the fortifications that had now been breached to the south and thus rendered useless, knowing that despite his victory, Pompeius would still not face him in an open battle until Metellus Scipio arrived and that when Metellus did arrive, if he held onto his position at Dyrrhachium, it would be he that was under siege. Furthermore, he had seen how a portion of his army would react to fighting on such terrain, when they broke. Thus Caesar clearly needed to change these dynamics and regain the momentum that Dyrrhachium had cost him.

The Caesarian Withdrawal

We find as much in Caesar's own words:

> Caesar, driven from his former plans, came to the conclusion that he must alter his whole method of campaign. And so simultaneously withdrawing all his garrisons, abandoning the siege, and gathering all his army together, he delivered a harangue before his troops.[35]

Thus Caesar determined to withdraw from his position at Dyrrhachium. The immediate destination was the Caesarian held port of Apollonia to the south, which would act as a staging post and temporary headquarters. Caesar himself states his reasons:

> It was necessary for Caesar to go to Apollonia for the purpose of depositing his wounded, paying his army, encouraging his allies, and leaving garrisons for the towns.[36]

Apollonia however was just a staging point and Caesar's ultimate destination was to link up with the portion of his army he had sent against Metellus Scipio, commanded by Cn. Domitius Calvinus, and then force Metellus Scipio into battle. Again, this was a risky manoeuvre stretching his supply lines to the limit and operating deeper into Macedonia.

In reality though Caesar had too few options. He could not retreat back to Italy, due to the Pompeian control of the Adriatic and even if he could have it would have been a signal to all that he had been defeated in Greece. If he stayed at Apollonia, then Pompeius and Metellus would have linked up and presented a more formidable force. Thus the only logical option was to try to knock Metellus out of the war before he could link up with Pompeius. Yet key to this strategy would be to ensure that he had a sufficient lead on Pompeius and thus Caesar ensured that he withdrew his army from Dyrrhachium under the cover of night.

> *And so, with only such delay as attention to the sick and wounded required, he quietly sent on all his baggage-train from the camp at nightfall to Apollonia and forbade it to stop for rest till the journey was finished, and one legion was sent to protect it. Having arranged these matters, he kept back two legions in camp and led out the rest at the fourth watch by several gates and sent them on by the same route.[37]*

Naturally enough at daybreak Pompeius' scouts reported that Caesar had indeed withdrawn, as Pompeius must have been expecting and so he gathered his legions and set off in pursuit. Again Pompeius would have wanted to avoid a set piece battle but would have wanted to inflict more casualties on Caesar's army and test their resolve once more, softening them up for the inevitable battle.

> *Nor, on the other hand, did Pompeius, when he learnt of his design, allow any delay in pursuit, but with the same object in view, hoping to overtake the foe in the confusion and alarm of a difficult march, led his army from the camp and sent forward his horse to delay the rearguard, but was unable to overtake them, because Caesar, being in light marching order, had gone far ahead. But when they reached the River Genusus [the modern Shkumbin], with its difficult banks, the cavalry following up engaged and hindered the rearguard. Caesar opposed his own horsemen to them, mixing with them four hundred light-armed front-rank men, who gained such success that, engaging in a cavalry skirmish, they repelled them all, slaying many, and withdrew unhurt to the main body.[38]*

According to Caesar' own account, Pompeius' pursuit of Caesar lasted for four days, but Caesar was able to put some distance between the two forces by unexpectedly breaking camp and marching through the night whilst Pompeius' forces were dispersed having set up their own camp. Stopping briefly at Apollonia, Caesar then marched east across Epirus to meet up with Domitius Calvinus in Macedonia.

> *And so Caesar sent on messengers and wrote to Cn. Domitius explaining what he wanted done; and leaving a garrison of four cohorts at Apollonia, one at Lissus, and three at Oricum, and depositing at various places those*

*who were suffering from wounds, he began his march through Epirus and
Athamania.*[39]

Thus Caesar had successfully extricated himself from the position he
found himself in at Dyrrhachium and gambled everything on marching
deeper into enemy territory to seek out the second Pompeian army and try
to resolve the issue in open battle. Pompeius too, soon discerned Caesar's
plan and set out to meet up with Metellus himself. Thus both Pompeius
and Caesar set out for Macedonia, with four armies (Pompeius', Metellus',
Caesar's and Calvinus') all converging for what they hoped would be the
decisive and final battle of the Third Civil War. This battle – the Battle
of Pharsalus – did indeed prove to be a decisive one, but did not lead to
the end of the civil war and if anything, merely inflamed it.

The Pharsalus campaign, battle and aftermath will be covered in
the next volume of this series, The Battle of Pharsalus (48 BC): Caesar,
Pompeius and the Third Roman Civil War.[40]

Summary – Caesar's Folly

What can be said in summary of the Battle of Dyrrhachium? As we
have seen it was a most unusual battle: a confrontation that lasted several
months punctuated by two brief periods of intense conflict, the first of
which (the Caesarian attack on Dyrrhachium and the Pompeian night
attack on Caesar's defences) ended in a stalemate, the second of which
(the Pompeian attack on Caesar's defences, the Caesarian counterattack
and then the Pompeian counterattack) ended in a Pompeian victory.

This months-long stalemate was the consequence of a clash of styles
and clash of battleplans between the main two commanders, Pompeius
and Caesar. As was so often the case, Caesar had seized the initiative and
invaded Pompeian controlled Epirus, yet aside from some early successes
in capturing minor cities found himself cut off from Italy, operating in
enemy territory and facing an opponent who was in no rush to meet in
battle. If anything the Dyrrhachium campaign was just one half of a
wider tactical clash, the other half of which (Metellus and Domitius) is
still obscure.

Pompeius was at first content to allow Caesar to pin his forces down
in the Bay of Dyrrhachium, especially with control of the sea, as he
waited for the arrival of Metellus Scipio and his eastern army. Likewise,

Caesar was eager to force Pompeius to commit to battle before Metellus' arrival. This dynamic was changed by the continued absence of Metellus Scipio, who was held up by the Caesarian forces of Domitius Calvinus. What is most unfortunate for anyone working on this clash is that it is this half of the campaign that we have almost no detail for. All we can discern is that by the aftermath of the Battle of Dyrrhachium both Caesar and Pompeius found Metellus and Calvinus locked in a stalemate in Macedonia, camped opposite each other.

Thus, in many respects, Caesar's unusual tactic of trapping Pompeius' army in the Bay of Dyrrhachium (despite them having open access to the sea) appeared to bear fruit, with the absence of Metellus forcing Pompeius into offensive action. With his attack on the central portion of the Caesarian lines of fortification being beaten off, Pompeius changed tactics and utilised his naval superiority by attacking and breaching the Caesarian defensive lines where they met the sea and furthest from Caesar's main camp. In hindsight it was this region that Pompeius should have focused on to begin with as it played to his strengths.

It was at this point that Caesar doubled down on his original tactic and, rather than admit defeat in besieging Pompeius' army (which was always questionable given that Pompeius held both the city and the sea), launched a trademark bold counterattack to dislodge the bridgehead that Pompeius had created through his lines. On this occasion his boldness backfired, thanks to the defiance of L. Manlius Torquatus and the Pompeian legion in the bridgehead and the quick thinking of Pompeius himself, who realised that Caesar was exposed and undermanned. The collapse of the Caesarian army was probably a shock to both commanders but showed that months of stalemate had taken their toll on the Caesarian forces as much as the Pompeian ones.

Despite Caesar's best efforts to gloss over the Battle of Dyrrhachium, it is clear that the battle was a Caesarian defeat both on the day and of the wider campaign. Not only had his forces been defeated, with the loss of up to four thousand men, but more importantly, Caesar had been seen to be defeated, shattering that air of invincibility that he had built up around himself since the Romano-Gallic Wars and the Spanish campaigns of the previous year. Furthermore, the very nature of the defeat, his forces breaking and routing at the sight of the enemy, was the very opposite effect of his intention at Dyrrhachium, to wear down the morale of the supposedly weaker Pompeian legions.

Nevertheless, as events were soon to show, the defeat was actually a blessing in disguise for Caesar as he had allowed himself to become completely enmeshed in a drawn-out and ultimately futile siege of Pompeius' army. For months now, Caesar had abandoned the one tactic that had seen such success in the civil war to date, his boldness and fluidity of movement, and had instead found himself conducting the war that Pompeius had dictated. By finally abandoning the siege, he gave himself the chance to regain the momentum in his campaign and though the odds were clearly against him, he was again fighting the war on his own terms. As events soon proved, by marching into Macedonia to link up with Calvinus and knock out Metellus, he forced Pompeius' hand and clearly jeopardised his masterplan, which until that point had been working well.

Thus, it is paradoxical that Caesar's defeat at Dyrrhachium did so much to change the nature to the wider civil war campaign and restored to him the initiative. By making a bold thrust into Macedonia to confront Metellus, he risked one of two outcomes: either knocking Metellus out of the war and destroying Pompeius' whole campaign and masterplan, or facing being confronted by the full unified force of the Pompeian Republic. Nevertheless, both outcomes would offer him the opportunity he sought; a high risk 'traditional' battle where he could deploy his skills of generalship, rather than the folly that had been Dyrrhachium.

Appendix I

Who's Who in the Third Roman Civil War (49–48 BC)

Given the continuous narrative of Caesar and the number of other surviving sources that comment on this period, we know the identities of a large number of Roman politicians and officers that were taking part in the conflict, in both major and minor roles. That being the case, the following is a brief Who's Who of those involved in the campaign across 49 and 48 BC up to the Battle of Dyrrhachium, along with their subsequent fates.

The Main Protagonists

Cn. Pompeius 'Magnus'   (Cos 70, 55, 52 BC)   Killed 48 BC

Son of a First Civil War general. Rose to prominence during the First Civil War as a supporter, and then son-in-law, of Sulla. Based his earlier career on the threat of force rather than the reality. Brought the First Civil War to an end in 70 BC in partnership with M. Licinius Crassus, and the two men's reforms ushered in a new period for the Republic (the Pompeian-Crassan). Carved out a large empire for Rome in the Great Eastern War (74–62 BC) and returned to Rome to convert his military prestige into lasting dominance. Reforged his alliance with Crassus in 60–59 BC and then the two men effectively seized control of the Republic in 55 BC (along with Caesar). In Crassus' absence and eventual death, helped to ferment the bloody chaos that engulfed the Republic in the late 50s BC and became Sole Consul (or Princeps) in 52 BC. With only one rival left, manipulated events forcing Caesar to attack his own country and became an enemy of the state, with the rest of the oligarchy having no choice but to turn to him to defend the state.

Victorious at Dyrrhachium, but defeated heavily at the subsequent Battle of Pharsalus, he nevertheless determined to regroup and fight on.

Murdered on an Egyptian beach on the orders of Pharaoh Ptolemy XIII to curry favour with Caesar, a ploy which failed spectacularly.

C. Iulius Caesar   (Cos. 59, 48, 46, 47, 45, 44 BC)   Killed 44 BC
Nephew of the great C. Marius, who was a leading general in the First Civil War and son in law of L. Cornelius Cinna, who ruled Rome between 87–84 BC. Came to notice in Roman politics in the 60s championing the Marian cause against the ruling Sullan faction, but still only a minor figure. Won the Consulship for 59 BC as an agent of Pompeius (and latterly Crassus) and was rewarded with a command in Gaul. Defied expectations by launching a war of conquest, backed by Pompeius and Crassus. Formed a fresh alliance with Pompeius and Crassus, whilst still being the junior member, remained in Gaul throughout the 50s BC. Identified by Pompeius as the last obstacle to his dominance in Rome and manipulated into invading Italy as an 'enemy of the state'.

Defeated at Dyrrhachium, he regrouped and won a major victory at the subsequent Battle of Pharsalus. Neither this victory, nor the subsequent murder of Pompeius brought the war to a conclusion and he fought further battles of Thapsus in 46 BC and Munda in 45 BC. Having finally defeated all his civil war opponents, he was preparing a major war of conquest against the Parthian Empire when he was famously murdered in the Senate, by a large group of Senators, composed of former enemies and many of his own officers, to prevent him becoming sole ruler of Rome.

Notable Leading Figures

M. Aemilius Lepidus   (Cos. 46 & 42 BC)
Son of a First Civil War general. One of the Caesarian faction. Left by Caesar in charge of Rome during 49 BC. Proposed Caesar as Dictator. Became one of the main leaders of the faction after Caesar's death but politically outmanoeuvred by M. Antonius and Caesar Octavianus after the Battles of Philippi in 42 BC. Left alive by Octavianus (Augustus) as Pontifex Maximus (Chief Priest). Died of natural causes in 13/12 BC.

L. Afranius   (Cos. 60 BC)   Killed 46 BC
A long serving Pompeian commander, having fought under Pompeius during the First Civil War and then in the Eastern Wars. Elected as

Consul under Pompeius' patronage (the year before Caesar). Commanded Pompeius' legions in Spain but was defeated by Caesar. Captured and pardoned, he immediately returned to fighting for Pompeius, being at both Dyrrhachium and Pharsalus. Murdered by Caesarian troops after the Battle of Thapsus.

T. Annius Milo   (Tr. 57, Pr. 55 BC)   Killed 48 BC
Former Pompeian agent and Roman gang leader in the 50s. Exiled following the murder of Clodius. Returned to Rome in 48 BC and started a rebellion against Caesar. Killed in battle in Italy in 48 BC.

C. Antonius   (Pr. 44 BC)   Killed 42 BC
Younger brother of M. Antonius and Caesarian officer. Was in command of Caesar's province of Illyria but was defeated and captured by Pompeius' forces in 49 BC. Caesarian governor of Macedonia following Caesar's murder but was overthrown and murdered by Brutus.

M. Antonius   (Tr. 49, Cos. 44, 34, 31 BC)   Suicide 30 BC
One of the two Tribunes who fled to Caesar at the beginning of 49 BC. Received an extraordinary Propraetorian command (which technically he could not hold as a serving Tribune). Held command in Italy during 49 BC and led the defence of Brundisium in early 48 BC. Took command of the Caesarian relief army which crossed into Illyria in early 48. Present at the Battles of Dyrrhachium and Pharsalus. Was Caesar's deputy during his Dictatorship and became one of the leaders of the Caesarian faction following Caesar's murder in 44 BC. Seized control of the Republic as one of the Second Triumvirate and took control of the Eastern Republic. Took command of the Second Romano-Parthian War and attempted to carve out his own familial empire in the east. Defeated by Caesar Octavianus at the Battle of Actium in 31 BC. Committed suicide following Octavianus' invasion of Egypt.

C. Asinius Pollio   (Cos. 40 BC)
Caesarian commander in Sicily and Africa, one of the few survivors of the African defeat. Commanded Roman forces in Spain in 44 BC against Sex. Pompeius. Supporter of the Second Triumvirate but retired before the final civil war between Octavianus and Antonius.

Later became a noted historian and wrote a history of the civil wars, which no longer survives, but is believed to have been used by many of the later (surviving) historians.

P. Attius Varus (Pr. c.53 BC) Killed 45 BC
Pompeian commander. Briefly fought Caesar's men in Italy before withdrawing. Seized command of Roman Africa and defeated the Caesarian invasion (with Numidian help). Fled Africa to Spain after the defeat at Thapsus. Killed during the final battle of Munda.

L. Caecilius Metellus (Tr. 49 BC)
Tribune who stayed in Rome in 49 BC. Attempted to prevent Caesar from seizing the state treasury but backed down when his life was threatened by Caesar. Nothing further is recorded about him.

Q. Caecilius Metellus Pius Scipio Nasica (Cos. 52 BC) Suicide 46 BC
Scion of two of Rome's leading families, became Pompeius' father in law and then fellow Consul in 52 BC and de-facto deputy. Sent to the Eastern Republic in 49 BC to raise an army, he returned to Greece in early 48 BC to fight Caesar's officers but too late to take part in the Battle of Dyrrhachium. He fought a significant part in the subsequent Battle of Pharsalus and retreated to North Africa in its aftermath, becoming commander of the Pompeian forces following Pompeius' murder in Egypt. Rebuilding these forces, he faced Caesar at the Battle of Thapsus (46 BC) but was defeated and committed suicide in the aftermath.

M. Caelius Rufus (Tr. 52, Pr. 48 BC) Killed 48 BC
Former supporter of Milo, who supported Caesar in 49 BC. Elected as Peregrine Praetor for 48 BC caused a political disturbance by proposing popular legislation on the issue of debt. Attempted to raise a revolt with former colleague Milo but was killed.

M. Calpurnius Bibulus (Cos. 59 BC) Died 48 BC
Caesar's colleague in the Consulship of 59 BC and long-time opponent. Commanded in Syria following Rome's defeat in the First Romano-Parthian War. Took command of Pompeius' fleet in the Adriatic and attacked Caesar's fleet trying to reinforce him in Epirus. Died of an illness in the Adriatic in early 48 BC.

C. Calvisius Sabinus   (Cos. 39 BC)
Caesarian commander dispatched to secure Aetolia in 48 BC. Backed the
Triumvirate after the murder of Caesar and supported Octavinaus in the
war against Sex. Pompeius. Supported Octavinaus against Antonius and
became part of the Augustan elite. Date of death remains unknown.

Q. Cassius Longinus   (Tr. 49 BC)   Died 47 BC
One of the two Tribunes who fled to Caesar at the beginning of 49 BC.
Received an extraordinary Propraetorian command (which technically he
could not hold as a serving Tribune) and fought in Spain with Caesar.
Became Caesarian Governor of Further Spain and ruled tyrannically,
sparking off a rebellion and his replacement. Died in 47 BC in shipwreck.

C. Claudius Marcellus   (Cos. 49 BC)
Pompeian Consul in 49 BC. Helped precipitate the final breach with
Caesar. Withdrew to Epirus along with Pompeius. Recorded as being
commander of Pompeius' Rhodian fleet, but then disappears from the
surviving sources. Date and cause of death unknown.

P. Cornelius Dolabella   (Tr. 47, Cos. 44 BC)   Killed 43 BC
Caesarian naval commander in Illyria, defeated by Pompeian forces in
49 BC. Stirred up political chaos in Rome as Tribune in 47 but pardoned
by Caesar. Succeeded Caesar as Consul in 44 BC and sided with Antonius
and Lepidus. Succeeded Caesar as commander of the proposed Romano-
Parthian War but fought several civil war campaigns in Asia Minor in
43 BC. Defeated and killed by Cassius.

L. Cornelius Lentulus Crus   (Cos. 49 BC)   Killed 48 BC
Pompeian Consul of 49 BC. Fled to Egypt after the Battle of Pharsalus
but was murdered on the orders of Ptolemy XIII.

P. Cornelius Lentulus Marcellinus
Caesarian Quaestor, who commanded the forces to the south of Caesar's
siege works at Battle of Dyrrhachium, where Pompeius focused his
successful attack. His subsequent career is not recorded, and he may have
been killed in the battle.

P. Cornelius Lentulus Spinther   (Cos. 57 BC)   Killed 48 BC?
Pompeian commander in Italy in 49 BC, captured by Caesar and pardoned, he re-joined Pompeius. Fled to Rhodes after the Battle of Pharsalus but is believed to have been murdered on the orders of Caesar.

F. Cornelius Sulla   Killed 46 BC
Son and heir of the late Dictator, and son in law of Pompeius. Held command of Pompeian forces in Macedonia and fought Domitius Calvinus. Withdrew to Africa after the defeat at Pharsalus. Murdered in the aftermath of the Battle of Thapsus.

P. Cornelius Sulla   (Cos. 65 BC)   Died 45 BC
Nephew of the late Dictator, and brother in law of Pompeius, but a Caesarian commander. Fought in both the Battles of Dyrrhachium and Pharsalus. Died, presumably of natural causes, in 45 BC.

L. Domitius Ahenobarbus   (Cos. 54 BC)   Killed 48 BC
Senatorial appointed successor to Caesar in Gaul. Defeated by Caesar at Corfinium. Commanded Massilia against a Caesarian siege. Re-joined Pompeius in Greece. Killed in the aftermath of the Battle of Pharsalus (48 BC).

Cn. Domitius Calvinus   (Cos. 53 & 40 BC)
Caesarian commander dispatched to face Metellus Scipio in 48 BC and later took part in the Battle of Pharsalus. He became an ally of Octavianus, following Caesar's murder and remained a key member of Octavianus' circle of supporters. His date of death is unknown.

Q. Fufius Calenus   (Cos. 47 BC)   Died 40 BC
Caesarian commander in Spain and Greece. Became Consul in 47 BC and joined M. Antonius in the aftermath of Caesar's murder. Died of (presumed) natural causes, in 40 BC, whilst commanding forces in Transalpine Gaul against Caesar Octavianus.

A. Gabinius   (Cos. 58 BC)   Died 48/47 BC
Former Pompeian commander, who sided with Caesar, after being discarded by Pompeius. Possible commander at Brundisium who marched a portion of the Caesarian army into Illyria by land but was defeated by

the local tribes. Fought in Illyricum in 48 BC, dying of (presumed) natural causes late in 48 or early 47 BC.

L. Iulius Caesar   Killed 46 BC
Son of the Consul of 64 BC and a member of the same family as Caesar, but a Pompeian supporter. Sent as an emissary by Pompeius in 49 BC, he was a naval commander in Africa. Killed in the aftermath of the Battle of Thapsus.

D. Iunius Brutus Albinus   (Pr. 45 BC)   Killed 43 BC
Caesarian commander placed in charge of the naval siege of Massilia. Went on to hold a Praetorship in 45 BC. Was one of the leading conspirators who murdered Caesar in 44 BC. Took up command in Cisalpine Gaul where he fought against M. Antonius in 43 BC, but was forced to flee when his army mutinied. Captured and murdered by a Gallic chief.

T. Labienus   (Pr. c.59 BC)   Killed 45 BC
Senior Caesarian commander in Gaul but defected to join Pompeius when Caesar invaded Italy. Became a senior Pompeian commander, fighting at both Pharsalus and Thapsus. Fled to Spain after Thapsus and (by default) found himself as joint leader of the Pompeian faction (along with Pompeius' sons). Killed in the Battle of Munda. His son became a Parthian client who conquered Asia Minor in 40 BC.

L. Manlius Torquatus   (Pr. 49 BC)   Killed 46 BC
Pompeian commander, who lost the city of Oricum to Caesar in 48 BC but commanded the Pompeian forces who were attacked by Caesar during the final battle of Dyrrhachium and seems to have played a key role in the victory. He retreated to North Africa after the Battle of Pharsalus but died in the aftermath of the Battle of Thapsus, after being captured; either executed or by his own hand.

L. Munatius Plancus   (Cos. 42 BC)
Caesarian commander in Spain, whose quick thinking saved two legions from destruction. Supported the Triumvirate in the aftermath of Caesar's assassination and became Consul in 42 BC, along with Lepidus. Proconsul of Syria during the Second Romano-Parthian War, he defected to Caesar Octavianus before his war with M. Antonius. Was appointed one of the

last two ever Censors in 22 BC, before that role became part of imperial power. Died of natural causes in c.15 BC.

M. Octavius
Pompeian naval commander in Illyria, who helped to defeat the Caesarian forces there in 49 BC. Continued his naval command in Africa in 47–46 BC. Subsequent career and fate unknown.

Q. Pedius   (Cos. 43 BC)   Died 43 BC
Caesarian commander, who served in Gaul and was a nephew of Caesar. Crushed Milo's rebellion in 48 BC. Fought in Spain in 45 BC. Named an heir in Caesar's will, along with his cousin Caesar Octavianus. Supported the Triumvirate and made Consul in 43 BC along with Octavianus but died in office.

M. Petreius   Suicide 46 BC
Fought in both the First and Second Civil Wars. Pompeian commander in Spain. Defeated by Caesar, he re-joined Pompeius in Greece. Retreated to North Africa after the Battle of Pharsalus, where he served as a commander. Committed suicide after the defeat at the Battle of Thapsus.

Sex. Pompeius   Killed 35 BC
Youngest of the two sons of Pompeius Magnus and an accomplished naval commander. He became joint leader of the Pompeian faction after the Battle of Thapsus and faced Caesar in Spain at the Battle of Munda in 45 BC. Becoming sole leader after the murder of his elder brother, he again took to the sea and opposed first Caesar and then the Caesarian Triumvirate, seizing control of Sicily. Fought civil war campaigns against Caesar Octavinaus and was ultimately defeated, before fleeing east to fight civil war campaigns against Antonius' forces. Captured and murdered in 35 BC by the Antonine general M. Titius.

M. Porcius Cato   (Pr. 54 BC)   Suicide 46 BC
More commonly known today as Cato the Younger. Contemporary of Caesar who opposed the various Triumvirs during the 60s and 50s. Pompeian supporter in the civil war. Commander in Sicily in 49 BC but withdrew rather than defend the island. Kept away from further military commands, withdrew to Africa after the defeat at Pharsalus. Famously

committed suicide after the defeat at Thapsus rather than compromise with Caesar.

C. Scribonius Curio   Killed 49 BC

Caesarian commander. Led the campaign to seize control of Roman North Africa. Defeated his Roman opponent but was killed in a battle with the Numidian army of King Juba, who had declared his support for Pompeius and the exiled Roman government.

L. Scribonius Libo   (Cos. 34 BC)

Pompeian commander who took charge of the Adriatic campaign in 48 BC. After the murder of Caesar he sided with Sex. Pompeius (his son-in-law), but after his defeat made peace with Caesar Octavianus (his brother-in-law). Became Consul in 34 BC and remained a part of the Senatorial elite who supported Caesar Octavianus. Date of death is unknown.

P. Servilius Isauricus   (Cos. 48 & 41 BC)

Son of a First Civil War general (Sullan faction). Caesar's fellow Consul in 48 BC. Defended Rome against Caelius and Milo. Named Caesar as Dictator after the Battle of Pharsalus. Sided with Caesar Octavianus after Caesar's murder and remained loyal throughout the subsequent civil war, earning another Consulship in 41 BC. Date and cause of death unknown.

C. Trebonius   (Cos. 45 BC)   Killed 43 BC

Caesarian commander, who had served with him in Gaul and was placed in charge of the siege of Massilia. As Praetor in 48 BC, opposed Caelus' measure on debt alleviation. Served in Spain as a Provincial Governor and went on to hold a Consulship in 45 BC. Became one of the conspirators in the murder of Caesar in 44 BC. Took up command in Asia where he fought against P. Cornelius Dolabella in 43 BC but was captured and murdered.

M. Tullius Cicero   (Cos. 63 BC)   Killed 43 BC

Famous political commentator and lawyer who held the Consulship in 63 BC and was central in the events of the Second Civil War. Remained in Italy during Caesar's invasion and only latterly joined Pompeius in Greece. Returned to Italy after the Battle of Pharsalus and was pardoned by Caesar. Murdered in 43 BC on the order of M. Antonius.

M. Tullius Cicero   (Cos. 30 BC)
Son of the Consul and writer, was a cavalry officer in the Pompeian forces. Pardoned after the Battle of Pharsalus by Caesar, he joined the faction of Brutus and Cassius after Caesar's murder, following the murder of his father on the order of M. Antonius. Pardoned again after the Battles of Philippi, by Octavianus, he supported the latter against M. Antonius. Was present at the Battle of Actium and as Consul in 30 BC announced the death of M. Antonius to the Senate.

Non Romans

Bocchus II (King of the Mauri 49–33 BC)   Died 33 BC
Bogud (King of the Mauri 49–31 BC)   Killed 31 BC
Joint Kings of the Maurian Kingdom in North Africa. Supported Caesar in opposition to their rivals in Numidia. In the subsequent civil war between Antonius and Octavianus the two brothers took opposing sides, with Bogud being deposed and dying during the prelude to the Battle of Actium.

Juba I (King of Numidia c. 85–46 BC)   Suicide 46 BC
King of Numida. Threw his whole support behind Pompeius. Defeated the Caesarian invasion of North Africa and butchered the survivors. Supported the Pompeian faction in the aftermath of Pharsalus. Was unable to take part in the Battle of Thapsus in 46 BC and fled in the aftermath, dying in a suicide pact with the Roman commander M. Petreius.

Raucillus and Egus   Killed 48 BC
Sons of an Allobrogian Chieftain and part of Caesar's Gallic allied contingent. Betrayed Caesar and defected to Pompeius before the final clash of the Battle of Dyrrhachium.

Lesser Figures

M. Acilius Caninus
Caesarian commander of Oricum in 48 BC.

M. Aurelius Cotta
Pompeian commander, driven out of Sardinia by a revolt in 49 BC.

L. Cassius Longinus   (Tr. 44 BC)
Caesarian commander dispatched to secure Thessaly in 48 BC but was heavily defeated by Metellus Scipio. Became a Tribune in 44 BC. His subsequent career is not known.

A. Clodius
Caesarian envoy in Greece in 48 BC.

C. Coponius   (Pr. 49 BC)
Pompeian commander of the naval forces at Dyrrhachium. Seems to have made peace with Caesar and returned to Rome.

C. Fabius   (Pr. 58 BC)
Caesarian commander in Spain. Nothing is known of his subsequent career or fate.

Fulvius Postumus
Caesarian commander at the Battle of Dyrrhachium. Possibly killed in Pompeius' final attack.

Licinius Damasippus
Pompeian Senator in North Africa.

C. Lucilius Hirrus
Pompeian commander in Italy, later sent as Pompeius' envoy to the Parthian court.

Q. Lucretius Vespillo
Pompeian officer, commanded a detachment of Pompeius' fleet at Oricum in 48 BC.

N. Magius
Pompeius' Chief Engineer, captured by Caesar in Italy but sent back to Pompeius, helped defend Brundisium.

Marcius Rufus
Caesarian officer, survivor of the Battle of Bagradas.

L. Minucius Basilus
Caesarian legate in Illyria, Caesarian assassin, murdered 43 BC by slaves.

Minucius Rufus
Pompeian officer, commanded a detachment of Pompeius' fleet at Oricum in 48 BC.

Q. Minucius Thermus   (Pr. c.53 BC)
Pompeian commander in Italy, withdrew rather than face Caesar.

L. Nasidius
Pompeian commander in charge of a relief fleet to Massilia. Withdrew from battle with D. Iunius Brutus to Spain. Later commanded further Pompeian naval forces and served with Sex. Pompeius in the 30s BC. Fate unknown.

Otacilius Crassus
Pompeian commander at Lissus.

T. Pulio
Former Caesarian soldier from the Gallic campaigns who switched sides in 49 BC and helped betray C. Antonius. Caesar names him as fighting for the Pompeians in the final clashes of the Battle of Dyrrhachium.

L. Roscius Fabatus   (Pr. 49+ BC)
Pompeian Emissary sent to Caesar in 49 BC.

P. Rutilius Lupus   (Pr. 49 BC)
Pompeian commander who defended Achaea from Caesarian forces in 48 BC.

C. Sallustius Crispus   (Pr. 46 BC)
Caesarian commander, who held a junior command in Illyria, but was defeated by Pompeian forces. Later became a famous historian.

Ser. Sulpicius
Pompeian Senator in North Africa.

L. Staberius

Pompeian officer in charge of Apollonia in 48 BC. Failed to defend the city when the locals rebelled. Fled to Pompeius.

M. Terentius Varro

Pompeian commander in Spain. Re-joined Pompeius after being defeated by Caesar. Pardoned after the Battle of Pharsalus, he retired and became one of Rome's' greatest academics, producing over seventy works. He died in 27 BC, in his late 80s.

Valerius Flaccus   Killed 48 BC

Grandson of the civil war general (Cinnan Faction) and a Pompeian commander. Killed during a Pompeian attack on the Caesarian defences at Dyrrhachium.

Q. Valerius Orca   (Pr. 57 BC)

Friend of Cicero and Caesarian commander who seized control of Sardinia in 49 BC. By 45 BC, he was seizing land for Caesar's troops in Etruria.

Vibius Curius

Caesarian cavalry officer in Italy in 49 BC.

L. Vibullius Rufus

Pompeian Prefect, captured in Italy and released, went to Pompeius in Epirus and then sent with Pompeius' orders to his legates in Spain. Captured again in Spain and held as a useful prisoner and sent by Caesar as a peace envoy in early 48 BC.

Appendix II

How Many Civil Wars?[1]

A s readers will note I have deliberately chosen to include the provocative sub-title of the Third Roman Civil War for this series of books. This deliberately challenges the cosy status quo that has emerged in modern historiography of the Roman civil war period, and which ignores a fundamental question for anyone studying this period of Roman history; namely, when is a civil war not a civil war? The short answer seems to be when it is a rebellion, revolt or even a conspiracy. There seems to have developed a very narrow and illogical definition of when a Roman army fighting a Roman army constitutes a civil war and when it does not.

Thus, we have the absurdity that a Consul marching his army on Rome itself in 88 and 87 BC constitutes a Civil War whilst a Proconsul doing so just ten years later (in 77 BC) does not. Throughout my various works I have sort to challenge this cosy and somewhat lazy consensus that has emerged, first by lengthening the duration of the First Civil War from its traditional 88–82 BC to 91–70 BC, which allows us to include the Lepidian, Sertorian and Marian campaigns, where again Roman fought Roman, as sequels to the events of the 80s BC.[2] Under this schema, the war only ended in 70 BC (with the last military campaign being fought in 71 BC) with the Consulships of Pompeius and Crassus and their political reform and general amnesty. This approach owes more to Appian, with his work on the civil wars covering 133–31 BC than to Florus, with each campaign being a separate war.

All too often modern historiography ignores this question and seems to follow the Florine route and wants to separate these various conflicts into nice self-contained wars. This is not just a problem with Roman history. Modern historiography seems to demand that civil wars be clearly defined between two opposing sides each with a different ideological standpoint.

Thus, English history only has one Civil War (1642–1651) with two clearly defined sides, each with separate ideological stand points (monarchy versus Parliament) and even clearly defined costumes. Yet this war was at least the sixth fought between the English in the last thousand years. We have the civil war between Stephen and Maud for the crowns of England and Normandy (1135–1153), the two civil wars fought between Kings John and Henry III and their rebellious nobles (1215–1217 and 1264–1267) and the two wars fought for the English crown between the various branches of the Plantagenet dynasty between 1399 to 1403 and 1455 to 1487 (the latter of which dubbed the War of the Roses).

Thus, English history has at least six civil wars in the last thousand years yet only one makes the cut as an 'official' Civil War. The obvious question is why are the others ignored and downgraded into non-civil wars each with a meaningless title (Baron Wars, Wars of the Roses)? Is it because they do not fit into a nice ideological framework or is it an unwillingness to admit that societies collapse more often that we would like to admit?

If we look at history, we can discern two broad types of civil war. One is the 'modern' version where we have a clash between two clearly defined sides, each with an ideological standpoint, usually centred on a question of governance. Thus, we have the classic English, American, Spanish and Chinese Civil Wars. Yet the second type is where there is a complete breakdown of government and a society collapses into anarchy with various competing warlords emerging and fighting for supremacy. These types can most commonly be seen in modern Africa.

Yet returning to Rome, which type of civil wars can we see? All too often modern historians want them to be the clear cut ideological civil wars, between optimates and populares (terms which have been grossly distorted). Thus, our two official civil wars of the period, Sulla versus Marius and Caesar versus Pompeius, are often painted in these terms. Yet having reviewed these events, such terms are meaningless. The various protagonists did not go to war over differing views of how to govern but turned to their armies to defend their own positions from the attacks of their enemies. The events of the 80s and 40s both snowballed out of everyone's control with the Republican system collapsing and leading to periods of anarchy where various Roman generals fought for supremacy amongst themselves until victorious individuals emerged who could rebuild central authority and calm the bloodshed, i.e. dominate without looking like they were doing so; Pompeius and Crassus in 71–70 BC and Octavianus in 30–27 BC.

Thus, modern Roman historiography leaves us with a Florine-like patchwork of different wars:

Social War	(91–88 BC)
First Civil War	(88–81 BC)
Sertorian Rebellion	(81–72 BC)
Lepidian Revolt	(78–77 BC)
Catiline Conspiracy	(63–62 BC)
Second Civil War	(49–31 BC)

The clear danger of following such an approach of course is that it shifts focus away from the underlying causes of these conflicts and onto the individuals and thus blurs the line between symptom and cause. Should we be focusing on Sulla, Lepidus, Catilina, Caesar or the underlying issues that were at work behind them. Clearly having read this volume, the reader will understand that focussing on the individuals at the expense of the wider picture is not a method I chose to pursue. Not one of these men woke up one morning and thought that they would like to march their army against their own state simply to gain power for themselves, but that the Republican politics had forced them to believe that they had no alternative and that what they were doing was for the benefit of the Republic.

Ultimately as these events proved, the Republican system did not provide a robust enough framework to keep the various tensions between the Senatorial oligarchy from spilling over into violence and civil war. Various attempts were made to modify the Republic, be it Triumvirate (official or unofficial) or sole rule (subtle or obvious). The one version that emerged victorious from this period was sole rule, with one figure guiding and overseeing the smooth running of the Republic and acting as arbiter to keep the others in check. Yet this too was flawed and laid the foundations for a role of Emperor, chosen first on a hereditary basis and then by merit or armed force.

Yet, if we are to reject the Florine version of the wars in this period; what are we to replace it with? Do we simply follow the Appianic version and state that all this period was one giant civil war, or do we reject the notion of a civil war in a society such as Rome altogether? I have and will continue to argue that within this period of Roman history there were distinct periods of civil wars, when the clashes and tensions within the Republican system boiled over into full blown military conflict and in two out of the three cases, total system-wide (and empire-wide) collapse.

Civil war within a country is one thing but civil war in a society that had a full-blown empire is another matter altogether and magnified the chaos and fighting on a Mediterranean-wide level. As we have seen in two out of three cases, Rome's empire became a battleground for the various parties of the civil war and led to the extinction of several independent kingdoms who became too closely associated with a losing side (namely Numidia and Egypt).

Having rejected the modern Florine notion of multiple separate wars, I would like to offer up a fresh scheme for the civil wars within this period, if only to stimulate further debate on a subject that can never have a right answer.

The First Civil War 91–70 BC

All too often, discussions of the First Civil War ignore the fact that Italy had been riven by civil warfare for three years with two rebel factions fighting the Republican government. This is the very reason that Sulla had an army of battle-hardened veterans in Italy within marching distance of Rome and citizen distribution was at the heart of the political manoeuvring which led to Sulla's loss of command. Thus, the war that broke out in 91 BC between the various societies that made up the Roman system, must be classed as a civil war, with neighbour fighting neighbour and, if we are to believe the more dramatic sources, brother fighting brother.

Thus, the First Civil War period saw a number of different phases, which were not neatly separate conflicts but were all intertwined. The war in Italy led to the Consular attack on Rome in 88 BC, both of which mixed together to spark off the war of 87 BC. There then followed a lull whilst at least two different Roman armies separately fought off a foreign invasion. When that invasion had been dealt with then all sides then engaged in a fight for supremacy which brought about another lull as Sulla consolidated his control of Italy and the Western Republic. Some regions were forcibly reunited (Sicily, Africa) whilst others (Spain and Gaul) were brought together through negotiation between warlords. Yet the faction that lost Italy soon stoked a rebellion in Spain where the civil war continued (mixed in with a native rebellion, as it had been in Italy) for another nine years. Whilst the civil war continued in the Western Republic (Spain), other elements of the faction that lost Italy spearheaded another foreign invasion of Rome's empire, again blurring the lines between civil war and foreign war.

Thus, we can see that during this period there were no neat delineations between civil war, native rebellion and foreign wars, but all became inexorably interlinked in one great collapse of the Republican system. It is also not a coincidence that the largest slave rebellion in Roman history happened during this period of chaos, when a certain slave named Spartacus took advantage of the devastation in Italy, disaffection with Rome and overseas wars to launch his rebellion.

By 71 BC there emerged another lull with the fighting ended in Spain, Italy and Asia. Yet it took the actions of Pompeius and Crassus who chose to unite, rather than continue the division (and personally benefit from it). Their Consulship did not only set an example that two oligarchs could work in a peaceful manner, especially if they cooperated and introduce a constitutional settlement, they removed a number of tension points (though some would say reintroduced them) and saw a very public recall of all Romans exiled during the previous twenty years of tumult. Thus, it can be argued that a lull became a definite end.

The Second Civil War 63–62 BC

That the events of 63/62 BC constitute a civil war should not be difficult to argue. Although the ancient sources and modern historiography chooses to focus on events in Rome, the key facts are that there were widescale rebellions against Rome throughout Italy and native rebellions in Gaul (again mixing the two) and two Romano-Italian armies fought one another in a set piece battle. That there was only one set piece battle, and that it was over relatively quickly should not disqualify this from being classed as a civil war. In fact, the surviving sources paint a picture of wider military action across Italy, but we only have the barest of detail for it. Had we fuller sources for this fighting then we would be able to see the true scale of the civil war in Italy.

The other question is that if this was a civil war, was it a continuation of the first war and, if so, can we extend the First Civil War down to 62 BC? As we have reviewed, the causes of this war do have their roots in the first war, be they disgruntled Sullan politicians and veterans or displaced Italian communities. Yet I would argue that it was a separate conflict from that of 91–70 BC and that the years 69–64 BC were not merely a lull in the first war, but that the Pompeian-Crassan Consulships did end the First Civil War. That a war can be finished but still leave matters unsettled can be seen frequently throughout history; most recently in the First and Second World Wars (at least in Europe). So, although the Second Civil War had its roots in the First, they were, I believe, separate conflicts. This can also be seen by the fact that the New Republic reconstituted out of the ashes of the First Civil War did not collapse as it had done in 91–70 or 49–30 BC.

The Third Civil War 49–27 BC

This is perhaps the most uncontentious of the three, with it being widely accepted that the events between the crossing of the Rubicon in 49 BC and the victory of Octavianus constitute another period of one civil war which again saw a total collapse of the Republican system and the emergence of various factions and warlords. It too saw the blurring between civil war and foreign war, again most easily seen in the east with the attack of the Parthian Empire being spearheaded by Roman generals. This period also saw lulls in the fighting between the various overlapping conflicts. There was no certainty that Octavianus' victory at Actium in 31 BC would be the final major battle of the war, any more than the Battle of Pharsalus in 48 BC or Philippi in 42 BC.

If there is one contentious issue, then it must be the end date of this civil war. It clearly did not end with the Battle of Actium in 31 BC as Antonius still fought on with his defence of Egypt, which only fell in 30 BC. Yet as we have explored above, winning a campaign did not bring about victory, especially in a civil war; it was winning the peace. This is where both Sulla and Caesar failed when they had military control of the Republic. Roman civil wars did not seem to end when one side was victorious in battle as new opponents soon emerged. Roman civil wars only ended when everyone agreed that there was no more need to fight and that the imbalances in the Republican system that they had believed were there had been righted. For that reason, I would argue that the Third Civil War did not end until the First Constitutional Settlement of the newly renamed Augustus in 27 BC, with the intervening years 30–27 BC being merely a lull in the fighting. Thus, Republican politics was both the cause of the civil wars and the solution (however temporary).

Notes

Chapter One

1. See G. Sampson (2019). *Rome. Blood and Power. Reform, Murder and Popular Politics in the late Roman Republic 70–27 BC.* (Barnsley).
2. 88, 87, 82, 77 BC
3. Both men had close connections to the attack on Rome in 87 BC, both having lost their fathers in the campaign (one on the attacking side and one on the defending side). In Crassus' case, he also lost his elder brother.
4. See G. Sampson (2018). *Rome. Blood and Politics. Reform, Murder and Popular Politics in the late Roman Republic 133–70 BC* (Barnsley).
5. See G. Sampson (2010). *The Crisis of Rome. The Jugurthine and Northern Wars and the Rise of Marius* (Barnsley).
6. See G. Sampson (2013). *The Collapse of Rome, Marius, Sulla, and The First Civil War 91–70 BC* (Barnsley).
7. Valerius Flaccus.
8. See A. Thein (2010). 'Sulla's Veteran Settlement Policy', F. Daubner. (ed). *Militärsiedlungen und Territorialherrschaft in der Antike* (Berlin), pp.79–99.
9. See T. Hillman (1992). 'Plutarch and the first Consulship of Pompeius and Crassus', *Phoenix* 46, pp.124–37.
10. See B. Marshall and J. Beness (1987). 'Tribunician Agitation and the Aristocratic Reaction 80–71 BC', *Athenaeum* 65, pp.361–378.
11. See G. Sampson (2021). *Rome's Great Eastern War: Lucullus, Pompey and the Conquest of the East, 74–62 BC* (Barnsley).
12. See G. Sampson (2021).
13. See L. Taylor (1941). 'Caesar's Early Career', *Classical Philology* 36, pp.113–132.
14. See R. Ridley (2000). 'The Dictator's Mistake: Caesar's Escape from Sulla', *Historia* 49, pp.211–229.
15. Dio. 37.24.3
16. Plut. *Cic.* 17.5
17. See G. Sampson (2021).
18. See G. Barnet (2017). *Emulating Alexander. How Alexander the Great's Legacy Fuelled Rome's Wars with Persia* (Barnsley).
19. See T. Rising (2013). 'Senatorial Opposition to Pompey's Eastern Settlement. A Storm in a Teacup?' *Historia* 62, pp.196–221.
20. See R. Williams & B. Williams (1988). 'Cn. Pompeius Magnus and L. Afranius. Failure to Secure the Eastern Settlement', *Classical Journal* 83, pp.198–206.
21. See G. Stanton & B. Marshall (1975). 'The Coalition between Pompeius and Crassus 60–59 BC', *Historia* 24, pp.205–219.
22. See S. Haley (1985). 'The Five Wives of Pompey the Great', *Greece & Rome* 32, pp.49–59.

23. See I. Shatzman (1971). 'The Egyptian Question in Roman Politics (59–54 B.C)', *Latomus* 30, pp.363–369; M. Siani-Davies (1997). 'Ptolemy XII Auletes and the Romans', *Historia* 46, pp.306–340.
24. See W. Tatum (1999). *The Patrician Tribune: Publius Clodius Pulcher* (Chapel Hill).
25. See E. Sanford (1939). 'The Career of Aulus Gabinius', *Transactions and Proceedings of the American Philological Association* 70, pp.64–92.
26. See E. Gruen (1966). 'P. Clodius: Instrument or Independent Agent?', *Phoenix* 20, pp.120–130.
27. See R. Evans (2004). 'Clodius and Milo; more equals than opposites', *Questioning Reputations* (Pretoria), pp.161–191.
28. Cic. *Att.* 4.1.7
29. Cic. *QF.* 2.3.2
30. See J. Lazenby (1959). 'The Conference of Luca and the Gallic War; A Study in Roman Politics 57–55 BC', *Latomus* 18, pp.63–76; E. Gruen (1969). 'Pompey, the Roman Aristocracy and the Conference at Luca', *Historia* 18, pp.71–108; C. Luibheid (1970). 'The Luca Conference', *Classical Philology* 65, pp.88–94; J. Ruebel (1975). 'When Did Cicero Learn about the Conference at Luca?' *Historia* 24, pp.622–624.
31. See G. Sampson (2020). *Rome and Parthia: Empires at War: Ventidius, Antony and the Second Romano-Parthian War, 40–20 BC* (Barnsley).
32. See G. Sampson (2008). *The Defeat of Rome. Crassus, Carrhae and the Invasion of the East* (Barnsley).
33. See J. Ramsey (2016). 'How and Why was Pompey Made Sole Consul in 52 BC?', *Historia* 65, pp.298–324.
34. J. Ruebel (1979). 'The Trial of Milo in 52 BC: A Chronological Study', *Transactions of the American Philological Association* 109, 231–249.
35. The idea of Pompeius wanting the role of Princeps in the Augustan sense is not a new one; see E. Meyer (1919). *Caesar's Monarchie und das Prinzipat des Pompejus* (Stuttgart).
36. See E. Hardy (1918). 'Caesar's Legal Position in Gaul', *Journal of Philology* 34, pp.161–221; H. Coffin (1926). 'Caesar's Command in Gaul', *Classical Weekly* 19, pp.176–182; F. Adcock (1932). 'The Legal Term of Caesar's Governorship in Gaul', *Classical Quarterly* 26, pp.14–26; G. Elton (1946). 'The Terminal Date of Caesar's Gallic Proconsulate', *Journal of Roman Studies* 36, pp.18–42; P. Cuff (1958). 'The Terminal Date of Caesar's Gallic Command', *Historia* 7, pp.445–471; A. Stocker (1961). 'The Legis Dies of Caesar's Command in Gaul', *Classical Journal* 56, pp.242–248; S. Jameson (1970b). 'The Intended Date of Caesar's Return from Gaul', *Latomus* 29, pp.638–660; R. Morstein-Marx (2007). 'Caesar's Alleged Fear of Prosecution and His "Ratio Absentis" in the Approach to the Civil War', *Historia* 56, pp.159–178.

Chapter Two
1. Plut. *Caes.* 32.8
2. See F. Sirianni (1979). Caesar's Decision to Cross the Rubicon', *L'Antiquité Classique*, 48, pp.636–638; C. Ehrhardt (1995). 'Crossing the Rubicon', *Antichthon* 29, pp.37–41; G. Stanton (2003). 'Why Did Caesar Cross the Rubicon?', *Historia* 52, pp.67–94; L. Fezzi (2019). *Crossing the Rubicon: Caesar's Decision and the Fate of Rome* (London).
3. See F. Sirianni (1993). 'Caesar's Peace Overtures to Pompey', *L'Antiquité Classique* 62 (1993), pp.219–237.

4. Plut. *Caes.* 32.1
5. See F. Vervaet (2006). 'The Official Position of Cn. Pompeius in 49 and 48 BC', *Latomus* 65, pp.928–953.
6. See F. Abbott (1917). 'Titus Labienus', *Classical Journal* 13, pp.4–13; R. Syme (1938). 'The Allegiance of Labienus', *Journal of Roman Studies* 28, pp.113–125; W. Tyrrell (1972). 'Labienus' Departure from Caesar in January 49 BC', *Historia* 21, pp.424–44; G. Wylie (1989). 'Why Did Labienus Defect From Caesar in 49 BC?', *Ancient History Bulletin* 3, pp.123–127.
7. Dio. 41.4
8. Cic. *Att. 8.11.2.* Though other letters contradict the pre-planned nature of this withdrawal. See K. von Fritz (1942). 'Pompey's Policy before and after the Outbreak of the Civil War of 49 BC' *Transactions and Proceedings of the American Philological Association* 73, pp.145–180; D. Shackleton Bailey (1956). 'Expectatio Corfiniensis', *Journal of Roman Studies* 46, pp.57–64.
9. Cic. *Att.* 9.10.6
10. R. Syme (1938). 'The Allegiance of Labienus', *Journal of Roman Studies* 28, p.114. Also see K. von Fritz (1942). 'Pompey's Policy before and after the Outbreak of the Civil War of 49 BC', *Transactions and Proceedings of the American Philological Association* 73, pp.145–180.
11. K. von Fritz (1941). 'The Mission of L. Caesar and L. Roscius in January 49 BC', *Transactions and Proceedings of the American Philological Association* 72, pp.125–156; D. Shackleton Bailey (1960). 'The Credentials of L. Caesar and L. Roscius', *Journal of Roman Studies*, 50, pp.80–83.
12. Caes. *BC.* 1.8
13. Ibid. 1.9
14. Caes. *BC.* 1.11
15. Ibid. 1.12
16. Caes. *BC.* 1.13
17. Ibid. 1.15
18. See G. Sampson (2013).
19. See A. Burns (1966). 'Pompey's Strategy and Domitius' Stand at Corfinium', *Historia* 15, pp.74–95.
20. Caes. *BC.* 1.16
21. Ibid. 1.17
22. Ibid.
23. Caes. *BC.* 1.18
24. Ibid.
25. Caes. *BC.* 1.19
26. Ibid. 1.23
27. Caes. *BC.* 1.14
28. Plut. *Caes.* 33.6–34.1
29. Dio. 41.6.2
30. Dio. 41.8.1–2
31. See G. Sampson (2021).
32. Caes. *BC.* 1.25
33. Ibid. 1.24
34. Plut. *Pomp.* 62.2
35. See L. Hayne (1996). 'Caesar and Lentulus Crus', *Acta Classica* 39, pp.72–76.
36. Ibid
37. Dio. 41.12.1

38. Caes. *BC.* 1.25–26
39. Ibid. 1.27
40. Caes. *BC.* 1.29
41. Cic. *Att.* 9.15
42. App. *BC.* 1.40
43. Cic. *Att.* 9.15
44. It is not known whether these two were deposed from office for such a transgression, given the timescales involved.
45. Plut. *Caes.* 4
46. App. *BC.* 2.41
47. Dio. 41.15.3
48. Caes. *BC.* 33
49. Plut. *Caes.* 5
50. Dio. 41.16.1
51. Ibid 41.16.4
52. App. *BC.* 2.41
53. Oros. 6.15.5
54. Plin. *NH.* 33.56
55. As in 310, 204 & 122 BC
56. A Tribune fleeing the city and his 'oath of office' could have resulted in his removal from office by the other Tribunes in the Assemblies and elections for their replacement (or co-option). Suffect Tribunes had been chosen in the past, but we are not explicitly told that this happened on this occasion, though it may have been likely.
57. Plut. *Caes.* 10
58. Caes. *BC.* 1.7
59. Caes. *BC.* 1.33
60. Cic. *Att.*10.4
61. Caes. *BC.* 1.33
62. App. *BC.* 2.41
63. His colleague Q. Cassius Longinus also received the same role.
64. See Dio. 41.17.3 & 18.1–2
65. Dio. 41.18.4–6
66. Plut. *Caes.* 63.1

Chapter Three
1. Caes. *BC.* 1.34
2. Dio. 41.19.3–4
3. Caes. *BC* 1.36
4. Ibid. 1.56–58 & 2.3–7
5. Caes. *BC.* 1.56
6. Ibid. 1.58
7. Ibid
8. Dio. 41.21.3
9. Caes. *BC.* 2.3
10. Ibid. 2.4
11. Ibid
12. Caes. *BC.* 2.7
13. Ibid.
14. Caes. *BC.* 2.2

15. Vit. 10.16.11
16. Caes. *BC.* 2.14
17. Ibid 1.39
18. Cic. *Att.* 8.3.7
19. Caes. *BC.* 1.39
20. Ibid. 1.40
21. Caes. *BC.* 1.40
22. Ibid. 1.85
23. Dio. 41.20.2
24. Caes. *BC.* 1.43
25. Ibid. 1.44
26. Dio. 41.20.5
27. Caes. *BC.* 1.47
28. Ibid. 1.51
29. Dio. 41.20.6
30. Caes. *BC.* 1.53
31. Dio. 41.21.1
32. Ibid. 41.21.2
33. Caes. *BC.* 1.60
34. Ibid. 1.61
35. Caes. *BC.* 1.63–64
36. Ibid
37. Caes. *BC.* 1.64
38. Ibid. 1.65
39. Ibid
40. Caes. *BC.* 1.69
41. Ibid. 1.70
42. Caes. *BC.* 1.75
43. Ibid. 1.76
44. Caes. *BC.* 1.78
45. Ibid. 1.79–82
46. Caes. *BC.* 1.83
47. Frontin. *Str.* 2.1.11
48. Caes. *BC.* 1.86–87
49. Ibid. 1.87
50. App. *BC.* 2.43
51. Dio. 41.23.1
52. Caes. *BC.* 2.18

Chapter Four
1. Case. *BC.* 1.30
2. Ibid.
3. Caes. *BC. 1.25.* See L. Morgan (2000). 'The Autopsy of C. Asinius Pollio', *Journal of Roman Studies* 90, p.51–69.
4. Ibid. 1.30
5. Caes. *BC.* 1.30
6. Plut. *Cat.* 53.1
7. App. *BC.* 2.40
8. Plut. *Cat.* 53.3
9. Plut. *Cat. 53.3,* Dio. *41.1, App. BC.* 2.40
10. Caes. *BC.* 1.30

11. Cic. *Att.* 10.16.3
12. T. Broughton (1951/2). *The Magistrates of the Roman Republic Volume* 2 (New York), p. 228.
13. Caes. BC. 1.31
14. See Sampson. (2010).
15. Dio. 41.41.3, Caes. BC. 2.25.4
16. App. BC. 2.44
17. Caes. BC. 2.26
18. Ibid. 2.27
19. Caes. BC. 2.31–32
20. Ibid. 2.34
21. Caes. BC. 2.35
22. Ibid
23. Caes. BC. *2.35, App. BC.* 2.44
24. Caes. BC. 2.37
25. Ibid. 2.38
26. Ibid
27. Caes. BC. 2.40
28. Ibid.
29. Caes. BC. 2.41
30. Ibid
31. Caes. BC. 2.42
32. App. BC. 2.45
33. Ibid 2.43
34. App. BC. 2.46
35. Caes. BC. 2.44
36. Ibid
37. Dio. 41.41.7
38. See D. Dzino (2010). 'The Construction of Illyricum: Caesar in Illyricum and the Civil Wars (59–44 BC)', in *Illyricum in Roman Politics, 229 BC–AD 68* (Cambridge), pp.80–98.
39. Oros. 6.15.8
40. Flor. 2.13.31–33
41. Dio. 41.40.1–2
42. Oros. 6.15.8–9
43. App. BC. 49.1
44. See G. Sampson (2021).
45. See G. Sampson (2008).
46. See G. Sampson (2020).
47. Ibid
48. Caes. BC. 3.32
49. Ibid. 3.31
50. See G. Sampson (forthcoming). *The Battle of Thapsus (46 BC). Caesar, Metellus Scipio, Cato and the Roman Civil War in Africa* (Barnsley).

Chapter Five
1. See F. Vervaet (2006).
2. See G. Sampson (2021).
3. Caes. BC. 3.3
4. Ibid. 3.4

5. App. *BC.* 2.49
6. Plut. *Pomp.* 64
7. Caes. *BC.* 3.5
8. App. *BC.* 2.50
9. App. *BC.* 2.52
10. Plut. *Pomp.* 65.1
11. Dio. 41.26–35
12. Dio. 41.26
13. App. *BC.* 2.47
14. Dio. 41.27–35
15. The sources are not clear on whether this measure was passed at this point or when Caesar returned to Rome in December 49 BC.

Chapter Six
1. Dio. 41.43.1–3
2. App. *BC.* 2.54
3. See I. Longhurst (2016) 'Caesar's Crossing of the Adriatic Countered by a Winter Blockade During the Roman Civil War', *Mariner's Mirror* 102, pp.132–152.
4. Caes. *BC.* 3.6, *App. BC.* 2.54
5. Caes. *BC.* 3.12
6. Ibid. 3.19
7. App. *BC.* 2.56
8. Ibid. 2.58
9. Dio. 41.47.2
10. Caes. *BC.* 3.19
11. Ibid.
12. Caes. *BC.* 3.14
13. Dio. 41.48.1
14. Caes. *BC.* 3.23
15. Ibid. 3.24
16. The Caesarian commander at the Siege of Massilia.
17. Vell. 2.68.1
18. Dio. 42.22.1
19. See Caes. *BC.* 3.21 vs. Dio. 42.23
20. Dio. 42.24.4. The assumption is that it was a Plebeian Tribune not a military one.
21. Caes. *BC.* 3.22
22. Ibid.
23. Ibid.
24. App. *BC.* 2.59
25. Plut. *Ant.* 7
26. Dio. 41.49.1
27. Caes. *BC.* 3.30
28. Ibid. 3.34
29. Caes. *BC.* 3.35
30. App. *BC.* 2.60
31. Dio. 41.51.2–3
32. Caes. *BC.* 3.36
33. Loeb Translation of the Greek
34. Faustus was married to Pompeia, Pompeius' daughter. Pompeius himself had previously been married to Aemilia, a stepdaughter of Sulla and thus Faustus' stepsister.

35. Dio. 41.51.3
36. Caes. *BC*. 3.37
37. See A. Powell & K. Welch (2002). *Sextus Pompeius* (London).
38. Ibid. 3.39
39. Caes. *BC*. 3.40
40. App. *BC*. 2.56, though much earlier in the campaign, before the stalemate at the Apsus.
41. Considered to be the dividing line between Illyria and Epirus.
42. Caes. *BC*. 3.42

Chapter Seven
1. Caes. *BC*. 3.42
2. See G. Veith (1920). *Der Feldzug von Dyrrhachium zwischen Caesar und Pompeius* (Wien), pp.5–12.
3. Caes. *BC*. 3.43
4. Ibid. 3.63
5. Caes. *BC*. 3.44
6. Ibid
7. Caes. *BC*. 3.45
8. Ibid. 3.47
9. Caes. *BC*. 3.45–46
10. See A. Anders (2015). 'The Face of Roman Skirmishing', *Historia* 64, pp.263–300.
11. Ibid. 3.49
12. Dio. 41.50
13. Caes. *BC*. 3.53
14. App. *BC*. 2.60
15. Caes. *BC*. 3.51
16. Ibid. 3.52
17. Caes. *BC*. 3.53
18. Dio. 41.50.4
19. Caes. *BC*. 3.55

Chapter Eight
1. Caes. *BC*. 3.59–60
2. See B. Kavanagh (2001). 'The citizenship and nomen of Roucillus and Egus.' *Ancient History Bulletin* 15, pp.163–171.
3. Ibid. 3.58 & 3.61
4. Caes. *BC*. 3.61
5. Ibid
6. Caes. *BC*. 3.63
7. Ibid
8. Caes. *BC*. 3.65
9. Ibid 3.69
10. Caes. *BC*. 3.70
11. Ibid. 3.71
12. Ibid.
13. Caes. *BC*. 3.72
14. Ibid.
15. App. *BC*. 2.61–62
16. Such as C. Asinius Pollio, see L. Morgan (2000), pp.51–69

17. Ibid. 2.63
18. Ibid
19. App. *BC.* 2.64
20. Dio. 41.51.1
21. Plut. *Pomp.* 65.4–5
22. Plut. *Caes.* 39.4–6
23. Ibid. 39.6–7
24. Plut. *Caes.* 39.8
25. Ibid. 39.9
26. Oros. 6.15.18
27. Luc. 6.292–299
28. Vell. 2.51.303–310
29. Flor. 2.13.39–40
30. Caes. *BC.* 3.71
31. App. *BC.* 2.63.1
32. Plut. *Pomp.* 66.1
33. Dio. 41.52.3
34. Caes. *BC.* 3.79
35. Ibid. 3.73
36. Caes. *BC.* 3.78
37. Ibid. 3.75
38. Ibid
39. Caes. *BC.* 3.78
40. Forthcoming

Appendix Two
1. This is a variation of the discussion found in G. Sampson (2019), pp.307–313.
2. See G. Sampson (2013).

Bibliography

Abbott, F. (1917). 'Titus Labienus', *Classical Journal* 13, 4–13.

Adcock, F. (1932). 'The Legal Term of Caesar's Governorship in Gaul', *Classical Quarterly* 26, 14–26.

——. (1966). *Marcus Crassus, Millionaire* (Cambridge).

Allély, A. (2012). *La déclaration d'hostis sous la République romaine* (Bordeaux).

Alston, R. (2015). *Rome's Revolution. Death of the Republic and Birth of the Empire* (Oxford).

Amela Valverde, L. (2003). *Cneo Pompeyo Magno. El defensor de la República romana* (Madrid).

Anders. A. (2015). 'The Face of Roman Skirmishing', *Historia* 64, 263–300.

Appel, H. (2012). 'Pompeius Magnus: his Third Consulate and the senatus consultum ultimum', *Biuletyn Polskiej Misji Historycznej* 7, 341–360.

Arena, V. (2012). *Libertas and the Practice of Politics in the Late Roman Republic* (Cambridge).

Armitage, D. (2017). *Civil War. A History in Ideas* (New York).

Badian, E. (1959). 'The Early Career of A. Gabinius (Cos. 58 B.C.)', *Philologus* 103, 87–99

——. (1965). 'M. Porcius Cato and the Annexation and Early Administration of Cyprus', *Journal of Roman Studies* 55, 110–121.

——. (1974). 'The Attempt to Try Caesar,' in J. Evans (ed.), *Polis and Imperium: Studies in Honour of Edward Togo Salmon* (Toronto), 145–166.

——. (1996). 'Tribuni Plebis and Res Publica', in J. Linderski (ed.) Imperium Sine Fine (Stuttgart), 187–214.

Balsdon, J. (1939). 'Consular Provinces under the Late Republic I. General Considerations', *Journal of Roman Studies* 29, 57–73.

——. (1939b). 'Consular Provinces under the Late Republic II. Caesar's Gallic Command', *Journal of Roman Studies* 29, 167–183.

——. (1957). 'The Veracity of Caesar', *Greece & Rome* 4, 19–28.

Baltrusch, E. (2004). *Caesar und Pompeius* (Darmstadt).

Barnet, G. (2017). *Emulating Alexander. How Alexander the Great's Legacy Fuelled Rome's Wars with Persia* (Barnsley).

Bartsch, S. (1997). *Ideology in Cold Blood. A Reading of Lucan's Civil War* (Cambridge).

Batstone, W & Damon, C. (2006). *Caesar's Civil War* (Oxford).

Bartsch, S. (1997). *Ideology in Cold Blood. A Reading of Lucan's Civil War* (Cambridge).

Bell, A. (1994). 'Fact and Exemplum in Accounts of the Death of Pompey and Caesar.' *Latomus* 53, 824–836.

Bellemore, J. (1995). 'Cato the Younger in the East in 66 BC', *Historia* 44, 376–379.

——. (2008). 'Cicero's Retreat from Rome in Early 58 BC', *Antichthon* 42, 100–120.

Billows, R. (2008). *Julius Caesar: The Colossus of Rome* (London).

Boak, A. (1918). 'The Extraordinary Commands from 80 to 48 BC: A Study in the Origins of the Principate', *American Historical Review* 24, 1–25.

Boatwright, M. (1988). 'Caesar's Second Consulship and the Completion and Date of the "Bellum Civile"', *Classical Journal* 84, 31–40.

Börm, H. Mattheis, M., & Wienand, J. (eds) (2015). *Civil Wars in Ancient Greece and Rome. Contexts of Disintegration and Reintegration* (Stuttgart).

Bosworth, A. (1972). 'Asinius Pollio and Augustus', *Historia* 21, 441–473.

Bosworth, A. (1972). Asinius Pollio and Augustus. Historia: Zeitschrift Für Alte Geschichte, 21(3), 441–473.

Breed, B, Damon, C & Rossi, A. (eds). *Citizens of Discord: Rome and Its Civil Wars* (Oxford).

Broughton, T. (1951/2). *The Magistrates of the Roman Republic Volume 1 & 2* (New York).

———. (1960). *Supplement to the Magistrates of the Roman Republic* (New York).

———. (1986). *Supplement to the Magistrates of the Roman Republic* (New York).

———. (1989). 'M. Aemilius Lepidus: His Youthful Career', in R. Curtis (ed.). Studia

Brunt, P. (1971). *Social Conflicts in the Roman Republic* (London).

———. (1988). *The Fall of the Roman Republic* (Oxford).

Burns, A. (1966). 'Pompey's Strategy and Domitius' Stand at Corfinium', *Historia* 15, 74–95.

Cairns, F. & Fantham, E. (eds.). *Caesar against Liberty? Perspectives on his Autocracy* (Cambridge).

Canfora, L. (2007). *Julius Caesar. The People's Dictator* (Edinburgh).

Chrystal, P. (2019). *Rome: Republic into Empire: The Civil Wars of the First Century BC* (Barnsley).

Coffin, H. (1926). 'Caesar's Command in Gaul', *Classical Weekly* 19, 176–182.

Collins, H. (1953). 'The Decline and Fall of Pompey the Great', *Greece & Rome* 22, 98–106.

Collins, J. (1972). 'Caesar as Political Propagandist', *Aufstieg und Niedergang der Römischen Welt* 1.1, 952–953.

Cornwell, H. (2014). 'The Construction of one's enemies in Civil War (49–30 BC)', *Hermathena* 196/197, 41–68.

———. (2017a). 'Negotiating Ideas of Peace in the Civic Conflicts of the late Republic', in E. Moloney & M. Williams (eds), *Peace and Reconciliation in the Classical World* (London), 86–101.

———. (2017b). *Pax and the Politics of Peace: Republic to Principate* (Oxford).

Coulter, C. (1931). 'Caesar's Clemency', *Classical Journal* 26, 513–524.

Cuff, P. (1958). 'The Terminal Date of Caesar's Gallic Command', *Historia* 7, 445–471.

De Ruggiero, P. (2013). *Mark Antony. A Plain Blunt Man* (Barnsley)

Driediger-Murphy, L. (2014). 'Cassius Dio 41.43: Religion as a liability in Pompey's Civil War', *Hermathena* 196/197, 99–120.

Drogula, F. (2019). *Cato the Younger: Life and Death at the End of the Roman Republic* (Oxford).

Drummond, A. (1995). *Law Politics and Power. Sallust and the Execution of the Catilinarian Conspirators* (Stuttgart).

———. (1999). 'Tribunes and Tribunician Programmes in 63 BC', *Athenaeum* 77, 121–167.

Duncan, M. (2017). *The Storm Before the Storm: The Beginning of the End of the Roman Republic* (London).

Dzino, D. (2010). 'The Construction of Illyricum: Caesar in Illyricum and the Civil Wars (59–44 BC)', in *Illyricum in Roman Politics, 229 BC–AD 68* (Cambridge), 80–98.

Ehrhardt, C. (1995). 'Crossing the Rubicon', *Antichthon* 29, 37–41.

Elton, G. (1946). The Terminal Date of Caesar's Gallic Proconsulate', *Journal of Roman Studies* 36, 18–42.

Epstein, D. (1987). *Personal Enmity in Roman Politics 218–43 BC* (London).

Evans, R. (1988). 'A Note on the Consuls from 69 to 60 BC', *Acta Classica* 31, 97–105.

——. (2004). 'Caesar's use of the tribuni plebis', *Questioning Reputations* (Pretoria), 65–92.

——. (2004). 'Clodius and Milo; more equals than opposites', *Questioning Reputations* (Pretoria), 161–191.

——. (2016). Pompey's Three Consulships: The End of Electoral Competition in the Late Roman Republic', *Acta Classica* 59, 80–100.

Ezov, A. (1996). 'The "Missing Dimension" of C. Julius Caesar', *Historia* 45, 64–94.

Fantham, E. (1975). 'The Trials of Gabinius in 54 BC', *Historia* 24, 425–443.

Fezzi, L. (2019). *Crossing the Rubicon: Caesar's Decision and the Fate of Rome* (London).

Field, N. (2009). *Warlords of Republican Rome: Caesar Versus Pompey* (Barnsley).

Flower, H. (2010). *Roman Republics* (Princeton).

Frolov, R. (2017). 'Better than (when) a Magistrate? Caesar's Suspension from Magisterial Functions in 62 BC', *Mnemosyne* 70, 977–995.

——. (2019). 'Lictoresque habent in urbe et Capitolio privati: Promagistrates in Rome in 49 BC', *Phoenix* 73, 114–133.

Fuller, J. (1965). *Julius Caesar: Man, Soldier, and Tyrant* (London).

Gagliardi, L. (2011). *Cesare Pompeo e la Lotta per le Magistra Anni 52–50 AC* (Milan).

Galassi, F. (2014). *Catiline. The Monster of Rome* (Yardley)

Gelzer, M. (1949). *Pompeius* (Munich).

——. (1968). *Caesar: Politician and Statesman* (Cambridge).

Gerrish, J. (2019). *Sallust's Histories and Triumviral Historiography. Confronting the End of History* (London).

Girardet, K. (2017). *Januar 49 v.Chr. Caesars Militärputsch. Vorgeschichte, Rechtslage, politische Aspekte* (Bonn).

Goar, R. (1987). *The Legend of Cato Uticensis from the First Century BC to the Fifth Century AD* (Leiden).

Golden, G. (2013). *Crisis Management during the Roman Republic: The Role of Political Institutions in Emergencies* (Cambridge).

Goldsworthy, A. (2006). *Caesar: Life of a Colossus* (Yale).

Goodman, R & Soni. J. (2012). *Rome's Last Citizen. The Life and Legacy of Cato, Mortal Enemy of Caesar* (New York).

Greenhalgh, P. (1980). *Pompey. The Roman Alexander* (London).

——. (1981). *Pompey. The Republican Prince* (London).

Girardet, K. (2000). 'Caesars Konsulatsplan fur das Jahr 49: Griinde und Scheitern', *Chiron* 30, 679–710.

——. (2001). 'Imperia und provinciae des Pompeius', *Chiron* 31, 153–209.

——. (2017). *Januar 49 v.Chr. Caesars Militärputsch. Vorgeschichte, Rechtslage, politische Aspekte* (Bonn).

Griffin, M. (1973). 'The Tribune C. Cornelius', *Journal of Roman Studies* 63, 196–213

Grillo, L. (2012). *The Art of Caesar's Bellum Civile. Literature, Ideology, and Community* (Cambridge).

Gruen. E. (1966). 'P. Clodius: Instrument or Independent Agent?', *Phoenix* 20, 120–130.

——. (1969). 'Pompey, the Roman Aristocracy and the Conference at Luca', *Historia* 18, 71–108.

——. (1969). 'Notes on the "First Catilinarian Conspiracy"', *Classical Philology* 64, 20–24.

——. (1971). 'Pompey, Metellus Pius, and the Trials of 70–69 BC: The Perils of Schematism', *American Journal of Philology* 92, 1–16.

——. (1974). *The Last Generation of the Roman Republic* (Berkeley).

Haley, S. (1985). 'The Five Wives of Pompey the Great', *Greece & Rome* 32, 49–59.

Hardy, E. (1917). 'The Catilinarian Conspiracy in Its Context: A Re-Study of the Evidence', *Journal of Roman Studies* 7, 153–228.

——. (1918). 'Caesar's Legal Position in Gaul', *Journal of Philology* 34, 161–221.

Harrison, I. (2008). 'Catiline, Clodius, and Popular Politics at Rome during the 60s and 50s BC', *Bulletin of the Institute of Classical Studies* 51, 95–118.

Hayne, L. (1996). 'Caesar and Lentulus Crus', *Acta Classica* 39, 72–76.

Heitland, W. (1909). *The Roman Republic Volumes 1–3* (Cambridge).

Henderson, J. (1998). *Fighting for Rome: Poets and Caesars, History and Civil War* (Cambridge).

Hillard, T. (1981). 'Crassus in 61', *Liverpool Classical Monthly* 6, 127–130.

——. (1982). 'P. Clodius Pulcher 62–58 BC: 'Pompeii Adfinis et Sodalis', *Papers of the British School at Rome* 50, 34–44.

Hillman, T. (1992). 'Plutarch and the first Consulship of Pompeius and Crassus', *Phoenix* 46, 124–37.

——. (1996). 'Pompeius ad Parthos?' *Klio* 78, 380–399.

Holland, T. (2003). *Rubicon: The Triumph and Tragedy of the Roman Republic* (London).

Holliday, V. (1969). *Pompeius in Cicero's correspondence and Lucan's Civil War* (Den Haag).

Holzapfel, L. (1904). 'Die Anfänge des Bürgerkrieges zwischen Cäsar und Pompejus', *Klio* 4 327–382.

Husband, R. (1915). 'The Prosecution of Milo', *Classical Weekly* 8, 146–150.

Huzar, E. (1978). *Mark Antony: A Biography* (Minneapolis).

Isayev, E. (2007). 'Unruly Youth? The Myth of Generation Conflict in Late Republican Rome', *Historia* 56, 1–13.

Jal, P. (1961a). 'La propagande religieuse à Rome au cours des guerres civiles de la fin de la République', *L'Antiquité Classique* 30.2, 395–414.

——. (1962). 'Les dieux et les guerres civiles dans la Rome de la fin de la République', *Revue des Etudes Latines*, 40, 170–200.

——. (1963). *La Guerre Civile a Rome: Étude littéraire et morale de Cicéron a Tacite* (Paris).

Jameson, S. (1970a). 'Pompey's Imperium in 67: Some Constitutional Fictions', *Historia* 19, 539–560.

——. (1970b). 'The Intended Date of Caesar's Return from Gaul', *Latomus* 29, 638–660.

Kavanagh, B. (2001). 'The citizenship and nomen of Roucillus and Egus.' *Ancient History Bulletin* 15, 163–171.

Keaveney, A. (2007). *The Army in the Roman Revolution* (London).

Kendall, S. (2013). *The Struggle for Roman Citizenship: Romans, Allies, and the Wars of 91–77 BC* (Piscataway).

Kraus, C. S. (2011). 'Caesar's Account of the Battle of Massilia (BC 1.34–2.22): Some Historiographical and Narratological Approaches', in J. Marincola (ed.) *A Companion to Greek and Roman Historiography* (Chichester), 371–8.

Lange, C. (2014). 'The Logic of Violence in Roman Civil War', *Hermathena* 196/197, 69–98.

——. (2018). *Triumphs in the Age of Civil War: The Late Republic and the Adaptability of Triumphal Tradition* (London).

Lange. C. & Scott. A. (2020). *Cassius Dio: The Impact of Violence, War, and Civil War* (Leiden).

Lange, C. & Vervaet, F. (2019) *The Historiography of Late Republican Civil War* (Leiden).

Lazenby, J. (1959). 'The Conference of Luca and the Gallic War; A Study in Roman Politics 57–55 BC', *Latomus* 18, 63–76.

Leach, J. (1978). *Pompey the Great* (London).

Lendon, J. (1999). 'The Rhetoric of Combat: Greek Military Theory and Roman Culture in Julius Caesar's Battle Descriptions', *Classical Antiquity* 18, 273–329.

Levick, B. (2015). *Catiline* (London).

Linderski, J. (1966). 'Were Pompey and Crassus elected in absence to their first Consulships?' M. Bernhard (ed.). *Mélanges offerts à K. Michalowski* (Warsaw), 523–26.

Lintott, A. (1967). 'P. Clodius Pulcher- 'Felix Catilina?' *Greece & Rome* 14, 157–169.

——. (1968). *Violence in Republican Rome* (Oxford).

——. (1971). 'Lucan and the History of the Civil War.' *Classical Quarterly* 21, 488–505.

——. (1974). 'Cicero and Milo', *Journal of Roman Studies* 64, 62–78.

——. (1999). *The Constitution of the Roman Republic* (Oxford).

Long, G. (1864). *The Decline of the Roman Republic Volumes 1–5* (London).

Longhurst, I. (2016) 'Caesar's Crossing of the Adriatic Countered by a Winter Blockade During the Roman Civil War', *Mariner's Mirror* 102, 132–152.

López Barja de Quiroga, P. (2019). 'The Bellum Civile Pompeianum: The War of Words', *Classical Quarterly* 69, 700–714.

Luibheid, C. (1970). 'The Luca Conference', *Classical Philology* 65, 88–94.

Mackay, C. (2009). *The Breakdown of the Roman Republic* (Cambridge).

Maguire, R. (2018). *Napoleon's Commentaries on Julius Caesar: A New English Translation* (Barnsley).

Marin, P. (2009). *Blood in the Forum. The Struggle for the Roman Republic* (London).

Marsh, F. (1927). 'The Chronology of Caesar's Consulship', *Classical Journal* 22, 504–524.

Marshall, A. (1972). 'The Lex Pompeia de provinciis (52 bc) and Cicero's Imperium in 51–50 bc: Constitutional Aspects', *Aufsteig und Niedergang der Römischen Welt* 1.1, 887–921.

Marshall, B. (1976). *Crassus: a Political Biography* (Amsterdam).

——. (1984). 'Faustus Sulla and Political Labels in the 60's and 50's bc', *Historia* 33, 199–219.

——. (1985). 'Catilina and the Execution of M. Marius Gratidianus', *Classical Quarterly* 35, 124–133.

Marshall. B and Beness, J. (1987). 'Tribunician Agitation and the Aristocratic Reaction 80–71 bc', *Athenaeum* 65, 361–378.

Masters, J. (1992). *Poetry and Civil War in Lucan's Bellum Civile* (Cambridge).

McDonald, W. (1929). 'The Tribunate of Cornelius', *Classical Quarterly* 23, 196–208.

Meier, C. (1995). *Caesar. A Biography* (London).

Meyer, E. (1919). *Caesars Monarchie und das Prinzipat des Pompejus* (Stuttgart).

Miączewska, A. (2014). 'Quintus Fufius Calenus: A forgotten career', *Hermathena* 196/197, 163–204.

Millar, F. (1994). 'Popular Politics at Rome in the Late Republic', in I. Malkin & Z. Rubinsohn (eds.) *Leaders and Masses in the Roman World: Studies in Honor of Zvi Yavetz* (Leiden), 91–113.

Mitchell, T. (1971). 'Cicero and the Senatus "consultum ultimum"', *Historia* 20, 47–61.

Morgan, L. (1997). 'Levi Quidem de re...': Julius Caesar as Tyrant and Pedant', *Journal of Roman Studies* 87, 23–40.

——. (2000). 'The Autopsy of C. Asinius Pollio', *Journal of Roman Studies* 90, 51–69.

Morrell, K. (2014). 'Cato and the Courts in 54 bc', Classical Quarterly 64, 669–681.

——. (2017). *Pompey, Cato, and the Governance of the Roman Empire* (Oxford).

Morstein-Marx, R. (2007). 'Caesar's Alleged Fear of Prosecution and His "Ratio Absentis" in the Approach to the Civil War', *Historia* 56,159–178.

Osgood, J. (2006). *Caesar's Legacy. Civil War and the Emergence of the Roman Empire* (Cambridge).

———. (2015). 'Ending Civil War at Rome: Rhetoric and Reality, 88 BC-197 AD', *American Historical Review* 120, 1683–1695.

Ottmer, H-M. (1979). *Die Rubikon-Legende. Untersuchungen zu Caesars und Pompeius' Strategie vor und nach Ausbruch des Bürgerkrieges* (Boppard am Rhein).

Parrish, E. (1973). 'Crassus' New Friends and Pompey's Return', *Phoenix* 27, 357–380.

Peaks, M. (1903). 'Caesar's Movements, January 21 to February 14, 49 BC', *Classical Review* 18, 346–349.

Peer, A. (2015). *Julius Caesar's Bellum Civile and the Composition of a New Reality* (London).

Phillips, E. (1976). 'Catiline's Conspiracy', *Historia* 25, 441–448.

Pocock, L. (1959). 'What Made Pompeius Fight in 49 BC?', *Greece & Rome* 6, 68–81.

Poletti, S. (2014). 'The flight from Rome in January 49 BC: Rhetorical patterns in the narratives of Lucan and Cassius Dio', *Hermathena* 196/197, 291–308.

Powell, A & Welch, K. (2002). *Sextus Pompeius* (London).

Raaflaub, K. (2003). 'Caesar the Liberator? Factional Politics, Civil War, and Ideology', in F. Cairns and E. Fantham (eds). Caesar Against Liberty? Perspectives on his Autocracy (Cambridge), 35–67.

———. (2010). 'Creating a Grand Coalition of True Roman Citizens: On Caesar's Political Strategy in Civil War', in B. W. Breed, C. Damon, & A. Rossi (eds), *Citizens of Discord. Rome and its Civil Wars* (Oxford), 159–170.

Rambaud, M. (1953). *L'Art de la déformation historique dans les Commentaires de Cesar* (Paris).

Ramsey, J. (1982). 'Cicero, pro Sulla 68 and the Catiline's Candidacy in 66 BC', *Harvard Studies in Classical Philology* 86, 121–131.

Ramsey, J. (2016). 'How and Why was Pompey Made Sole Consul in 52 BC?', *Historia* 65, 298–324

Rice Holmes, T. (1923). *The Roman Republic and the Founder of the Empire Volumes 1–3* (Oxford).

Ridley, R. (1981). 'The Extraordinary Commands of the Late Republic: A Matter of Definition', *Historia* 30, 280–297.

———. (1983). 'Pompey's Commands in the 50's: How Cumulative?' *Rheinisches Museum für Philologie* 126, 136–148.

———. (2000). 'The Dictator's Mistake: Caesar's Escape from Sulla', *Historia* 49, 211–229.

———. (2004). 'Attacking the World with Five Cohorts; Caesar in January 49', *Ancient Society* 34, 127–152.

Riggsby, A. (2006). *Caesar in Gaul and Rome: War in Words* (Austin).

Rising, T. (2013). Senatorial Opposition to Pompey's Eastern Settlement. A Storm in a Teacup?' *Historia* 62, 196–221.

Rosenblitt, A. (2014). 'The Turning Tide: The Politics of the Year 79 BC', *Transactions of the American Philological Association* 144, 415–444.

———. (2019). *Rome After Sulla* (London).

Rossi, A. (2000). 'The Camp of Pompey: Strategy of Representation in Caesar's Bellum Civile.' *Classical Journal* 95, 239–256.

Rowland, R. (1960). 'Crassus, Clodius, and Curio in the Year 59 BC', *Historia* 15, 217–223.

———. (1964). *Roman Grain Legislation 133–50 BC* (Michigan).

———. (1966). 'Caesar's Fear of Prosecution in 49 BC', *Liverpool Classical Monthly* 2, 165–166.

Ruebel, J. (1979). 'The Trial of Milo in 52 BC: A Chronological Study', *Transactions of the American Philological Association* 109, 231–249.

Sabin, P. (2000). 'The Face of Roman Battle', *Journal of Roman Studies* 90, 1–17.

Sage, E. (1920). 'The Senatus Consultum Ultimum', *Classical Weekly* 13, 185–189.

Salmon, E. (1935). 'Catiline, Crassus, and Caesar', *American Journal of Philology* 56, 302–316.

Sampson. G. (2005). *A re-examination of the office of the Tribunate of the Plebs in the Roman Republic (494 – 23 BC)* (Unpublished Thesis).

——. (2008). *The Defeat of Rome. Crassus, Carrhae and the Invasion of the East* (Barnsley).

——. (2010). *The Crisis of Rome. The Jugurthine and Northern Wars and the Rise of Marius* (Barnsley).

——. (2013). *The Collapse of Rome, Marius, Sulla and The First Civil War 91–70 BC* (Barnsley).

——. (2017). *Rome, Blood and Politics. Reform, Murder and Popular Politics in the Late Republic 146–70 BC* (Barnsley).

——. (2019). *Rome, Blood and Power: Reform, Murder and Popular Politics in the Late Republic 70–27 BC* (Barnsley).

——. (2020). *Rome and Parthia: Empires at War: Ventidius, Antony and the Second Romano-Parthian War, 40–20 BC* (Barnsley).

——. (2021). *Rome's Great Eastern War: Lucullus, Pompey, and the Conquest of the East, 74–62 BC* (Barnsley).

Sanders, H. (1932). 'The So-Called First Triumvirate', *Memoirs of the American Academy in Rome* 10, 55–68.

Sanford, E. (1939). 'The Career of Aulus Gabinius', *Transactions and Proceedings of the American Philological Association* 70, 64–92.

Santangelo, F. (2014). 'Roman Politics in the 70s BC: a Story of Realignments?', *Journal of Roman Studies* 104, 1–27.

Seager, R. (1979). *Pompey. A Political Biography* (Oxford).

Shackleton Bailey, D. (1956). 'Expectatio Corfiniensis', *Journal of Roman Studies* 46, 57–64.

——. (1960). 'The Credentials of L. Caesar and L. Roscius', *Journal of Roman Studies*, 50, 80–83.

Shatzman, I. (1971). 'The Egyptian Question in Roman Politics (59–54 B.C)', *Latomus* 30, 363–369.

Siani-Davies, M. (1997). 'Ptolemy XII Auletes and the Romans', *Historia* 46, 306–340.

Sirianni, F. (1979). 'Caesar's Decision to Cross the Rubicon', *L'Antiquité Classique*, 48, 636–638.

——. (1993). 'Caesar's Peace Overtures to Pompey', *L'Antiquité Classique* 62, 219–237.

Smith, R. (1957). 'The Lex Plotia Agraria and Pompey's Spanish Veterans', *Classical Quarterly* 7, 82–85.

——. (1957b). 'The Conspiracy and the Conspirators', *Greece & Rome* 4, 58–70.

——. (1977). 'The Use of Force in Passing Legislation in the Late Republic', *Athenaeum* 55, 150–174.

Southern, P. (2002). *Pompey the Great* (Stroud).

Stanton, G. (2003). 'Why Did Caesar Cross the Rubicon?', *Historia* 52, 67–94.

Stanton, G. & Marshall, B. (1975). 'The Coalition between Pompeius and Crassus 60–59 BC', *Historia* 24, 205–219.

Steel, C. (2012). 'The 'Lex Pompeia de Provinciis' of 52 BC. A Reconsideration', *Historia* 61, 83–93.

——. (2014a). 'Rethinking Sulla: The Case of the Roman Senate', *Classical Quarterly* 64, 657–668.

——. (2014b). 'The Roman Senate and the post-Sullan res publica', *Historia* 63, 323–339.

Stocker, A. (1961). 'The Legis Dies of Caesar's Command in Gaul'. *Classical Journal* 56, 242–248.

Sumner, G. (1963b). 'The Last Journey of L. Sergius Catilina', *Classical Philology* 58, 215–219.

Syme, R. (1938). 'The Allegiance of Labienus', *Journal of Roman Studies* 28, 113–125.

——. (1939). *The Roman Revolution* (Oxford).

——. (1963). 'Ten Tribunes', *Journal of Roman Studies* 53, 55–60.

Tatum, W. (1999). *The Patrician Tribune: Publius Clodius Pulcher* (Chapel Hill).

——. (2008). *Always I Am Caesar* (London).

Taylor, L. (1941). 'Caesar's Early Career', *Classical Philology* 36, 113–132.

——. (1942). 'Caesar and the Roman Nobility', *Transactions and Proceedings of the American Philological Association* 73, 1–24.

——. (1957). 'The Rise of Julius Caesar', *Greece & Rome*, 4, 10–18.

——. (1949). *Party Politics in the Age of Caesar* (Berkeley).

Thein, A. (2010). 'Sulla's Veteran Settlement Policy', in F. Daubner. (ed). *Militärsiedlungen und Territorialherrschaft in der Antike* (Berlin), 79–99.

Twyman, B. (1972). 'The Metelli, Pompeius and Prosopography', *Aufsteig und Niedergang der Römischen Welt* 1.1, 816–874.

Tyrrell, W. (1972). 'Labienus' Departure from Caesar in January 49 BC', *Historia* 21, 424–440.

Van der Blom, H. (2011). ' Pompey in the Contio', *Classical Quarterly* 61, 553–573.

—— (2012). ' Cato and the People', *Bulletin of the Institute of Classical Studies* 55, 39–56.

Van Ooteghem, J. (1954). *Pompée le Grand, bâtiseur d'Empire* (Bruxelles).

Von Ravensburg, A. (1961). *Burgerkrieg Zwischen Casar Und Pompejus, Im Jahre 50/49 V. Chr. Und Die Kampfe Dei Dyrrhachium Und Pharsalus*.

Veith, G. (1920). *Der Feldzug von Dyrrhachium zwischen Caesar und Pompeius* (Wien).

Vervaet, F. (2006). 'The Official Position of Cn. Pompeius in 49 and 48 BC', *Latomus* 65, 928–953.

——. (2009). 'Pompeius' career from 79 to 70 BC: Constitutional, political and historical Considerations', *Klio* 91, 406–34.

——. (2010). 'Arrogating Despotic Power Through Deceit: The Pompeian Model For Augustan Dissimulatio', in A. Turner, K. On Chong-Gossard & F, Vervaet. (eds). *Private and Public Lies. The Discourse of Despotism and Deceit in the Graeco-Roman World* (Leiden), 131–166.

Von Fritz, K. (1941). 'The Mission of L. Caesar and L. Roscius in January 49 BC', *Transactions and Proceedings of the American Philological Association* 72, 125–156.

——. (1942). 'Pompey's Policy before and after the Outbreak of the Civil War of 49 BC', *Transactions and Proceedings of the American Philological Association* 73, 145–180.

Ward, A. (1972). 'Cicero's Fight Against Crassus and Caesar in 65 and 63 BC', *Historia* 21, 244–258.

——. (1977). *Marcus Crassus and the Late Roman Republic* (Columbia).

Warde Fowler, W. (1900). *Julius Caesar and the Foundation of the Roman Imperial System* (London).

Watts, E. (2019). *Mortal Republic: How Rome Fell into Tyranny* (London).

Welsh, K. (1998*). Julius Caesar as Artful Reporter: The War Commentaries as Political* (London).

Westall, R. (2015). 'The Sources for the Civil Wars of Appian of Alexandria', in K. Welch (ed.). *Appian's Roman History. Empire and Civil War* (Swansea), 125–167.

——. (2016). 'The Sources of Cassius Dio for the Roman Civil Wars of 49–30 BC', in C. Lange and J. Madsen (eds.). *Cassius Dio. Greek Intellectual and Roman Politician* (Leiden), 51–75.

——. (2017). *Caesar's Civil War. Historical Reality and Fabrication* (Leiden).

Williams, R. (1978). 'The Role of "Amicitia" in the Career of A. Gabinius (Cos. 58)', *Phoenix* 32, 195–210.

——. (1985). 'Rei Publicae Causa: Gabinius' Defence of His Restoration of Ptolemy Auletes', *Classical Journal* 81, 25–38.

Williams, R. & Williams, B. (1988). 'Cn. Pompeius Magnus and L. Afranius. Failure to Secure the Eastern Settlement', *Classical Journal* 83, 198–206.

Wirszubski, C. (1968). *Libertas as a political idea during the Late Republic and Early Principate* (Cambridge).

Wistrand, E. (1968). *Sallust on Judicial Murders in Rome. A philological and historical study* (Gothenburg).

Wylie, G. (1989). 'Why Did Labienus Defect From Caesar in 49 BC?', *Ancient History Bulletin* 3, 123–127.

——. (1992). 'The Road to Pharsalus', *Latomus* 51, 557–565.

Yakobson, A. (2010). 'Traditional Political Culture and the People's Role in the Roman Republic', *Historia* 59, 282–302.

Yarrow, L. (2006). *Historiography at the End of the Republic: Provincial Perspectives on Roman Rule* (Oxford).

Yates, D. (2011). 'The Role of Cato the Younger in Caesar's "Bellum Civile"', *Classical World* 104, 161–174.

Index